Aug/03

START UP STAY UP

AND

IN THAILAND

Stories, Insight and Advice from Enterprising Expats

Roy Tomizawa

 Alpha Research Co.,Ltd.

Start Up and Stay Up in Thailand

Third Printing

Cover designed by
Manfred Winkle

Printing management by
Xerox DocuTech 6135
Thai Fuji Xerox Co., Ltd.
Tel. 02-617-6700-24 Ext. 2140-5

Published by
Alpha Research Co.,Ltd.

Alpha Research Co.,Ltd.
289/8 Lad Prao 35 Rd., Jatujak, Bangkok 10900
Tel. 02-939-0764, 02-939-0765 Fax: 02-939-0763
e-mail:*info@alpharesearch.co.th*
web site:*www.thailandinfiguresupdate.com*

National Library of Thailand Cataloging in Publication Data
Tomizawa, Roy.
Start Up and Stay Up in Thailand. -- Bangkok :
Alpha Research, 2003
224 p.
1. Entrepreneurship. I. Title
338.04
ISBN 974-86580-8-2

Dedication

For my mother, Sayoko, who desires much for her children and gives with great compassion, and in memory of my father, Thomas, whose wit, kindness and integrity made him a journalist and father to greatly admire.

CONTENTS

INTRODUCTION
Thailand -- An Entrepreneurial Paradise

Trouble is only opportunity in work clothes. -- Henry J. Kaiser

"You haven't lived until you've raced to your destination on a motorcycle taxi," said one long-time expat in Thailand. On most lanes leading up to major roads in Bangkok, you're bound to find troops of young men on motorcycles who are ready to help you beat what many consider the world's worst traffic. Is it safe? Well, not really. Accidents happen routinely. Is it fast? You bet. Motorcycles are capable of zipping between, behind and in front of cars, trucks and buses that sit and wait for traffic to lumber forward. Slipping into the narrowest windows of opportunity and storming ahead of their more cumbersome four-wheeled cousins, motorcycles are the fastest way of getting from point A to point B in Bangkok.

Motorcycle taxis are exciting, especially with a skilled driver who can twist and turn through a maze of fenders and mirrors, moving at a sprightly speed while cars are motionless. Motorcycle taxis are gritty, epitomized by the tough, weather-beaten young men on weather-beaten bikes, people who can joke, swear, smile and curse with the best of them. They are flexible, symbolized by their insistent requests for passengers to wear old, not particularly hygienic, poor-fitting helmets which would do little to prevent one's skull from cracking open in a crash just so the police would have one less excuse to pull them over. And motorcycle taxis are practical, as they will employ every shortcut and every meter of free space, whether it be on the roads or on the sidewalks, to get the passenger to his destination.

1

Bangkok, the center of business in Thailand, shares these qualities with motorcycle taxis: it's an exciting, gritty, flexible and practical town -- ideal for entrepreneurs. If the Chinese-influenced, almost-anything-goes type of entrepreneurialism is alive anywhere, it's alive in Bangkok, a haven for people with ideas, drive, ability and smarts.

This is a book about entrepreneurs in Thailand, people who seek opportunity, freedom and independence in their lives in a country willing to give it. It is a book of true stories given from the perspectives of successful foreign business people, people whose tales offer insight into how one could or should go about forming a company, deal with the Thai bureaucracy, manage local staff and market one's products. There are more comprehensive guides available on doing business in Thailand, but this book aims to give you a "feel" for what starting up a business in Thailand would be like. Imagine sitting at a bar with an old Thai hand, a savvy lawyer, and a successful foreign entrepreneur exchanging tips, war stories, and explanations into the deeper cultural reasons for certain Thai business practices, and you may have a better understanding of what this book is about.

This is not a book for people who only **think** about doing big things, but never get around to **doing** them, or who always find a reason not to. But even if entrepreneurial blood is flowing through your veins, starting up a business in Thailand, or anywhere for that matter, may be a rude introduction to some of the harsher facts of life -- that life is unfair, and that whatever can go wrong, may very well go wrong. As Vincent Swift, the head of an executive search firm in Thailand, put it, "By definition, you wouldn't start a business if you weren't overly optimistic."

And Thailand, at the dawn of the next millennium, is certainly in short supply of optimism. The second half of 1997 was an economic disaster for Thailand. This is quite a reversal in fortune from the ten-year period of 1985 to 1995 when Thailand was the fastest growing economy on the planet. But booms never last forever. In the mid-1990s, exports, the engine of Thai economic growth, were steadily declining as Thai industrial competitiveness began to erode in comparison with other lower-cost countries in the region. A property market that blazed to glory in the late 1980s and early 1990s, thanks primarily to cheap overseas credit and a thirst for easy gain by foreign and local investors alike, fizzled and crashed in 1997, leaving the Thai financial sector drowning in a sea of unperforming loans. The government eventually had to close down over fifty finance companies. With money tight and confidence low, Thailand's stock market lost over forty percent of its value in 1997.

One of the great advantages of doing business in Thailand was the stability of the Thai currency, the baht, which was pegged to the generally steady US dollar. But the Bank of Thailand lost over US$20 billion in valuable foreign currency reserves in order to defend a weakening baht. On July 2, 1997, the Thai government was forced to remove the umbilical cord that connected the baht to the dollar, and implemented what was called a managed float of its currency. The baht went into a free fall, devaluing from 26 baht to the dollar to a little over 50 six months later, a devaluation of about 50%. Even a US$ 17 billion bailout of the Thai economy led by the International Monetary Fund could not prevent the Thai economy from worsening.

And yet, as the number of bankruptcies increased and pessimism reigned, entrepreneurs continued to look for opportunities. If opportunity was deemed better elsewhere, entrepreneurs took their savings and sought fortune elsewhere. But many entrepreneurs in Thailand chose not to leave. Stories abound of foreigners who have come to Thailand on vacation or short trips and decided that living and working in Thailand was their dream all along. One of the MD's of a company interviewed for this book explained, somewhat sheepishly, that not much thought went into starting up a factory in Thailand. "Actually there wasn't any strategy," the MD said. "Our chairman came to Thailand, he liked the country, found a building and started production." Another entrepreneur profiled in this book, Andrew Clark, had lived and worked in Japan for several years when he decided to take a break and visit a Thai friend. "I thought, "Wow! Thailand has great food and great weather, and the people are friendly. They're my style -- easy-going and laid back. What am I doing in Japan?"

Many foreigners, including the author, have fallen in love with Thailand -- its people, its food, its heat, its colors, its culture. To many, Thailand is paradise found, and will not be lost in this economic crisis without a fight. In fact, the crisis only spurs some entrepreneurs on to greater heights of optimism. Claes Ostrom, an entrepreneur also profiled in this book, wrote to the author in early 1998, a time of great economic pessimism in Thailand, that his export clothing business was booming. He understands that the cheap baht is the engine behind his sudden spurt of profits, but he also believes that this crisis will be the opportunity that Thailand has needed -- a chance to recognize its problems and to improve.

> Business is exciting. This ought to be the time when honesty, reputation, hard work, and not just luck, pay off. I might be the only one who thinks Thailand will benefit from the present downturn, but it's like a second chance, to improve quality and increase productivity and service to compete internationally. I have customers now from Spain, Portugal and Italy who are very interested in buying from Thailand, not necessarily because of price, but because of service and quality. They are thinking long term. And we all need to as well.

Times are tough in Thailand. But for the dyed-in-the-wool entrepreneur, tough times mean opportunity. And those who can best spot opportunity are not those wallowing in despair, but those with the energy and the optimism to take control of their own lives and see problems only as challenges.

As someone once said, "When it is dark enough, you can see the stars."

ONE

THE "SABAY-NESS" OF IN-HOUSE
Starting Up the Easy Way

Starting up in Thailand can be easy for foreigners, especially for those with the right service and the right attitude. And if you know the basic laws and how to interpret them, or know someone who does, you'll probably be able to spend more time marketing your business and less time worrying about the technicalities of starting up in Thailand.

I was in business for twenty years in Canada and I never made a farthing. My business here in Thailand has made me a lot of money. And I have a very nice lifestyle. I spend as much time as possible in my beautiful home on the sea. I commute every week. I couldn't possibly dream of going back. -- Richard Murray, MD of Distri-Thai, a wholesaler/retailer of foreign publications

A COOL PLACE TO WORK

On April Fool's Day of 1993, Andrew Clark and Robbie Gilchrist started up an advertising agency called Creative In-House Limited out of the home they shared, hoping for a chance to live the entrepreneur's dream -- to succeed in business as one's own boss. Today, they are no joke. With a reputation for creativity, quality, efficiency and client responsiveness, In-House is becoming a small but potent force in an industry dominated by big international firms.

However, In-House is less an advertising firm as it is a way of life. It is a close approximation of many people's ideal work situation -- relaxed atmosphere, close relationships, respectful professionalism and success.

Clark, a Canadian, and Gilchrist, an Australian, share a strong affinity with what they feel is the easygoing nature of the Thais -- their "sabay-ness"[1] as Clark calls it. If you were to meet them at In-House, you'd enter a house surrounded by palm and mango trees on a quiet, nondescript residential street, not another office in another office building. The people of In-House work their magic in a Thai-style house, tastefully constructed to their design. Stepping into the entrance, you are greeted by open space as the two-story structure has no second floor, just a loft at the front and a ceiling that doubles as an arching terra cotta roof. In the middle

---

[1] The word "sabay" in Thai is used in many different ways, with general English translations being "comfortable", "feeling good", "easy", "enjoyable". It is so commonly used that even foreigners who don't speak Thai would very likely know this word.

of this space, people are busy getting their work done in apparent comfort around big tables. At the back, you might find Clark and Gilchrist sitting on planter's chairs in T-shirts and jeans, hashing over ideas for their latest work.

Their work is to provide a wide range of advertisement services from producing collaterals (brochures, menus, timetables) to direct marketing, to print and television advertising. Because of their small size and capable creative talent, In-House can fill the niche of smaller budget jobs that the big advertising companies simply won't look at. "The big international agencies don't want to touch anything under ten million baht," said Clark. "They aren't interested in doing menus or brochures. All they want to do is place their TV ads."

Thanks to their skillful mining of this niche, the money rolled in during the first four years of In-House's existence. Clark and Gilchrist never really experienced cash flow problems, and as a result, were able to pay their 10 or so Thai staff above average rates and bonuses, and give themselves two or three months off a year on holidays or trips. A maid cooks lunch and they often eat together. In fact, they even take trips to the beach together. The Thais they hired not only recommend others to join, they resist the urge to look for bigger, greener pastures. To the casual observer, it is a casual place where friends happen to be working together. In-House has made it all look so simple, and would certainly deserve the wrath of the Patron Saint of Failed Entrepreneurs and Frustrated Wage-Earners if not for the modesty and aplomb with which they have achieved success. In the vernacular of the young, In-House is a cool place to work.

IT AIN'T THAT EASY, IS IT?

In early 1993, Clark was creative director for KL&P Asia and Gilchrist was creative director for McCann-Erickson. Unfortunately, they felt that their creative abilities were not being fully utilized. That's when their friend, the head of a major airlines, called. Because this airlines had only eight million baht a year to do their collateral work, they were forced to go to Thai design companies where they would end up with brochures in English that would have typos, and Thai directors who couldn't really communicate well with their foreign clients. Their friend asked Clark and Gilchrist if they could put together a simple timetable for him on the side. At the same time, Minor Group asked them to produce brochures for their new condos in Chiang Mai. "That's when Robbie and I started thinking, 'Wow, we could just quit our jobs and go full-time with this business.'" And that's what they did.

Clark and Gilchrist were practically broke when they started up In-House. But with a deposit from Minor Group for their freelance work, they rented used office equipment, bought office supplies and acquired the services of a good lawyer, all for about 80,000 baht. From that time on they never looked back.

Is it really that easy? Not according to William Heinecke, the head of Minor Group who was there at the birth of In-House.

> Starting up on very little money? I gotta tell you maybe thirty years ago, great. But today? No. If you're like the guys at In-House, and you got a service to sell, you have a chance to get away with it if you're lucky. But they had some credibility with us because we knew them from their old jobs. But to come square, it ain't easy. If you're coming in cold, and you just got a good idea, and you think Thailand is a great, exciting market because you read about it in Fortune Magazine, unless you've got a lot of money, forget it. For every guy with a success story, there are twenty five of them who have bit the dust. Believe me, it's tough. If you look at when I started in Thailand over twenty years ago, housing was 2,500 baht a month for a very nice apartment. You could buy a car for 25,000 baht. Now you can't do it any more. There aren't any more bargains here.

KNOWING THE ROPES

In-House was able to get away with a very low-cost start up.

However, In-House had to deal with important basic legal requirements, written and unwritten, that need to be understood by almost all would-be entrepreneurs in Thailand. Fortunately, they hired a very competent lawyer who knew the ropes.

All foreigners working in Thailand are required to have a work permit as well as an appropriate visa to allow them to stay for the duration of their work permit. Here are two basic, but unwritten rules of thumb for foreigners starting up their own firms:

1) In order to get one work permit, the Labor Department currently requires your company to be capitalized at a minimum of 2 million baht; and

2) In order to get a visa to stay in the country, the Immigration Department currently requires that your company have at least 4 employees for every long-term visa you request.

According to the law that controls the formation of companies, at least 25% of the company's capitalization must be paid in upon incorporation. If you're an entrepreneur in your own country, legal capitalization requirements are not going to be that high. The same is true for Thais starting up in Thailand.

However, if you're a foreigner starting up in Thailand, then you need to capitalize at 2 million baht in order to get the work permit. Obviously, In-House did not have the 500,000 baht, or 25%, required by the letter of the law to be initially paid up on the capital, much less the two million baht that must be paid up to be eligible for one work permit. In a similar situation, you could lie and say that you are paid up, which means that you would have to file a false statement when your books are audited. According to one lawyer, the Ministry of Commerce used to require that you go down to their offices and prove that you had paid up your capital, but for some reason stopped requiring this check in the early 1990's. Thus, theoretically, you could get away with the lie.

For those who feel uncomfortable about blatantly fabricating the truth, lawyers or accountants may arrange it so that the capital is placed on the books, but quickly placed out as a loan to the director or the shareholders of the company. As one lawyer stated, "You put two million into the company and you give yourself a loan for two million. Essentially, as long as you accrue the interest on the loan, your books are balanced. You show money in and where it went, so your auditor's happy and it's capitalized. The interest isn't even being paid. It's being accrued on the books. That's one way to do it if you don't have any money." If that doesn't make total sense to you, don't worry. It seems to make perfect legal sense to lawyers and accountants here in Thailand.

The second barrier is the Immigration Department's requirement for a long-term visa. For every long-term visa desired (which usually means one year), the company needs to have four Thai employees. Many small foreign start-ups do not have or need that many Thais on staff in the initial stages. Fortunately for foreigners, according to a lawyer, this four-to-one rule may be negotiable, especially for small consultancy and service businesses. However, if you feel that you may not have an adequate number of Thai employees, it has not been unheard of to place Thai names on the payroll, a slight case of legal legerdemain. Thais such as your friends, your maid or your girlfriend could be listed as your employees, but in actuality would not be receiving salaries. However, it has to be clear on the books that their withholding taxes are being paid.

Somehow, all foreigners eventually find out about these unwritten rules. If they have a lawyer handling the formation of their company, they may have only a fleeting awareness of these rules. If not, they stumble over them in the process. Some entrepreneurs may feel the methods to deal with these rules stated above are against the letter of the law. If so, they should follow what could be interpreted as the letter of the law by depositing 500,000 baht into a bank account and hiring four Thais. For most other business people struggling to get their company off the ground, if business is good, then they will have the money to eventually meet the capitalization requirements and hire the required number of staff. If business is bad, they may have much bigger concerns than unpaid capital and imaginary staff.

REGISTERING AS A THAI COMPANY

The first step towards setting up a private limited company, the most popular structure in Thailand for the small to medium-sized business, is to register a Memorandum of Association with the Ministry of Commerce. The following information is required for this document:

1) The name and address of the company;
2) The objectives of the company;
3) The registered capital of the company, divided into shares and par value; and
4) The names, addresses, occupations and signatures of a minimum of seven people who will be the promoters (in essence, your founding shareholders) of the company, as well as the number of shares subscribed by each promoter.

According to one lawyer, the Ministry of Commerce began to tire of the wide-ranging and eclectic listings of business objectives that many Thai business people wished to have for their companies, so the Ministry now provides a standard form for the Memorandum of Association. If this standard form is used, the application process can proceed fairly quickly. However, the listing of business objectives is somewhat laughable. In-House, as a result, has a list of 40 objectives which allows the company to get involved in such businesses as real estate, manufacturing, publishing, hotels and restaurants, law, hairdressing, accounting, engineering, pharmaceuticals and massage parlors. (See entire listings in Appendix 1.) You name it, you got it. And yes, buried in business objective number 34 is In-House's mandate to provide advertising services, their only real business purpose. Obviously this sort of listing gives the entrepreneur tremendous flexibility to diversify in the future.

To the non-lawyer, this incredible listing of objectives seems to fly in the face of the Alien Business Law. The Alien Business Law, otherwise known as the Announcement of the National Executive Council No. 281, is the law that dictates what kind of businesses foreigners can own and operate in Thailand. And it clearly lists advertising as one of the businesses closed to "alien" majority ownership. (See entire listings in Appendix 2.) So how were Clark and Gilchrist, two definite non-Thais, able to start-up and operate an advertising firm?

The answer is, they weren't. The "juristic person", or legal entity known as Creative In-House Limited was. In-House is a Thai entity, not a foreign one, and therefore is not restricted by the Alien Business Law in terms of what businesses it can engage in. The Alien Business Law states that an "alien" company is defined by foreign ownership of 50% upwards. The Land Code states that an "alien" company is defined by foreign ownership of more than 49%. As most foreigners investing in Thailand would like to have their companies eligible to purchase land, they usually decide to create a company in which 51% of the shares are Thai-owned and 49% are foreign-owned. In this manner, foreigners become directors in a Thai company, which consequently allows them to avoid the restrictions of the Alien Business Law.

WHEN OWNING IS NOT NECESSARILY CONTROLLING

Which brings us to the question: Who are the Thai shareholders and what role do they play? Ideally, foreigners go into business with Thais and they are able to synergize each other's strengths into a formidable partnership: the foreigners, for instance, bring in expertise and international business standards while the Thais provide understanding of the local business laws and customs, as well as connections. (See Chapter Three.) However, many foreign entrepreneurs wish to limit the number of their business partners so as to maximize the control they will have over the company. This usually means having at least four Thai partners.

All private limited companies in Thailand must have at least seven shareholders. In order to be recognized as a Thai entity, the majority of shareholders must be Thai, and as stated before, the majority of shares must also be owned by Thais. Thus, a private limited company that has six foreigners and one Thai, in which each foreigner holds one share each and the lone Thai holds 94 shares, is considered "alien" because the majority of shareholders are foreign. Thus, a foreigner must have at least four Thai share holders if he has a minimum of seven shareholders in his company. In the case of In-House, one of the first Thai shareholders was Clark's girlfriend at the time. These Thai shareholders could actually invest in the company. They may even borrow money from the foreign shareholders and promise to pay back the loan with a percentage of their salaries or their dividends. Many don't actually invest any of their money, and simply sign their names as subscribers of shares out of friendship, in a sense, receiving the shares as a gift without expectation of any real financial reward. All you need are four Thais, and those four will technically own 51% of the company. Three non-Thais can make up the remaining 49% share of the company.

However, since the foreign entrepreneur who starts up a small-to - medium-sized business usually is the one investing most or all of the capital, he naturally wants to control his own destiny as much as possible. The way the company is structured can provide the legal mechanisms for the foreign minority shareholders to exert control in varying degrees. There are a great number of such structures of varying legality. Explanations of two basic and legally firm structures follow.

Share Voting Structure: In this particular structure, Thais legally own 51% of the shares in a private limited company, while foreigners own the remaining 49%. However, the Articles of Association, the by-laws which dictate how the company operates and makes decisions, can be drafted in a way that gives the minority shareholders, the foreigners, the ability to elect a majority of the board of directors and so block any of the following board of director resolutions that any Thai director(s) may wish to pass:

1) acquiring or disposing of any assets of the company of a value greater than an amount decided upon in the Articles of Association;

2) entering into any agreement on behalf of the company except in the ordinary course of business to pay a sum in excess of an amount decided upon in the Articles of Association;

3) causing the company to enter into any new line of business.

13

This is possible because the Alien Business Law does not dictate that members of the board of directors have to be Thai. In fact, all of the directors may be foreign. The Articles of Association can instruct a foreign shareholder to appoint a majority of the directors. It can also provide that in board of director meetings, at least one of the directors nominated by the foreign shareholder must be present, that resolutions can be passed only with a certain percentage of the votes, and that resolutions can be passed only if a director nominated by a foreign shareholder agrees to a given resolution.

Other more significant resolutions can only be passed by a specified majority of the shareholders. Such resolutions include decisions to :

1) increase or reduce capital;
2) amend the Memorandum of Association or the company by-laws;
3) merge with another company; or
4) dissolve the company.

Termed special resolutions, shareholders, not the board of directors, need to pass any of these resolutions in two successive meetings by a majority of not less than three-fourths, and then a majority of not less than two-thirds. In a nutshell, control over the company is dependent on garnering at least 75% of the votes of all shareholders for the above resolutions. Since the Thais possess 51% and the foreign partners possess 49%, they each have *negative control* over each other, and thus need the cooperation of the other party to make major decisions.

Preference Share Structure: After careful examination of the Alien Business Law, some law firm somewhere introduced the concept of preference shares to Thailand, which enabled the minority foreign shareholder to have legal and *total control* over the management of the company, not just negative control as explained in the Share Voting Structure. This is made possible by creating two sets of shares: ordinary shares and preference shares. The foreigners would possess 49% of the shares and the Thais would have 51%, but the type of shares they possess would differ.

The Articles of Association would then be drafted so that the voting rights of the shareholder would differ depending on what type of share he holds. For example, it can be stated that ordinary shares would have one vote per share, whereas preference shares would have one vote for every five or ten shares. In fact, In-House is set up so that the Thai shareholders possess preference shares that equal one vote per ten shares. If you add up the votes, the foreign shareholders have 49 votes, while the Thai shareholders have 5.1 votes. This effectively gives Clark and Gilchrist over 90% of the votes, enough to pass any major resolution unilaterally.

Although the Preference Share Structure has been challenged by certain areas within the Thai government, it is still one of the safest legal ways for foreign interests to have control over a Thai private limited company. As one prominent lawyer has said, the Alien Business Law never explicitly states that foreigners must be in the minority in terms of voting rights. "The ABL speaks only about percentages of ownership," he said. "It does not speak about the values of the Thai and the foreign investment or the ability to vote in a company."[2]

GROWING PAINS

> *And he looked up at me, and stared at me, this stare that only Steve Jobs has, and he said, 'Do you want to sell sugar water for the rest of your life, or do you want to come with me and change the world?' And I gulped because I knew I would wonder for the rest of my life what I would have missed.* -- John Sculley, former head of PepsiCo and Apple Computers

Perhaps it is a slight exaggeration to say that George Romanyk went through the same angst as John Sculley did before Sculley decided to leave his position of prestige and power with PepsiCo, one of the biggest companies in the world, for an unproven up-start called

---

[2]   At the time of this book's printing, a draft of a new law called the Foreign Business Law, which will probably replace the ABL, was being considered by the Thai government. Wording of the draft available in October, 1998 indicated that the preferred share structure may still be a valid corporate structure in the new law, although that issue will be heavily debated.

Apple Computers which was established in a garage four years before. But Romanyk was the number two at The Regent Bangkok, one of the leading hotels in the world according to one recent rating, and after twenty years in the hotel industry with the very best in the business, he decided with some hesitancy to join In-House.

In-House was growing. Clark and Gilchrist felt that while they were good creative people, they were not necessarily good managers. After getting to know Romanyk through work that In-House did for the Regent Chiang Mai, a hotel Romanyk opened, Clark and Gilchrist began to court the hotelier. In-House was getting to the point where they just didn't have a handle on their internal systems, financial systems and legal matters. They needed a professional manager who could bring some control to the business as well as credibility, especially since most of In-House's clients were hotels. "Basically, we needed a suit," said Clark.

There was obviously something quite persuasive about Clark's and Gilchrist's laidback style, as well as their devotion to quality, that appealed to Romanyk, persuasive enough for him to take over a fifty percent cut in salary in exchange for shares in the firm. Tired of moving from position to position and locale to locale in the ever-proper, ever-restrained hotel industry for so many years, Romanyk thought that at the age of forty this would be a great chance to break the cycle. Although he wouldn't be embarking on a mission to "change the world", it would be a chance for him to be his own boss. Echoing Sculley's words, Romanyk thought, "If I didn't make the move, I'd probably be kicking myself for a long time."

In Romanyk's first few months with In-House, he actually was kicking himself as he had to get used to the fact that he wasn't going to have a staff of 800 "bowing and scraping" as he had in the Regent. In fact, he was placed in a small area under the stairwell when he first joined, and ended up using his own money to buy his own desk. "My ego wasn't being stroked."

On top of that, he still fights against In-House's seeming disregard for clear and prompt communication. He's trying hard to convince people that the simple acts of having an In-Tray/Out-Tray system, or even buying and using telephone message pads can make a world of difference. "You know I got three phone calls from China today, but no one even mentioned this to me," said Romanyk. Clark replied, "I also don't get messages, but I'm not as serious about it. However, I do realize that a message could mean ten million baht."

Ten million baht is big money as the Thai economic engine continues to sputter. When a new hotel in Bangkok was partially gutted by fire a day before its opening in 1997, In-House lost about 8 million baht in expected revenue. When foreign management of a major toy company left the country the same year, they lost another projected 12 million baht in fees. The bigger the company becomes, the bigger the stakes. But Gilchrist isn't worried. He's very happy with In-House's culture that prioritizes quality of life over money. He feels that his arrival in Thailand has united his soul with a people whom he believes feel that life's too short to get worked up over the game of business. "We've been to zero in the bank before," said Gilchrist. "But the phone will ring. This is Thai positive thinking. It will get you through."

Sabay sabay indeed.

TWO

THE DOCUMENT STORAGE COMPANY'S ROCKY ROAD TO SUCCESS
Starting Up the Hard Way

Starting up a successful business is tough enough in your home country, where you probably have a better idea of how to get things done. But to start up in a foreign land can be stressful because gaps in knowledge cannot so easily be filled by common sense guesses. To be an entrepreneur is to be an optimist, but more than optimism is needed to be successful in a new land. Competition can be fierce, and sometimes foreigners have to be tough to withstand the unique pressures that face them in Thailand. But with drive, hard work and a bit of luck, barriers can be overcome.

I'd seen it so many times. People bring a lot of money to invest in a place where they don't know anybody or anything, and the money goes just like that. If you come with a limited amount of money, you have to be careful. You have to build it up slowly. And if you're lucky, it can happen quickly. -- Claes Ostrom, M.D. of Poliville

SUCCESS!

One day Frank Crocker was pulling his BMW onto the expressway. A policeman stopped him at the toll, telling him that there was something wrong with his insurance. Crocker insisted that his insurance was fine and didn't expire until September. The police man said, "Wrong. Pull over." That's when Crocker lost his temper, angry at what he perceived to be another unwarranted shakedown by the police. He got out of the car and locked the doors. "You want the car? You can have it," he shouted as he started walking up the expressway ramp. As the cars honked their horns behind the abandoned car that blocked their path, the policeman rushed up to Crocker. Crocker offered him the keys to his car, but the policeman knew it was no use reasoning with this person, and let Crocker get back in his car and drive away.

Crocker is a nice guy, a musician, a pilot, a designer, a painter. He's got a great laugh and a belly that his Thai staff can kid him about. But he's a tough guy and he's not one to back down from a fight. In over five years in Thailand, he has had plenty of opportunities to give up. But like his fight with the traffic cop, he's ended up on top again -- big time.

Crocker accomplished what so many entrepreneurs dream about -- building up a company and selling out at a hefty profit. In September of 1996, he and his partners sold his company, The Document Storage Company (TDSC), for a 970% return on investment in a little over four years. Crocker personally owned over 40% of the company, and as a result, is now a US$ millionaire. Although he is still a director, Crocker finally believes he can end thirty years of six-day work weeks and relax.

PROBLEMATIC PARTNERS

In 1991, Crocker was in Hong Kong and he wasn't very happy. He had been asked by his boss to go to Hong Kong and break up a five-year joint venture between his company, an old and prestigious British freight forwarding firm, and a large Hong Kong firm. If not for a personality conflict between the two chairmen, Crocker believes this joint venture could have thrived. "After ten days in Hong Kong I realized it was very stupid, that I was being asked to smash a very beautiful piece of glass," he said. "Breaking glass is easy, but putting the pieces back together is really difficult."

So after Crocker was forced to break up the relationship, he spent twenty months trying to pick up the pieces and salvage his company's half of the joint venture. In the end, both operations lost heavily as they tried to make it on their own. Crocker was miserable -- and ripe for a change.

One day, a friend asked Crocker to join him for dinner. At that dinner, Crocker met a Thai man named Somchai[1], who would change his life. According to Crocker, Somchai was a charming gentleman who was also in the freight-forwarding business. The two men got along right from the start. Somchai knew Crocker wasn't happy in Hong Kong, and began a persistent courtship to woo Crocker to Bangkok to run his own faltering firm. After several visits to Hong Kong, Somchai finally convinced Crocker to move to Thailand.

Crocker was so happy to be leaving Hong Kong and the agony of a healthy company ripped in half that he gladly accepted a 100% cut in salary. He also agreed to buy five percent of the company, Siam Movers, every year for five years, and thus eventually own 25% of the firm. There was one problem. This company was in poor shape. When Crocker arrived, staff weren't being regularly paid, morale was low, company property ownership was highly questionable, and business was bad. After bringing in his own people, Crocker said he increased revenues by 100% within the first three months and started Siam Movers on the road to recovery.

---

[1] The name of this man and the related companies are aliases.

Unfortunately, overall progress was slow and Crocker himself received only a small part of his promised income, although he used his own money to buy into the company. This state of affairs worried Crocker desperately, especially since he suspected that Somchai wasn't as clean as he had originally thought. Crocker wanted out of Siam Movers, but he also wanted his money. And he knew he wasn't going to get it unless Siam Movers suddenly became very profitable, or unless he could start up another business that was successful enough to enable him to get his money back and turn his luck around.

Document storage was an idea waiting to happen. Companies are legally required to keep records, particularly financial records, for up to ten years. For many companies during the expansive boom years, boxes and boxes of files began to take up too much valuable office space. Crocker thought that a company with a well-placed and well-secured warehouse at the edge of the city could do pretty brisk business with companies looking to find a less expensive home for their old documents. So in order to get his money back from Somchai, Crocker started up another company with Somchai called SecuriFile, in which he had to invest up to 800,000 baht of his own money. Unfortunately, Crocker and Somchai couldn't agree on certain matters of confidentiality and other operational criteria required for SecuriFile's clients' possessions.

After a year of trying to run SecuriFile, Crocker decided to give up. An accounting firm hired by Crocker to look into the true value of Somchai's companies told Crocker that Somchai was in "serious personal debt", and that Crocker should get out. An Englishman who's set foot in 98 different nations and lived in 26 countries, Crocker had one of the most frustrating 20-month periods of his life in Thailand as he struggled to figure out what kind of relationship he was going to have with his Thai partner. After a final spat, Crocker said enough was enough, and left. Although Somchai paid back some of the money owed to Crocker in salary, Crocker still lost over US$100,000 of personal savings invested in another man's companies. "I was so upset I gave my shares back to him for nothing."

Obviously, this was not a partnership made in heaven. Perhaps Crocker had wanted out of Hong Kong so badly he didn't really check into the background of his future partner. Bryan Baldwin, the 20-year managing director of Castrol Thailand and former shareholder in TDSC said that finding the right partner is very often the difference between success and failure. "In my time here, I would say that the key to doing business in Thailand, the number one consideration, has got to be identifying the right Thai partner." And yet, according to Peter Williams, a former consultant for start-up businesses in Asia and managing director of International Specialty Products (ISP), this is a common phenomenon. "A guy will arrive here and, amazingly, will simply not take as much care in setting up a business and doing the due diligence required to determine the correct partner as he would do in his home country."

RISKY BUSINESS

The evening after Crocker decided to walk away from Somchai and his companies, a Thai male visited Crocker's apartment with a gun. "This man suggested that I leave Thailand because he represented people who liked me and knew me for a long time," said Crocker. "He said they wanted me to have a long and happy life, and to do that I would have to be taking in oxygen. If I was here by next Thursday, I wouldn't be taking in any more oxygen."

It is very likely that many major Western cities have higher murder rates than Bangkok, a relatively safe big city. However, stories about Thais hiring assassins to settle business disputes are not unheard of. And the occasional sensationalized story in the media about assassinations may tend to have a great impact on the psyche of some foreign residents of Thailand and may lead them to believe that the hiring of assassins is a fairly popular way for a Thai to settle a grudge with another person. Non-Thais probably tend to believe that conflict between two business parties can and should be solved through dialogue or the courts of law, and that assassination is more of a crime of gangland intrigue and political conflict. This is probably how most Thais think as well.

And yet some have made cultural arguments for the prevalence of violence in Thai society, despite the stereotypical view of Thais as smiling, calm and tolerant people. It is generally accepted that Thais naturally prefer to avoid conflict and open displays of emotion. A smile, a change of subject, or an expression of agreement with the confrontor are just three ways in which Thais will restrain their emotions and attempt to turn a potentially stressful interaction into one of emotional equilibrium. Thus, Thais are famous for their **jai yen** ("cool heart") approach to life. Unfortunately, as a prominent author on Thai culture, William Klausner, noted, keeping your emotions bottled up can sometimes result in violence.

> To fully understand the Thai personality, we must appreciate that the "cool heart" and the ubiquitous smile are quite often merely cultural masks covering emotional concerns related to dignity, face, perceived status. There is strain and tension; and release is sought, at least initially, through indirect methods. When these latter techniques are no longer psychologically satisfying or effective, extreme forms of violence may well result.[2]

Perhaps, the gunman was sent to Crocker's home by Somchai, as Crocker speculates. If that were the case, somehow Somchai took great offense with Crocker and sought to express his anger in a violent way. Klausner explains that there are a couple of good reasons why Somchai may have resorted to violence. Thais who live in villages are restrained from committing acts of violence by the desire to maintain the close relationships and interdependencies between villagers. But for Thais who live in a rapidly expanding city like Bangkok, Klausner suspects that "increased crime and violence may be seen as a result of these too abrupt and disruptive socioeconomic changes." Klausner also believes that the ineffectiveness of the police and judicial systems to act swiftly and fairly encourage people to consider violence as their only means to receiving justice.

> Other controls and restraints associated with an impersonal urban society, including police and court systems, have not proven to be as effective to maintaining social peace and avoiding violence. The

---

[2] Klausner, William, *Reflections on Thai Culture*, The Siam Society, 1993, page 325

court system, an institutional mechanism for restitution of wrongs and conflict resolution, may itself, actually contribute to violence. There have been accusations of increasing corruption within the judicial system. Disgruntled and wronged businessmen have sometimes taken the law into their own hands convinced they cannot get a fair and impartial hearing in the courts.[3]

Perhaps Somchai felt that no other method of settling the conflict was viable.

There is another way to view this incident, however. Aggressive behavior by one can result in aggressive behavior by another. Dr. Henry Holmes, an authority on cross cultural management in Thailand, said that there is a great need in Thailand to work hard in building up rapport and loyalty with Thais, a culture that on the most part prioritizes the value of building and maintaining relationships over the value of task accomplishment. Being sensitive to the feelings and motivations of the Thais, or of anybody for that matter, is of paramount importance to a good relationship. "An ability to create rapport and loyalty would go a long way toward discouraging their (Thais) hidden and rapacious instincts," said Holmes.

For whatever reasons, the partnership between Crocker and Somchai failed. What he didn't know, though, was that this business divorce was just the break he needed.

A STORMY START UP

Only two days after a stranger threatened his life with a gun, Crocker was ready to start up another document storage company, which he decided, simply enough, to call The Document Storage Company. People told him to take the death threat seriously, but he replied, "If it's going to happen, it's going to happen very quickly, so it doesn't really matter."

Crocker rented out 500 square meters of a new, foreign-owned

---

[3] Klausner, William, *Reflections on Thai Culture*, The Siam Society, 1993, page 325, 326

warehouse in Bangna, a district on the eastern edge of Bangkok. A large finance company was about to agree to become TDSC's first customer, but first wanted to see the lease that TDSC had with the owner of the warehouse in order to determine if TDSC was really going to be around for years. The first lease Crocker received from the foreign firm that owned the warehouse was not satisfactorily drafted. This lease mentioned nothing about insurance, about when rent was to be paid, or about any process for termination of the lease. When Crocker got the revised lease, it still did not mention insurance.

That's when the roof fell in. Literally.

A storm tore off the roof of Crocker's section of the warehouse, deluging his brand new company with water. When Crocker arrived at his company the next day, thousands of his specially designed storage boxes were waterlogged and ruined, his new computers useless. Crocker went back to his foreign partners and asked them to help him cover the 400,000 baht needed to replace his damaged goods and equipment, confident that he would get the money back through the warehouse owner's insurance company. Unfortunately, the reason why insurance was never written into the first two drafts of the lease was because the owners of the warehouse had not yet insured the building.

The warehouse owner's real estate agent, a large foreign firm, seemed very sympathetic to Crocker's problem. Crocker needed a signed lease so that he could get his first customer. However, he wanted to make sure that the lease made it clear that insurance would cover the recent damage to his property, as well as any future insurable troubles. The foreign manager of the real estate agent told Crocker not to worry, that if Crocker signed the lease, the agent would not send the lease to the warehouse owner until the warehouse owner sent Crocker a letter stating that TDSC would be compensated by their insurance company for damages to its property. But no letter was forthcoming. When Crocker called the warehouse owner, he learned that the real estate agent had already sent the signed lease to the warehouse owner, making the agreement official. TDSC was in fact not covered by insurance. When Crocker called the real estate agent for an explanation as to why the agent sent the signed lease prematurely, according to Crocker, the agent said, "You have to understand. They pay my bill." Crocker, feeling betrayed for a second time in Thailand, learned a great lesson: "Farangs can be just as likely as the Thais to screw people."

Unfortunately, the betrayals didn't end there.

KILLER COMPETITION

After recovering from this early anguish, business was pretty good that first year in 1992. TDSC was able to sell some 55,000 boxes. After two years, TDSC had eighty firm customers and many potential customers. The staff also began to grow. Even so, Crocker was doing what all entrepreneurs have to do -- everything.

> I did the marketing. I drove the Jeep. I would deliver something here, go into the toilet and change into a suit, make a sales call, put my jeans and t-shirt back on, jump back in my Jeep and move some other client's boxes around. Sometimes it was embarrassing because I would go to a company to deliver boxes in my work clothes only to realize that I had been to meet with the MD in my suit the day before.

At the end of TDSC's second year, a 28-year old Chulalongkorn University graduate knocked on Crocker's door asking for a job. He said that he was an accountant but that he had been away in Australia so long that nobody in Thailand would give him a job because he was behind the times in terms of tax law. "He said he needed a break," said Crocker, "so I gave him a job." After four months, the accountant told Crocker that he had to leave. According to Crocker, the accountant explained that "I'm a good boy and my family is up north. My brother left home and my father is too old to milk the cows. I don't want to give up my job because you've been so kind to me, but I've got to go." Crocker thought this was terrible and arranged a nice party for the poor accountant, gave him a gift of gold, and wished him luck. Three weeks later, one of his staff told Crocker that the accountant who supposedly had returned to his farm in the North had actually opened up a document storage company, complete with copies of TDSC's contracts and writs, TDSC's box design, and a bunch of TDSC's customers. And this former accountant was offering a rate up to 50% lower than Crocker was. "That was my first taste of competition." Six months later, two of Crocker's supervisors left and started up a document storage company with a bank. Competitors seemed to be springing up left and right.

One evening, Crocker was in the parking lot of a supermarket opening his car door when a Thai male threatened Crocker with a gun and told him to leave the country. Another evening, Crocker got a death threat over the phone, again telling him to leave the country. "I was told that this business was not something farangs should be involved with -- that this was a Thai business. And I thought, 'Well that's bloody amazing because two years ago I was the first one doing this. Suddenly it was a Thai business!'"

TIMING IS EVERYTHING

Now that The Document Storage Company is owned by a company called Brambles, enemies will have to send their death threats to Australia because that's where the owners are. In 1996, security companies were looking to expand in Asia through acquisition. TDSC was pursued by several companies, but Brambles made Crocker and his fellow shareholders an offer they couldn't refuse.

But what a difference a year makes. In July of 1996, TDSC had only about 1.4 million baht receivable over 90 days. In 1997, the Thai economy came to a crashing halt. Companies tightened up and simply stopped paying their bills. Cash stopped flowing and TDSC was hit hard. Accounts receivable increased many fold and TDSC's ability to close new customers decreased ten times. No one knew it at the time, but when Crocker and his partners sold out to Brambles in September of 1996, the Thai economy was riding at the top of the wave, only to come crashing down in 1997. "Right now, I don't think I could sell the company."

Luckily, for Crocker and his partners, he was able to sell it. And after all he's been through, maybe he deserves the break.

THREE

EXCEL-LENT PARTNERS
A Trusting Relationship

Some foreign entrepreneurs choose to start up small to medium-sized businesses in ways that allow them to avoid active participation by their Thai partners. Using nominees as shareholders is a not-uncommon, although illegal, method practiced by foreigners who value independent control of resources over local expertise and knowledge. However, finding the right Thai partners and integrating them into your business can mean the difference between success or failure in Thailand.

It is better to suffer wrong than to do it, and happier to be sometimes cheated than not to trust. -- Samuel Johnson

THE BENEFITS OF REAL THAI PARTNERS

Chanya Kamolchaikaimoog and David Quine are excellent partners. Although they didn't realize that a friendship that started in a Thai restaurant in London many years ago would blossom into such a healthy business relationship, Excel Computers Thailand is the product of a complementary mixture of overseas expertise and local know-how. This is a not-so-common amalgam in the world of foreign entrepreneurs in Thailand.

Excel is a consultancy that advises companies on a variety of software and hardware systems, and specializes in selling, installing and maintaining a comprehensive and sophisticated accounting software system. Since 1992, Excel has been digging itself a niche that still has great room for growth as more and more organizations in Thailand are seeing the need to computerize and systemize. With Quine concentrating on the marketing of Excel's products and Chanya anchoring the Thai staff, a strong sense of cross-cultural teamwork has emerged, allowing Excel to grow, as well as weather a crisis that threatened to close down the company.

Quine and his English partner Steven Foster Davis were already operating a similar company in London in 1990 when they decided to move to Thailand and replicate the business in Bangkok. In doing so, however, their thinking was different from that of many foreign small business operators. In order to get around the legal requirement for majority Thai ownership, many foreigners start up companies with nominee Thai shareholders: girlfriends, wives, maids, or people procured through lawyers for a fee. The objective of these foreign investors is to maintain control of the company while maintaining the illusion of the existence of Thai shareholders holding a controlling interest in the company.

From the very beginning, the nominee method didn't sit well with Quine and Davis. They couldn't imagine setting up in a foreign environment without the help of local partners they could trust. They instead decided to find Thai partners who would be a part of the Excel family. According to Quine, "We wanted to build relations. We felt we would achieve much more if we were fully involved with our Thai partners."

Quine's search for Thai partners began near Excel's office in London, at a Thai restaurant on Belmont Road called *Tup Tim*. After spending several vacations in Thailand, Quine and Davis had become quite enamored with Thai food and would often have meals at *Tup Tim*. One of the owner's Thai friends, Chanya, was helping out at the restaurant on weekends. After Chanya got to know Quine and Davis, she asked Quine whether her son could work for them. He said yes, and that, as they say, was the beginning of a beautiful relationship.

When Quine and Davis started making investigative forays into Thailand in 1991, Chanya and her family had, coincidentally, also decided to end 18 years of life in England and move back to Thailand. Thankful for the opportunity they had given her son in England, Chanya, before leaving for Thailand, told Quine and Davis, "If there's anything I can do for you in Thailand, let me know." Quine and Davis had gotten to know Chanya and liked her, and so they asked her if she would be interested in becoming a partner in the business they were planning to set up in Bangkok.

Chanya responded that she and other family members would agree to be shareholders if her uncle, a prominent officer in the military, approved of Excel. Once in Bangkok, they all gathered for a Sunday lunch, and Quine and Davis had the opportunity to meet with Chanya's uncle. A tad nervous, Quine said that they were on their best behavior. The uncle asked about the business. Quine and Davis answered. In the end, the uncle endorsed the idea, took up a token share in the company, and told the other family members to help Excel whenever possible. "We could see that they were honest people," said Chanya. The feeling was mutual.

From that point on, Chanya's family has been a key factor in Excel's success. Before Chanya had even moved back to Thailand, she had her daughter, Priya, who was already working for another organization, help Quine and Davis cope with the masses of paper-work that banks and government demand. This sort of work is maddening for a foreigner and difficult for a Thai, but Priya offered her services for free.

About a year into Excel's operations, Chanya decided to call Quine and Davis to see how they were coping with their venture. According to Chanya, she asked again, "Is there anything I can do?" Quine once again said yes to this question. "At that time, they had started with maybe two or three Thais, and I think they were having difficulty fully communicating with them," said Chanya. Quine and Davis agreed that they needed someone in administration, and they needed someone right away. Chanya was hired.

Chanya came in and ran the show, almost as if the position was designed for her. In a hierarchal society like Thailand, a person's social status is often measured by power, wealth, professional rank, age, merit and birth.[1] She was older than the other Thais and came from a good family, and thus had great influence over the staff. When there was a problem with the staff, she would already have worked it out satisfactorily before explaining it to Quine and Davis. She hired excellent staff when they were needed, and cleared up misunderstandings between the foreigners and the Thais. Not only that, Chanya took care of Excel's dealings with the Thai government, having mastered the art of getting and renewing visas and work permits, among other things bureaucratic. Said Quine, "Chanya has been an absolute key person to have in our company."

Vincent Swift, MD of The Wright Company, an executive search firm, understands exactly how lucky Excel is.

> One of the key reasons why some businesses generally fail here or anywhere is that the managing director gets buried in administration. When you set up a small company, you're out selling. You're the face. You have the knowledge. If possible, that's all you want to do and all you feel you have time for. In reality, what

---

[1] Holmes, Henry and Tangtongtavy, Suchada, *Working with the Thais*, White Lotus, page 26

really happens is that you spend about a third of your time on marketing, a third on admin, and a third on doing the business: the consultancy, the writing of the reports, whatever. Even though in and of itself it is not a revenue generating activity, administration is critical. Unfortunately, you can get bogged down in it.

Today Chanya is an executive director of the company and her daughter Priya is also a key member of the management team. This particular arrangement was not planned or even imagined by either the foreign or Thai partners, but it is a development that both sides are pleased with. In fact, in the early days of the venture, Quine and Davis were basically advised to go the nominee route by their lawyers, but the two Englishmen couldn't see Excel building a business in Thailand without Thai expertise.

REAL PARTNERS VS. NOMINEE PARTNERS

According to the Alien Business Law, it is illegal to have nominee shareholders in a company. Clause 29 states that

> Any person of Thai nationality, holding shares in a partnership which is a juristic person or in a limited company as an agent for an alien so that the juristic person can engage in a business in violation of this Announcement of the National Executive Council, or an alien, who causes a Thai to act in such way, shall be liable to a fine from 30 thousand baht to 500 thousand baht; and the Court shall order the cessation of the business.

In other words, if a foreigner recruits the minimum four Thai shareholders in order to give the appearance that his company is 51% Thai owned, and thus legal, and both foreign and Thai parties form this company with the understanding that the only ones who can vote or receive dividends in the company are the foreign interests, this could be interpreted as illegal by the Thai courts. The Thais would be considered agents, or nominees, and the company could be shut down.

But the fact of the matter is there are probably more than a few foreigners who have started up small to medium-sized Thai limited companies using nominee Thai shareholders. Very simply, the foreigner gets his Thai shareholders, whether they be friends, acquaintances, spouses or servants, to sign a **blank share transfer sheet**. A share transfer sheet is a legal document that is used when one person transfers his or her shares to another person. This happens, for example, when one buys shares from another person, or when a person gives the shares to a family member. However, when a Thai shareholder is asked to sign a blank share transfer sheet, the space for the name of the person who is supposed to be the recipient of the shares is left blank. The foreign shareholder would actually hold this blank share transfer sheet and have another Thai sign the blank space when the original shareholder is deemed unnecessary or a threat. In this manner, the foreign shareholders maintain **illegal** control over the Thai shareholders.

Lawyers will tell you that this is a blatant violation of Clause 29 of the Alien Business Law. However, they will also tell you that no foreigner or Thai has ever been prosecuted under this clause. One reason is that the Thai nominee shareholders would also be liable under the law and, therefore, generally would not go to the police for fear of punishment. Another reason is that the Ministry of Commerce, among other government agencies, is not eager to attack foreign investors openly, first because the illegality would be fairly difficult to definitively prove, and second because they don't want to rattle the business community.

Even more than the threat of prosecution, lawyers say that the problem with the nominee shareholder route is that the Thai shareholders can turn the tables on you. Apparently there have been cases where the Thai nominee shareholders have used the threat of revealing the illegality to gain control of the company, and some-times kick the foreigners out. A very common method used by foreigners in previous years was having legitimate Thai and foreign shareholders hold 49% of the shares each, with a Thai nominee holding 2% in favor of the foreign shareholders. There have been times when the Thai nominee shareholders have decided to switch allegiances to the paid-up Thai shareholders. By threatening to reveal the illegality of the situation, the Thai shareholders can put pressure on the foreign investors to give in to the Thai demands. In this way, *de jure* Thai companies have become *de facto* Thai companies. "These people can take over your business," said one lawyer. "It does happen. Starting up with nominee shares is just stupid business practice."

So why do so many small to medium-sized businesses have nominee shareholding structures? Why not set up the company under the preference share method as described in Chapter One, a legally safe method for foreigners to control their companies in Thailand? The biggest reason is the nominee system's simplicity. Lawyers and their high fees may not be required to set up under such a system. It is common for entrepreneurs of small businesses to have an aversion to lawyers. In fact, Quine and Davis were very upset with the lawyers they initially dealt with. According to Quine,

> By the time we finished talking to our lawyers, all this mysticism about doing business in Thailand was being put on so thickly we were getting really scared about doing anything. We actually ended up paying over US$5,000 over a period of six months. And this didn't even include work permits and visas. They got us started, but in retrospect, we could have done all that in a few weeks for nothing, apart from the registration fees.

Lawyers work out very well for some, but not for others. In Quine's case, he admits to having an anti-lawyer bias and is glad that he now has the personnel to handle the initially daunting administrative tasks that lawyers get paid for. He might not have had that personnel if he had followed his lawyer's recommendation to have the Thai shareholders sign blank share transfer sheets. But after Excel dropped the law firm, somehow the blank share transfer sheets never got drawn up and signed. Explained Quine, "The simple reason why we never had our Thai partners sign the blank share transfer sheets is because we didn't want to go to the Thais who worked with us and say, 'Look, we don't actually trust you so we want you to sign these papers.'"

As a result, but probably not by intention, Excel is an uncommon example of a Thai private limited company started up by foreigners in which the Thai investors invested no capital and yet have the majority number of shareholders, shares and most importantly, votes. In essence, the Thais have more control than the foreigners.

But that doesn't overly concern Quine.

> The company is dependent on a two-way relationship, i.e. if they somehow kicked us out, the company would fail because the Thai shareholders are very much dependent on our IT skills and overseas product agreements. They would not only lose our expertise, they would lose the key products that the company is selling. There are many businesses such as the restaurant or hotel trade where the Thais might feel confident enough to run it themselves. This sort of corporate structure is not an acceptable risk for some. On the other hand, we need to be a Thai entity, and thus must have Thai shareholders. Second, our Thai shareholders are invaluable in dealing with the government and because of their understanding of the culture.

REAL INVESTMENT

The Thai law requires Thai majority share ownership in most businesses that foreigners wish to start up. Some Thais offer to become non-active shareholders for a fee. Some actually wish to invest, and maybe play an active role in the success of the company. But some will do it out of kindness, as a favor to a friend in need, with the hope of having a good long-term relationship, and not necessarily for financial gain. As Chanya said when explaining her family's decision to take up shares without investing any capital,

> The law requires 51% Thai ownership so we decided to help them. But we never wanted any financial return from them. Apart from our taking up shares, they were supposed to take care of the business. We knew there weren't going to be any problems with

the company and that they weren't going to treat us disrespectfully because we trusted David and Steve.

When Excel in Thailand was first formed in 1991, Quine, Quine's father and Davis were the only people who had actually invested capital into the company. And in 1997, Excel needed more money. The weakened economy following the devaluation of the baht in July, 1997 was certainly a blow to their revenues, but it wasn't as big a problem as the dilemma they faced at the hands of their long-time supplier.

For nearly a decade, about six years in England and three in Thailand, Excel sold a very good accounting system from a company called Helios Systems.[2] In Excel's first few years in Thailand, sales were quite good as many international companies using the Helios accounting system found it quite natural to use the same system when they started up in Thailand. However, after about three years, sales peaked and then started declining mysteriously. First, leads from Helios became fewer and fewer. Then corporations that Excel had been pursuing would suddenly be signed up to purchase the Helios accounting system, although not through Excel. It wasn't long before Quine discovered that Helios had secretly set up an office in Bangkok to sell their product directly to the Thai market.

> Helios probably first thought was that we were mad to set up shop in Thailand. But as sales went up and up, they probably sat up and thought, "They're doing pretty good business in Thailand." Instead of thinking how they could strengthen their existing affiliation in Thailand, they began to wonder if they couldn't do the deal themselves.

Quine's problem was that he was never able to convince Helios to agree to a contract that would give Excel exclusive rights to sell the Helios accounting system in Thailand. But the product was good, Helios was generally quite encouraging, and in the end, Helios's system was the only one that Excel really knew -- so Quine and his

---

[2] This is not the company's real name.

partners took a chance. Since they could not get exclusive rights to sell Helios in Thailand, they, in retrospect somewhat naively, believed that Helios would honor an oral agreement to let Excel know what plans Helios had for Thailand so that Excel could balance their marketing and investment accordingly. But that's exactly what Helios didn't do.

Quine decided to drop Helios Systems from their slim product line. I suddenly thought, "God, I'd been dealing with Helios Systems in the UK and here for nine years," said Quine. "I only know that product. This is going to be a hell of a change." Apparently, the Thai staff were even more devastated to hear the news because they had trained long and hard to learn Helios. They had visions of losing their jobs and having nothing to do. It was a difficult time. Fortunately, though, no one left.

No one left because management was able to convince the staff that Helios' replacement was even better. After examining three global accounting systems that Excel had previously considered competitors, Quine thought that Solomon Software, an American company, had an accounting systems product that had a very strong future. While the accounting world was still locked into the computer language of Cobol, Solomon had the vision several years back to develop their accounting system in visual basic, a language ideal for Windows. As everybody knows today, the Windows operating system is the fastest growing in the world. "We're learning tomorrow's software now, and we'll be one step ahead of everyone next year," Quine told his staff. When an agreement for Excel to exclusively market the product in Thailand was signed, and one of the VPs from Solomon came to visit Excel in Bangkok in October of 1996, the staff began to realize that maybe this wasn't such a disaster after all.

However, accounting systems like Solomon's aren't like the computer programs you might buy and install on your own. Solomon's system is very big and demands a great deal from the staff who implement the product, and from the management who market it. Understanding all of the components to the system and being able to customize the system to each customers needs requires a great deal of training. Educating the Thai market well enough to get them to switch accounting systems requires a great deal of effort and ingenuity. Translations of the product manuals and software have to be completed. Promotional materials have to be developed. Open seminars have to be held to inform potential clients that Solomon's is the future of corporate accounting systems. Because of the work that needed to be done to prepare the product for the Thai market, Quine anticipated that it would take one year before anything was really sold (starting from December, 1996), and two years before Excel would be fully operational for this product.

This was a major problem as Excel was generating very little revenue since it dropped Helios. And all of the retooling, training and marketing was costing Excel a lot of money. Where would they get all the operating capital from? Quine couldn't borrow money from the banks even if he wanted to the way the economy was in 1997. Instead, he got a fresh infusion of cash from his investors.

In mid-1997, Quine's original partner, Davis, decided to leave Excel to pursue another line of business, which meant that Quine not only had to source funds for his shift to Solomon, but he also had to come up with enough cash to buy Davis' shares in the company. But two Swiss men, one who had worked closely with Excel for about two years, bought Davis shares and a considerable bit more. In addition, Chanya and her daughter Priya decided to help out as well by paying up for some shares. This inflow of cash was vital to Excel's continued push into a Windows-based accounting world.

There is a concern however. Whenever real money enters the picture, real partners have the potential to squabble. Up till mid-1997, the Thai shareholders were content to merely offer their signatures as a sign of friendship. Now two of them are actual paid-up shareholders who have a financial stake in the success of the company. The trust factor especially comes into play since the shareholders have all agreed **orally** to parcel out future dividend payments along these prescribed lines: Quine contingent 52%, the Swiss contingent 40% and Thai contingent 8%. These percentages were agreed to by all parties as they reflect the percentages of real capital investment in the company, despite the official 51/49, Thai/foreign shareholder ratio.

A cynical foreigner might say that in this case, the Thai partners may get jealous of the greater financial gain of the foreign partners and may try to exert their power as majority shareholders. In Excel's case, Quine disagrees.

> It's true the Thais' proportion of shares is significant if they wanted to vote on something in the company. And it's true I could've done it with bits of paper, with nominees who have names I'd never heard of. But we've got to the stage where our confidence is right, their confidence is right, and the course of the business is right. If you're ultimately going to succeed here, and live here and enjoy working here, don't you want involvement from your Thai partners? The nominee system might suit some people. It doesn't suit us. I believe we've got a very good relationship with our Thai partners and we wouldn't have it any other way.

FOUR

BREAKING UP IS VERY HARD
The Meaning and Meaninglessness of the Alien Business Law

The Alien Business Law is the most significant law for foreigners and foreign entities conducting business in Thailand. It restricts the business activities of foreigners and allows the Thai government to determine what businesses foreigners can invest in. And yet, it is a law open to fairly flexible interpretations, interpretations which actually allow foreigners to enter and control almost any business of their choosing. A historical overview offers some clues as to why the law can seem both restrictive and flexible at the same time.

*If you get right down to it, the Alien Business Law is
in a way meaningless.* -- A foreign lawyer with over
twenty years of experience with Thailand

FROM BAD TO WORSE

Gerhardt Schmidt knew his marriage was in trouble. But business
was business. He had already paid for a booth to display his
new products at an exhibition in Europe, so he felt he had no choice
but to leave Bangkok and hope that his new offerings would
take off, and that his wife would not.

When the exhibition ended and Schmidt came back to his office in
Bangkok, his fears were justified. His wife, Malee, and their children
were gone. All the money in the company bank account -- gone
as well. Schmidt had just been robbed by his own wife, the
managing director.

Schmidt, a German national, had built up a fairly successful clothing
export business called Bangkok Traders, initially selling low-cost
goods to European clients, and then shifting upwards to high-quality
fashion over his eight years in Thailand. However, with no money
in the bank, he suddenly found himself fighting a fire that
threatened to put him out of business. He dropped a new line of
clothing. After taking stock of all his clients, their size and their
ability to pay promptly, he passed clients on to other clothing export
agents. In addition, Schmidt had to be on guard against raids by
Malee, who would sneak into the office and home while he was out,
taking furniture and various other possessions.

Malee refused to divorce him. According to Schmidt, she bought
two condos with the money she took out of the company, and as
managing director, wanted continued access to company revenues.
After months of harassing phone calls from his wife and her
relatives, and constant vigilance against further loss of company and
personal property, Schmidt finally convinced her to sign the divorce
papers. He told her that if she didn't divorce him, he would go
into her house, take anything he could pile into a truck, and give it
away to the poor people in Klong Toey. He would claim the same

right that she was claiming in terms of shared ownership of property belonging to either person. Malee knew that this was no idle threat, so she reluctantly agreed to sign the divorce papers, as well as relinquish ownership and position in Bangkok Traders.

But Schmidt's troubles weren't over. Bangkok Traders lost a lot of money when the currency of a major client's country was devalued by 30%, forcing Schmidt to reduce his workforce by two-thirds. Divorce settlement payments and legal fees further added to his financial woes. But it was the Immigration Bureau that threatened to put him out of business. When Schmidt's visa was about to expire, he went in to Immigration to reapply for his one-year visa. This time, the authorities told him that due to changes in the company structure after the divorce, he was now undercapitalized by two million baht and that he needed to hire two more Thai employees. If he didn't comply, he would have to leave the country in seven days. "I was in shock," he said. After eight years of bringing foreign currency into Thailand, Schmidt did not appreciate the government's method of showing thanks. In a letter to The Bangkok Post, Schmidt explained that he could not hire any more Thais nor find an extra two million baht. As a result, he said that in a matter of days he would have to stop paying bills, fire five Thais, find other places or countries for his customers to go, and shut down a company that he believed only benefited Thailand. "Is it still safe to invest in Thailand?," questioned Schmidt.

FORMING A THAI COMPANY IS EASIER

Fortunately for Schmidt, he was able to renew his visa, stay in Thailand and continue his export business. Very often, the Thai bureaucracy will give Thais and non-Thais alike some reason to fret, and then, for some other reason, will react the next day as if there had never been a problem. With a few visits to the authorities, all "misunderstandings" were cleared up, the appropriate papers signed, and Schmidt's visa extension was approved as if nothing had happened.

But indeed, things did happen. For a few months, Schmidt's life was turned upside down. His wife took custody of the children.

WHAT IS THE ALIEN BUSINESS LAW?

The Alien Business Law is officially known as the "National Executive Council's Announcement 281", otherwise known as NEC 281. Since 1972, this law has been, the main set of legal guidelines that help the Thai bureaucracy control the establishment of businesses in Thailand by foreigners or foreign entities. The Alien Business Law (ABL) basically divides the types of businesses barred to foreigners or for which foreigners need permission into three categories.

Category A: Businesses listed in Category A of the ABL are forbidden to foreign entities, with the exception of American businesses that are protected under the Treaty of Amity and Economic Relations. (See Chapter Five.) Thus, business entities with "half or more of its total shares belonging to aliens," or "half or more of its shareholders, partners or members being aliens, regardless of the amount of capital invested by aliens", cannot enter such diverse businesses as rice or salt farming, land trade, accounting, law, advertising, building construction or hairdressing.

Category B: Foreign entities cannot engage in businesses listed in ABL's Category B unless the company's project is promoted by the Board of Investment. (See Chapter Six.) If BOI promotion is approved, then foreign firms can operate businesses in such areas as animal husbandry, fishing, manufacturing of flour, sugar, beverages or matches, casting of Buddha images, newspaper publication, tour agencies, laundering, and transportation. An Alien Business License for Category B businesses from the Commerce of Ministry is fairly easily attained after BOI approval is granted.

Category C: Businesses listed in ABL's Category C are open to foreigners, with the condition that the Ministry of Commerce approves the company and its project and grants the business an Alien Business License. Some businesses included in this annex are wholesale trade, exporting, manufacture of textiles, glassware, crockery and animal feeds. Since January, 1996, it has been possible to apply for BOI promotion for businesses in Category C. However, the owners must comply with BOI regulations that require at least 10 million baht in share capital be paid up, and that the business have at least 10 million baht in operating expenses every year.

It is often officially stated that any businesses, usually manufacturing, that the Ministry of Commerce agrees do not fall under the three categories, can be formed with majority foreign ownership pretty much without any special permission or conditions, and this is generally true. (See Appendix 3 for the full listing of the Alien Business Law.)

She also sent the company into financial crisis and almost forced him to close down the business. Who's to blame? An argument can be made that Thailand's Alien Business Law was partially to blame.

When Schmidt first came to Thailand, his clothes were exported to Europe from Thailand, but his clients' invoices were sent from his company in Hong Kong, which is where the checks were sent to as well. However, after a short while, Schmidt knew that if he was going to continue doing business in Thailand, he had to have a legal presence in this country. When he formed Bangkok Traders, he probably didn't look closely at the Alien Business Law. No one really does. If he had, he would have learned that his business, exporting, was considered at that time a restricted business under the law. In order for Bangkok Traders to get an Alien Business License to export goods, Schmidt would apparently have had to undergo a fairly intrusive and somewhat lengthy process to get approval, much like the process to get BOI promotion, except without the privileges. Not only that, an Alien Business License lasts only up to about five years, requiring regular renewal procedures to continue operating under the license.

It is most likely that people experienced in doing business in Thailand recommended to Schmidt that he form a Thai company and avoid applying for an Alien Business License. Forming a Thai company allows a foreigner to get involved in practically any business he or she wants, provided the company is majority Thai owned. Even the most restricted businesses in the ABL are open to foreigners who set themselves up as Thai companies with Thais holding over 50% of the shares. A case in point is the company featured in the first chapter of the book, In-House, an advertising firm most definitely controlled by foreigners, but legally established as a Thai entity.

So even though Schmidt had the option of forming a foreign company with an Alien Business License, this was a less attractive option than establishing a Thai company. But in order to form a Thai company, he needed Thai shareholders. Schmidt, out of convenience, had his wife and her relatives sign up as owners of shares, although they did not invest any capital. Perhaps in foresight, Schmidt might have been wise not to make his wife a director, which may have prevented her from taking money out of the company.

But when Schmidt was asked why he gave Malee the managing director position, he said, "She was supposed to be my life partner, right? I trusted her."

In a nutshell, if the Alien Business Law had never been legislated, Schmidt would have simply formed a German company. That's what people and companies did before the the ABL was created in 1972. This structure would have made sense to Schmidt since he was the only one investing and he was the only one who had the foreign clients, and thus, he reasoned, had relatively little need for Thai partners. As the law does exist, and he did not wish to conform to the restrictions and bureaucratic procedures required to get an Alien Business License to export, he formed a Thai company and gathered Thai shareholders. Although Schmidt's wife was an exception, Thai shareholders can easily be relegated to a position of powerlessness in the company, leaving foreigners in control, avoiding any of the negative implications of the law, and basically rendering the "spirit of the law" meaningless.

So the question begs: Why does this law exist at all?

WHY DOES THE ALIEN BUSINESS LAW EXIST?

If the purpose of the Alien Business Law is to create greater opportunities for Thais to get involved in commerce, why make it so easy for foreigners to seemingly get around the law? As is often the case, laws that appear out of synch with the times often have their origins in rationales no longer relevant to society today. In the case of the Alien Business Law, there is evidence that the law was formed more as a political statement than as the best method for creating greater business opportunities for Thais.

Although foreigners were surprised to learn about the Alien Business Law when they saw their English newspapers on November 27, 1972, the law had been in the works since September, 1969. Foreigners weren't aware of this bill probably because Thailand was ruled by a military government that kept its internal workings confidential and censored the press. This may have been a fairly normal state of affairs at the time, considering that America was fighting a war in Vietnam, a country neighboring Thailand, and that the Thai government was seeking out communists. In the early 1970's, there were people in Thailand who wanted the American military bases out of Thailand, and there were others who saw the communist threat seeping in from Vietnam and China. The economy was also fairly unstable in this period. It is the consensus of some that the political and economic environment produced fertile ground for feelings of nationalism among many Thais.

On September 8, 1971, a little over a year before the implementation of the Alien Business Law, and its companion law, the Alien Occupation Law (NEC 322), the Thailand Management Association (TMA), an organization that strongly represented Thai government and business interests, held a seminar to provide participants with an overview of the proposed bills. Some of the reasons given for the necessity of such laws were:

a) that at least 80% of Thais were involved in agriculture and very few of them had enough knowledge or experience to conduct commerce;

b) that the previous law, the Act for the Assistance of Occupations and Vocations (1941), only focused on labor, not business, and never provided a definitive description of what an alien was;

c) that if Thais were required to hold 51% or more of shares in a company, this would "promote the long-range participation of Thai people in business enterprises";

d) that other countries were restricting the business activities of foreign businesses;

e) that Thai people would have more work to do and that the problems of unemployment would decrease; and

f) that foreigners tended to avoid paying taxes by transferring money out of the country, something that Thais would or could not do;

In short, the purpose of these proposed laws, according to a director of the Thai Chamber of Commerce at the TMA seminar, was to ensure that "the economy and trade will fall into the hands of the Thai people, completely or for the most part."

(With these new laws), the status of the country will become stronger. Thai people will be the producers, the buyers, the consumers, and the sellers. This would be as it once was in former times, when the government tried to encourage Thai people to favor Thai-produced items and to become aware of the importance of using items produced in Thailand itself. However, as soon as the Second World War ended, the products of foreign countries poured into Thailand and were sold at cheap prices. The Thai people who were already partial to foreign products then turned to buying these foreign products again. If the government had been really in earnest about its campaign to promote Thai-produced products and had followed up this policy to this date, then trade and the economy would be in the hands of Thai people today, more so than is now the case.

SCAPEGOATS

It was an anti-Chinese phenomenon. The concept of limiting foreign participation in certain professions originated with the laws to prevent the rising tide of Chinese immigrants in the early 20th century. At some point the Thai government felt threatened because of the hold the Chinese had on the economy. Because of that, they introduced limitations to areas of business that Chinese were engaging. That may be the genesis of the Alien Business Law. -- Michael Vatikiotis, Bangkok Bureau Chief, Far Eastern Economic Review

If not in the hands of Thais, whose hands were Thai trade and the economy in? The answer was overwhelmingly the Chinese. Of the over 100,000 registered businesses in 1973, 88% were considered Chinese. (See Table 1.) The Vietnamese and the Indians were the only two other ethnic groups that were of any significant size in the Thai business community. It is true that although Japanese and American companies were few in number, they also possessed

47

some of the highest concentrations of registered capital. However, Chinese companies were also a dominant force in terms of capitalization. (See Table 2.)

Table 1:	Nationality Breakdown of Alien Firms Doing Business in Thailand in 1973		
Nationality		No. of Firms	%
1.	Chinese	92,128	88
2.	Vietnamese	8,071	7
3.	Indian	2,473	2
4.	British	380	-
5.	Japanese	252	-
6.	American	122	-
7.	German	18	-
8.	Others	2,146	2
	Total	**104,590**	**100**

Source: Board of Investment

Table 2:	Registered Capital of Industrial Activities Already Promoted as of April 30, 1973		
Nationality of Ownership		Total Registered Capital	%
1.	Japan	957	37.0
2.	Republic of China	411	15.8
3.	U.S.A.	356	13.8
4.	United Kingdom	135	5.2
5.	Malaysia	101	3.0
6.	France	60	2.4
7.	Netherlands	50	1.9
8.	West Germany	48	1.8
9.	Others	471	18.2
	Total	**2,589**	**100.0**

Source: Board of Investment

Throughout the 20th century, the Chinese have been the target of various laws that have somewhat restricted their businesses. Fortunately, because of the relative ease of Chinese assimilation into Thai society, Thailand has never experienced the deadly race riots common in Malaysia and Indonesia. However, the Chinese were considered an alien force that was perceived to have tremendous control over the economy. Economic nationalism found its greatest booster in Field Marshal Plaek Phibunsongkram, Thailand's right-wing prime minister from 1938 to 1944, and then again from 1948 to 1957. In the 1920s and 1930s, the business-minded Chinese were emigrating to Thailand at a rate of over 35,000 per year. And in contrast to previous waves of immigration, they were bringing their Chinese wives, thus avoiding inter-marriages with Thais. With the Chinese in Thailand becoming more nationalistic as the Japanese increased their aggressions on China, Phibunsongkram, an ally of the Japanese, felt he needed to crack down on these potentially harmful aliens. During World War II, for example, Phibunsongkram moved Chinese out of border provinces, closed Chinese schools and newspapers, as well as Chinese community organizations. When China turned communist, Phibunsongkram, allied with the U.S., raided what were rumored to be communist Chinese organizations. Hundreds of these organizations were Chinese businesses.[1]

In a confidential report entitled, "Report on the Status, Effects and Implications of the Alien Business Bill and Alien Occupation Bill on the Thai Economy"[2], a Thai writer fairly intimate with the inner workings of the government of the early 1970s stated that the then new alien laws were in large part directed at minority groups in Thailand. A casual glance at the Alien Business Law that was in force until late 1998 will reveal that businesses such as hairdressing, manufacturing of alms bowls and lacquer ware, manufacturing of casting of Buddha images, and laundering are still restricted under the three categories. There's no doubt that multi-national firms in recent years were not all that upset with these barriers to trade. However, these type of restrictions probably had much greater meaning in the 1970s,

---

[1] Laothamatas, Anek, *Business Associations and the New Political Economy of Thailand*, p.22-26

[2] This document was provided by Tilleke & Gibbins. Although the author is unknown, it seems apparent that it is a translation of a document written by a Thai.

although in the end, very little effectiveness. As the report states,

> One strong motivation behind the issuing of (the Alien Business Law and the Alien Occupations Act) is to limit the job opportunities of the few large ethnic groups already settled in Thailand, more obviously the Chinese, Indians and Vietnamese. This is obvious from the facts that many occupations restricted have been the struggles between the Thais and these ethnic groups. Many occupations restricted contribute little to the economic development of the whole country. And the (laws) themselves are not effective because these ethnic groups can easily change nationality and transfer business to family members who have already been nationalized. The (Thai) employment increase resulting from minimizing competition in this direction is also insignificant.

Tilleke & Gibbins, the oldest law firm in Thailand, was asked in early 1971 to analyze an English translation of a draft of an early incarnation of the alien laws. This law firm saw these laws as a manifestation of fears of government leaders over economic difficulties, and thus questioned their appropriateness. The analysis states that some of the problems attributed to foreigners in general were spiraling land prices due to speculation, an increase in the cost of meat and vegetables, the scarcity of servants, higher home rental costs, higher bus fares, corruption of government officials, greater demand for "luxury" living, and the higher price of farm and consumer credit. On the other hand, Tilleke and Gibbins saw these problems in terms of a more affluent Thai society that "desired more comforts of life and demanded more from its government".

In fact, Tilleke & Gibbins, although not entirely supportive of the government bills, saw the government reaction to the economic difficulties as natural.

> Every country and every era of history have had their scapegoats. Thailand is presently facing an unfavorable balance of payments situation in which it is suffering a deficit, not to mention a highly volatile

regional political situation, not of its making but in
which its commitments could be embarrassing and
dangerous. People are always receptive to blaming
such a situation on the foreigner. Human nature and
anxieties fuel such thoughts.

Based on the cited source documents, there seems to be consensus
that the alien bills were created more for political reasons than for
an actual desire to create more business opportunities for Thais.
In fact, the confidential report insisted that if certain laws (eg: the
Foreign Exchange Law, the Tax and Excise law, the Company Law,
the Promotion of Industries Act, the Immigration Law and International Treaties) were implemented with any "subtlety and conceptual
skill" by certain agencies (eg: the Bank of Thailand, the Labor
Department, the Revenue Department and Immigration), then the
alien laws should have had no reason to exist. But, according to the
confidential report, they do have a reason to exist.

The alien bills serve their good purpose to present
the state of thinking and the comfortable feeling
that the Thais are being protected, and something
is being done. What is really happening is not significant. The political value of these bills are well perceived by their original proposers.

THE FUTURE LIBERALIZATION OF THE ALIEN BUSINESS LAW

The Thai business community had long believed that it was time to
take the ABL out of the Cold War 1970s and into the global 1990s.
After Prime Minister Chuan Leekpai assumed power in late 1997, he
sought to liberalize the ABL. In late 1998, a draft of a new law called
the Foreign Business Law, which will eventually replace NEC 281,
was approved by the Cabinet and submitted to Parliament. As of this
printing, the law had not been approved and was expected to undergo
lengthy debate.

Some of the proposed major changes include a significant decrease in
the number of activities which are restricted or barred to foreigners.

Previously, 68 types of businesses required Thai majority ownership or special permission from the Board of Investment (BOI) and/or the Ministry of Commerce. That number may be narrowed to about half. Although it was reported that such businesses as firearms manufacturing, harbor or international maritime carriage business and engineering may in the future be restricted for the first time to foreign entry, other previously restricted businesses may be completely liberalized. A few of the significant businesses in which foreigners may have majority shareholdings include garments, hotels, beverages, and retail establishments with over ten million baht ($250,000) in capital. (See Appendix 5 for the tentative listing of the proposed restrictions in the Foreign Business Law draft.)

The way the restricted businesses are categorized will also be changed. The current ABL has three schedules or categories: businesses barred to majority foreign ownership (Category A), businesses that require BOI promotion status (Category B), and businesses that require approval by the Ministry of Commerce. Drafts of the new law indicate that there will only be two categories in the future. Category 1 businesses are those that are said to have an impact on national security and safety, culture and tradition, traditional handicrafts, natural resources and the environment, while Category 2 businesses will be reserved for Thai ownership with the understanding that Thai firms in these areas still need more time to be competitive in the global market. Whereas foreigners currently have zero chance of owning a majority of the shares in Category A businesses, in the future they may be able to receive permits to operate in Category 1 businesses if the Cabinet grants approval. Foreigners who wish to own and control Category 2 businesses will probably require approval from the director-general of the Ministry of Commerce.

According to Kiat Sittheeamorn, a member of a committee commissioned by the Chuan administration to submit recommendations for changes to the ABL, if a business is not interpreted as falling within the revised categories 1 and 2, then approval from the Ministry of Commerce or the BOI will not be needed for foreign majority ownership. Kiat, a director of the Board of Trade, also stated that a system may be set up whereby these restricted businesses would be reviewed every two years, leaving open the possibility of further liberalization in the future. This biennial review may be conducted by a committee made up of the private and public sector, which, Kiat said, would help ensure that the ABL stays relevant to changing times. Eventual changes would probably fall along the lines of the World Trade Organization's program to liberalize world trade. "The ABL will definitely be more liberal," said Kiat.

Some foreigners are cynical about the new draft, believing that it will still be far easier and better to avoid the restrictions of the new law simply by forming a Thai corporate entity. Kiat, however, is optimistic about the future of business in Thailand, seeing the new draft as the next step in the evolution of the Thai business culture. He believes that liberalizing the ABL will certainly make Thailand more attractive to foreign investors. But he also believes that amending the ABL is just the tip of the iceberg. The economic slump Thailand is experiencing, in Kiat's opinion, is a great opportunity to transform the country into a business environment of international standards and excellence.

> This economic crisis actually has given us a lot of good things. As a result, we are forced to look at ourselves. We have to reform our industries. We have to relook at our BOI incentives and decide what areas we really need to promote. We need to examine the trade blocs and determine what our competitive advantages are. And we have to reform our political system to take us to that next level. And I think we'll get there. We will have to pay for it, but we're learning very fast.

FIVE

AN AMERICAN ADVANTAGE
The Treaty of Amity and Economic Relations

The Treaty of Amity and Economic Relations between the United States and Thailand frees Americans and American entities from many of the restrictions listed in the Alien Business Law. In other words, Americans can legally own 100% of their businesses in Thailand while other foreign entities can do so only under much more limited circumstances. This is no doubt a great advantage for Americans, as well as an occasional lightning rod for controversy as other nationalities clamor for equal status.

> *For this purpose the Siamese and the citizens of the*
> *United States of America shall, with sincerity, hold*
> *commercial intercourse in the Ports of their respective*
> *nations as long as heaven and earth shall endure.* --
> From the opening paragraph of the Treaty of Amity
> and Commerce between Siam and the United States,
> signed on March 20th, 1833

FEAR OF FLYING INTO JAIL

Peter Williams didn't like it all.

As far as he was concerned, he was at risk representing International
Specialty Products (ISP), an American multi-national that primarily
manufactures chemical products for pharmaceuticals and skin care
products. Williams believed that as the sole manager of ISP's
representative office in Thailand, he would be the only available
target for any legal entanglements that ISP might get involved in.
As he had heard that there was a thin line between criminal and
civil law in this country, he was worried about being held personally
accountable, and maybe thrown in jail, for any legal charge that is
leveled towards the company.

When Castrol Thailand was two hours late submitting a routine
monthly oil stocks report of alleged strategic importance to the
Ministry of Commerce one time in the early 1980's, ex-Castrol
managing director, Bryan Baldwin, was carted off to the police
station where he had his fingerprints taken. Baldwin said that he
was eventually given a six-month jail sentence suspended for two
years. To this day he's not quite sure why he and many others in the
oil industry were forced to have their day in a "courtroom filled with
guys in handcuffs and leg irons on rape, murder and drug charges".
In fact, Baldwin never even saw the reports that were filled out
automatically by his finance and admin people. But he suspects that
for some reason, someone got upset enough with the oil industry
and looked for a way to ruffle feathers.

Lawyers today say that fears of company executives being arrested
for such un-criminal reasons are unfounded. However, Peter

Williams still felt insecure as the head of a representative office. From the very beginning, when ISP established a rep office in Thailand in 1991, Williams lobbied the board of directors in New Jersey to consider changing ISP's structure in Thailand to a private limited company. Williams believed that a private limited company would afford him greater legal protection.

In addition, he also knew of an easy way ISP could form a perfectly legitimate 100% American-owned-and-controlled company-- through the controversial Treaty of Amity and Economic Relations between Thailand and the United States. This treaty gives Americans and American entities the privilege of forming American companies in almost every business that other foreigners or foreign entities are restricted from entering. And in the early 1990s, dissent towards this treaty by much of the foreign business community was growing. Since the treaty seemed to be on precarious ground, Williams convinced his bosses in America that this was their last window of opportunity to take advantage of the treaty.

Today, thanks to the treaty, ISP is 100% American-owned.

OBTAINING TREATY PROTECTION

However, OS/CM is not. Dr. Bennett Robinson, an American, started up this computer network consulting company in Bangkok in 1993. He was investing a significant amount of his own money and he understandably wanted to be able to control how that money was going to be used. There were very few people in Thailand who understand the complexities of high bandwidth local and wide area computer communications systems, so he was concerned about putting his money in the hands of unknowledgeable strangers who would legally own 51% of his company. He started up the company as a Thai private limited company, but when he heard about the Treaty, he decided he wanted to be 100% American-owned.

In his first year of business, Robinson was busy marketing his services. He was new to Thailand and was averse to using lawyers, so he asked his secretary to figure out how to go about filing for protection under the Treaty. Consumed by the everyday rush of

THE PROS AND CONS OF REPRESENTATIVE OFFICES

Rep Offices are a convenient structure for companies wishing to dip their toes into the hopefully warm waters of the Thai business environment. The laws permitting the establishment of Rep Offices were created in order to promote export businesses in Thailand. Thus the purposes of the Rep Office as defined by the government are to:

a) find suppliers, goods or services in Thailand for its head office,
b) check the quality and quantity of goods purchased from local manufacturers,
c) provide advice or consultation to the local agent and purchaser who purchases goods from the head office,
d) promote goods, services or information from the head office, and
e) report to the head office on movements of business in Thailand.

However, a Rep Office cannot involve itself in any profit-generating operations. In fact, one of the few times that the Thai government has cracked down on foreign businesses is when the Alien Business licenses of 30 firms were revoked in a period from November 1992 to August, 1994 because these companies were said to be illegally generating income through their Rep Offices.[12]

But the ISP board of directors in America liked the representative office structure because of its convenience. With a Rep Office, there is no need to worry about finding shareholders, losing control of a part of the business, nor any fuss about parting with partners if they thought a presence in Thailand wasn't worth it. In addition, it allowed them to have a non-taxable presence in Thailand. The Rep Office in Thailand was designed to make sure that ISP's products made it smoothly to distributors in Thailand. As far as the board was concerned, ISP's presence in Thailand didn't need to do any more than that. But Williams patiently made his arguments, and persuaded ISP to replace the Rep Office with a private limited company.

First, with a private limited company, Williams would become one of several directors. As the head of the Rep Office, he was the only one signing documents. As one of several directors signing documents, Williams believed that his share of any liability ISP might face in Thailand would be diluted.

Second, an Alien Business license for a Rep Office is good for only five years, and it is sometimes difficult to continually renew the license. After all, from

---

[12] Lyman, David, "A New Alien Business Law -- Is This Good or Bad?", a speech delivered on September 1, 1994

the government's perspective, the underlying purpose of the Rep Office is to conduct an investigation as to whether Thailand is indeed a place in which you wish to invest. The argument is that if you haven't found out in five years, then perhaps you shouldn't be here at all.

Third, ISP ultimately needed a legal vehicle to export and sell goods in Thailand. ISP was subcontracting the manufacturing of certain products to a company in Thailand in order to export to ISP operations in Singapore, which would then distribute the goods to its clients. However, ISP had difficulty selling these made-in-Thailand products to clients in Thailand. In order to prevent direct contact between the subcontractor and ISP's Thai clients, and consequently the possible elimination of ISP as a middle man, ISP needed to have a legal structure that would allow them to buy and sell. The Rep Office structure would not allow for that.

Fourth, a Rep Office still has to pay Value Added Tax (VAT) on utilities such as telephone, petrol, rent and purchases. According to Williams, a private limited company can claim back a portion of that VAT. "Depending on the size of the operation, this claim can be considerable," he said.

starting up a business, he could see that his secretary was not having success obtaining Treaty protection for the company, but he didn't really have the time or the sense of urgency to do anything about it.

Lawyers will often explain that if you or your company is clearly American, it is pretty easy to get Treaty protection. Even though Williams is Australian, all he had to prove was that a majority of ISP's shareholders and directors are American citizens. "To apply, there is a system," said Williams. "You follow the system and you get your approvals step by step. It's logical and it's 100% legal. The whole process for us took about six months."

One lawyer speculated that perhaps the reason that OS/CM didn't get it was because its business may have been interpreted as being one of the six restricted areas in the Treaty that neither Americans nor Thais can enter in the other country:

> communications
> transport
> fiduciary functions
> banking involving depository functions

      the exploitation of land or other natural resources
      domestic trade in indigenous agricultural products

Perhaps, the lawyer thought, the company business was described as it was in the OS/CM brochure, as a firm that provides clients with "digital communication business solutions." Such a description may have given any bureaucrat a reason to reject the application. The lawyer went on to explain that filling out the paperwork for Treaty protection, like anything else, is in the wording. "Instead of the word 'communications', you just say 'computers' " said the lawyer. "That's fine. That may be just bad draftsmanship on the application."

As it turns out, Robinson's secretary had never even made it to the application stage. The secretary, inexperienced in dealing with the government, found it very hard to get proper information from the related bureaucracies. She would go to a certain office and ask for specific information and they would say they didn't have it. She would call if they had this document or form and then go in, and they would still say they didn't have it. If you don't know the ropes, dealing with civil servants is not for the weak-willed.

As business picked up, Robinson no longer concerned himself with getting Treaty protection. His Thai company turned out to be a totally adequate business structure and caused him little concern. In fact, he took heart in the remarks of another person who told him that wholly-owned American companies may sometimes be at a disadvantage. Bidding on government contracts as an American company, he was told, may do him more harm than good. Williams, though, disagreed with that assessment. He found no stigma attached to being a Treaty-protected 100% American firm, and said that a reasonably-priced lawyer or consultant who can take care of everything for you could easily be found. As an official of the American Embassy stated, "We have no idea why an American firm would not want Treaty protection."

THE CONTROVERSIAL AMERICAN ADVANTAGE

Americans and American organizations have what many feel is

a significant advantage over every other foreign nationality in Thailand. American entrepreneurs and companies can take advantage of a privilege granting them the right to be exempt from the Alien Business Law. Even in the highly restricted Annex A businesses of the Alien Business Law (described in Chapter Four), if an American entity wanted to own 100% of a law firm, or an accounting firm, or an advertising firm, it could. Under Thai law, no other foreign individual or corporate entity can do that.

On June 8th, 1968, The Treaty of Amity and Economic Relations Between The Kingdom of Thailand and the United States of America went into effect.[1] The Treaty allows Thai citizens and organizations as well as American citizens and organizations to receive national treatment in each other's country. National treatment means that an American entity enjoys practically the same rights that a Thai entity would get in Thailand. For all intents and purposes, the Alien Business Law is non-existent for Americans and American companies that seek protection under the Treaty.

As a result of this privilege, the United States Embassy claims that over 400 American companies have received protection under the Treaty of Amity from 1994 to 1997. A few of the big names that are 100% owned by their American parent companies thanks to the Treaty are Coca Cola, IBM, Digital, General Electric and Esso Standard.

As one might expect, this state of affairs has not sat well with some parts of the foreign business community. The Treaty is seen as an unfair advantage for Americans. As the head of one of the foreign chambers of commerce commented,

> Well I don't see why they should have a beneficial position compared to every one else. Once, when the Thai government was hinting that they might abrogate the Treaty, the Americans wrote the other chambers asking them to issue a statement supporting their right to have their treaty, while every one else didn't. And I said, "I don't know about other people but there's no way you're going to get me to sign anything like that."

---

[1] The Treaty was actually signed on May 29, 1966.

The Thai government has predictably been under pressure by foreign chambers of commerce and embassies. In an American Chamber of Commerce memo of August, 1992, the writer expressed concern over the government's stance in regards to the Treaty. Although low-level bureaucrats had been known to comment critically about the Treaty, this time the Deputy Minister of Commerce was quoted as saying that "the treaty was a problem". Michael Vatikiotis, Bangkok Bureau Chief of the Far Eastern Economic Review has heard even harsher language by Thai authorities. "The Thais hate this treaty and want to get rid of it," he said. "As far as they're concerned it gives everybody else unequal treatment. They don't like that kind of situation."

The reply from the American business community has been fairly consistent through the years. It is not the Treaty that is at fault, but the Alien Business Law which has created this unequal footing. If the Alien Business Law is revoked, the argument goes, then the entire foreign business community would be playing the same rules on the same field regardless of the Treaty. And although the American business community realizes the sensitive nature of the issue, Americans who know the history of the Treaty feel that they have every right to protect their privilege.

FAIRNESS IS IN THE EYE OF THE BEHOLDER

A fact that Americans like to bring up is that the Treaty of Amity and Economic Relations precedes the promulgation of the Alien Business Law by over four years. In other words, the American and Thai governments had negotiated the clause about national treatment at a time when there was practically no reason to have national treatment. Before the Alien Business Law, there were very few laws restricting business practices by foreigners in Thailand. But for some not entirely clear reason, national treatment ended up becoming a clause in the Treaty. Only four years later when the Alien Business Law came into effect did the national treatment clause have any real meaning. Although one might suspect that the American government perhaps knew about the coming alien laws, it is likely they did not as the Thai government had not begun their feasibility studies into the alien laws until September, 1969. (See Chapter Four.)

It may have instead been a case where the American negotiating team was merely implementing US policy. As a Fulbright scholar based at Chulalongkorn University wrote,

> The history of the so-called FCN (Friendship, Commerce and Navigation) treaties is that they were part of a US State Department initiative to enter into bilateral commercial arrangements with other countries after World War Two which guaranteed "national" treatment with certain exceptions to citizens of each of the signatory countries in their economic relationships.[2]

Implementing this policy may have been made easier by the immense influence that America wielded as Thailand's number one source of aid and its military ally against communist forces during the Vietnam War era.

The 1968 Treaty, the one that is currently in effect, replaced a Friendship, Commerce and Navigation treaty established between the two countries in 1937. Perhaps the most significant aspect of the 1937 Treaty was its allowance for individuals and organizations to "acquire, possess and dispose of immovable property" in the other party's country. "Immovable property" is lawyer-speak for land.

In the nationalistic 1960's, foreign ownership of land in Thailand was becoming less and less tolerable to the government. Unfortunately, Thailand had treaties with seventeen foreign nations[3], allowing nationals and national entities of those countries to buy land, a situation most undesirable by the Thai powers that be. According to Harold Vickery, an American lawyer who has been consulting foreign businesses in Thailand since the late 1960's, Thailand really wanted to renegotiate the 1937 treaty with America. They believed that if America could be convinced to drop the right to land ownership, then other nations could be convinced to do the same.

---

[2] Delaney, Andrew, The Bangkok Post, September 1, 1992
[3] Besides the US, Thailand had treaties that allowed foreign ownership of land with Belgium, Burma, Republic of China, Denmark, Germany, India, Italy, Japan, Luxembourg, Netherlands, Norway, Pakistan, Portugal, Sweden, Switzerland, and the United Kingdom.

The Treaty of Amity and Economic Relations, which no longer allows land ownership in Thailand by Americans, entered into force on June 8, 1968. On February 27, 1970 the Thai government notified the sixteen other countries that their treaties would be null and void a year later.[4] Thus, from February 27, 1971, no foreign entity or individual was able to buy land in Thailand.

Americans who know will remind other foreigners in Thailand that for all the claims of unfairness in regards to the current Treaty, sixteen other nations had the "unfair" advantage of being able to buy land in Thailand for over two-and-a-half years while Americans could not.

FRIENDS SINCE 1833

When the Alien Business Law was announced to the public in late 1972, the foreign business community, as Vickery recalled, went into shock as 40,000 businesses suddenly found themselves under restriction. For many months, confusion reigned as government officials tried to interpret the new laws for the business community. Naturally, the American Embassy quickly asserted that Americans and American companies were exempt from the new laws because of the clause in the Treaty of Amity and Economic Relations that grants national treatment. Embassy officials quoted paragraph 2 of the Alien Business Law, which states that "the law does not apply to aliens who enter the Kingdom to operate...under an agreement made between the Government and any foreign governments."

According to Vickery, The Ministry of Commerce, which was primarily responsible for the passage of the alien laws, was somehow caught unawares by the existence of the Treaty. Moreover, the Foreign Ministry, which negotiated the Treaty, insisted that the Treaty superseded the alien laws. The Ministry of Commerce would have liked to have canceled the Treaty, but by law were unable to do so until ten years after the Treaty was established. It appeared that the Thai government, reluctantly, would have to wait until June, 1978 before they would have a chance to get America to conform to the new alien laws.

---

[4] Investor Magazine, May 1970

Reaction to America's insistence in maintaining Treaty privilege seems to have sparked some anti-American sentiment, if the newspapers of the time are any barometer. In an article entitled, "Ugly American Revisited?", an editorial explains, "Neither we nor the US wants us to be tied to their apron-strings but isn't it unfair on the part of the United States to seek preferential treatment from Thailand when it should be the other way round considering that the United States is the world's biggest economic power?"[5] An editorial in another newspaper stated, "No America, even if the Treaty justified you to concessions in our decree (the Alien Business Law), this is Thailand and the majority of people are for the maintenance of this decree without amendment."[6]

In the end, the Treaty was honored by the Thai government although relations with America deteriorated in the 1970s. Student protests against the military regime supported by American aid was a prelude to the eventual eviction of American military bases from Thai soil in 1975 and 1976.[7] This period was arguably one of the lowest points in Thai-American relations, adding some stress to what had been a very long and cordial relationship.

The Treaty of Amity and Economic Relations is actually the fifth in an unbroken chain of treaties that started over 160 years ago. On March 20, 1833, representatives of the United States and Thai governments signed The Treaty of Amity and Commerce. Since Thais were doing practically no business in the United States, this treaty concerned Americans doing business in Thailand. Similar to a treaty Britain negotiated with Thailand in 1826, Americans were given permission to free trade in all areas of Thai commerce except for rice, firearms and opium.[8]

Unfortunately, as people today have difficulty dealing with Thai Customs, Americans and English, even with their treaty privileges of tax-free trade, could not evade the demands of the so-called tax

---

[5] The Nation, January 23, 1973
[6] The Bangkok Post, April 27, 1973
[7] Indorf, Hans, *Thai-American Relations in Contemporary Affairs*, 1982, p. 149-150
[8] Much of the information on the treaties preceding the current one was culled from a book called *The Eagle and the Elephant -- Thai-American Relations Since 1833*

farmers. These people were given concessions by the government to trade in certain goods, and could not be persuaded that any treaty should prevent them from exacting their 10 to 30%.

Constant complaints from their nationals about the lack of free trade and dissatisfaction with the failure of their treaties to increase trade with Thailand led to demands by the British and American governments to renegotiate the treaties. Desiring greater power and influence in the region, Britain was able to secure a treaty in 1855 that was quite disadvantageous to Thailand. The following year, Townsend Harris, the American Consul General-designate to Japan, settled a similar treaty to Britain's, one that compromised the Thai government's authority in setting tariffs and settling matters of jurisprudence.

First, the new treaty insisted that Americans be charged an import duty of only 3% for any goods shipped into Thailand. Second, any Americans that had a legal entanglement with a Thai had extraterritorial rights. In other words, according to Vickery,

> If an American or a British merchant got into a dispute with a Thai, the case would be tried in a British or an American consular court, and the British or American consul would decide the case, and that would be the end of it. And if a Thai allegedly injured a British or an American or a French or a Portuguese or whatever, the Thai would be hauled before the appropriate foreign consular court, and if convicted would be placed in the foreign consulate's jail here in Bangkok. (Thanks to the new treaties) foreigners ran their own judicial system here.

The Thai rulers accepted these terms because they could see the Western powers, particularly France and England, taking over nations and territories all around Thailand. Flexibility in such matters may have contributed to Thailand's ability to remain uncolonized in those colonial times. But for decades the Thai government felt the pain of lost sovereignty.

Although America was one of the first countries to sign an unfair treaty with Thailand, it was also the first to give Thailand back its sovereignty. Thailand had employed foreign advisors since 1866. The most important position that a foreigner could hold was the General Advisor to the Government, designed for a person from a neutral country. Except for the very first one, who was Belgian, all general advisors had been American. And the American advisors who served the Thai monarchy in the first half of the 20th century had a great impact on Thai international relations.

From 1903 to 1940, seven Americans served as top foreign advisor to the Thai government. All of them possessed strong academic and professional backgrounds which undoubtedly helped Thailand reach its goal of renegotiating what they perceived as unfair treaties. Little by little, such people as Edward Strobel, Jens Westengard and Eldon R James were able to negotiate deals with Britain, Denmark and France that would lessen extraterritorial rights their nationals held in Thailand. But the breakthrough came when James helped convinced then President Woodrow Wilson to negotiate a new treaty with Thailand. Wilson, pleased that Thailand had sent volunteer troops to fight for the Allies at the end of WWI, dropped all claims to extraterritoriality for American citizens and allowed the Thai government to fix its own import and export tariffs in a landmark treaty signed in December of 1920. This led to the efforts of President Wilson's son-in-law, Francis B. Sayre, who was somehow able to convince ten European nations to negotiate new treaties, and give back Thailand its judicial and fiscal autonomy.

In World War II, the Thai government collaborated with the Japanese, and the French and British governments wanted Thailand to pay dearly for that when the war ended. The American government sympathized with the Thai government and was able to convince the British and the French to ease their demands considerably, a move which "impressed the Thai people."[9] This sympathy continued as an abundant amount of American military and police aid supported successive Thai military regimes through the 1950s and 1960s, culminating in permission to allow 50,000 American combat troops to be stationed in Thailand in 1963.[10]

---

[9] Indorf, Hans, *Thai-American Relations in Contemporary Affairs*, 1982, p. 147
[10] Indorf, Hans, *Thai-American Relations in Contemporary Affairs*, 1982, p 141, 142

THE FUTURE OF THE TREATY

The Treaty of Amity and Economic Relations is still in effect. From June 1968 to June 1978, neither side could unilaterally annul the Treaty. But there was a great deal of speculation that the Thai government would cancel the Treaty when 1978 rolled around. They never did. And now, the Treaty continues on until either side decides that the cons outweigh the pros. The American Embassy provides information stating that agreements reached at the Uruguay Round of the GATT multilateral trade negotiations will require Thailand to offer Most Favored Nation status to all member-states of the World Trade Organization by January 1, 2005.[11] In other words, by that time, all countries should be placed on equal footing with America whether the Treaty or the Alien Business laws are eliminated or not.

As stated before, some in the Thai government would prefer to see the Treaty canceled as soon as possible so that complaints about unfairness by other foreign governments and organizations would stop. The Thai government has made their discomfort with the Treaty known, but simply find it difficult to take the step of possibly offending a country that is the biggest market for Thai products and that has been so supportive of Thailand for so long.

In the very first treaty between the US and Thailand, it was written that the commerce between the two countries was to last "as long as heaven and earth shall endure." The melodrama of the words aside, Americans of influence do feel justified in protecting America's Treaty rights based on this long friendship the two nations have had. After all, they gave up the right to extraterritoriality in 1920 and their rights to land ownership in 1968, years before anyone else. While non-Americans may consider the Treaty unfair, Americans view it as the logical product and well-earned fruit of a relationship that has been worked at in good faith since 1833.

---

[11] Procedures for Receiving Rights under the Treaty of Amity and Economic Relations between the United States and Thailand, by the Commercial Service of the U.S. Department of Commerce, May 1997

SIX

SOFRAGEM IN CONTROL
The Benefits of BOI

One of the few ways to form a completely legitimate, foreign-owned and controlled company in Thailand is through the Board of Investment (BOI). This government agency has one of the best reputations in the entire Thai bureaucracy and provides many incentives for foreigners who have the technology, skills and capital that Thailand needs. Advantages outweigh disadvantages when working hand in hand with the BOI. As one foreign entrepreneur said, receiving BOI approval is like receiving a "stamp of good housekeeping."

*As for BOI I see no disadvantages. I'm 100%
foreign owned. I can do what I want.* -- Herve Mouly,
managing director of Fee Thai, a French electronics
parts manufacturer

THE BOSS ISN'T ALWAYS RIGHT

Patrick Saliou came to Thailand with US$10,000 and the desire to
show his former boss in France that he too could be successful in
business.

"I worked for a company manufacturing jewelry in France," said
Saliou. "After ten years, I got the feeling that I was as clever as my
boss, maybe even cleverer. When I gave him advice, he didn't seem
interested. So I thought, 'Why don't I keep my advice to myself and
start my own business. If I am successful it will be prove that my
ideas were correct.' And that's what I did."

After studying investment opportunities in Southeast Asia, Saliou
decided that Bangkok was the best place to start up a jewelry
factory. In the mid-1980's, to set up a jewelry factory in Bangkok
was to be "in the middle of tons and tons of sapphires and rubies
available at any price and any quality," said Saliou. "Whatever we
wanted to find, we could find." Since Saliou had very little money
to buy gold and precious stones, and thus could not maintain an
inventory of raw materials, he was pleased that he could buy any
type of stone any time he wanted.

Saliou's company, Sofragem Co. Ltd., was established in October of
1985. In the beginning, it produced low-cost jewelry at the request
of overseas buyers, copying other designs for cheaper prices than
the original designs. Starting with so little capital forced Saliou and
his partners to produce only what they knew would sell. Sofragem
was in no position to experiment with original designs for fear of
getting stuck with unsold, high-priced jewelry products. However,
after five years of building up capital, they began to design their
own jewelry and establish a name for themselves. In 1989, Sofragem
won the Thai Expo Award, a government award that goes to high

quality exporters of goods manufactured in Thailand. Today, according to Saliou, Sofragem is one of the twenty biggest exporters of jewelry in Thailand, sending its products to France, Japan, Switzerland, Germany and the US.

When Sofragem was formed, it was a typical 51/49, Thai/French joint venture. Saliou's main Thai partner, Khun Sakhon, is from a family of high-ranking civil servants, people who had been friends of Saliou's family for many years. Saliou realized that he would need a real Thai partner, a Thai on whom he could depend for dealings with the government, particularly in regards to the maze of official and unofficial rules that the government may have. "In these cases, it is better to send a Thai to negotiate with Thais," said Saliou. Khun Sakhon became the principle shareholder in the company, while three of Sakhon's family and friends rounded out the required four Thai shareholders holding 51% of the company, although none of the four actually invested any money at that time.

Saliou wasn't too happy with the structure of his company. Even though he trusted Sakhon very much, he still felt uncomfortable putting in 100% of the capital and yet being recognized only as a minority partner. To Saliou, it did not feel like an entirely legal or fair structure. And if there is any hint of illegality in Thailand, there is a greater threat of blackmail than of government prosecution. Competitors may try to exploit such suspicions by informing the authorities. Or even the Thai partner may try to use a perceived illegality as leverage against the foreign investor. "In Thailand, when you establish a joint venture, as long as the business is not profitable, it is no problem," said Saliou. "But when you are profitable, you can sometimes be forced out of the company."

Based on this perception, Saliou believed he needed greater control. But he also wanted to be able to sleep at night with a clean conscience.

CONTROL AND THE SPIRIT OF THE LAW

It's human nature to want to be in control -- whether it is control over one's personal affairs, one's job, one's company or one's destiny. And despite the seemingly restrictive nature of Thailand's Alien

Business Law, (see Chapter Four), many foreigners and Thais have found a variety of inventive methods that allow foreigners to have a minority stake in a company, and yet still be able to control it as if they owned a majority of the shares, all in apparent compliance with the Alien Business Law (ABL). Some of the methods are, according to the lawyers, perfectly legal. Other methods are more legally dubious. The bottom line is that control over the management and finances of a restricted business can easily be placed in the hands of foreigners.

It is also human nature to want to be morally upstanding, to be recognized as clean in the eyes of the law and society. As former M.D. of Castrol Thailand, Bryan Baldwin, said, structures where the nominee route is being used to get around the law or where there are shareholding arrangements whereby a percentage is held by a Thai who has insignificant voting rights "are against the spirit of the law and I would not recommend anyone to do that. If the law of the land says that the majority of the shareholding has got to be Thai, then so be it." In other words, why else would the Thai government require majority Thai ownership if not to have Thais control certain businesses.

Thus human nature's desire to be in control and to be morally correct seem to come into conflict for the foreigner in the Thai business world. Even if the lawyer assures you that your company structure has legal integrity, you may experience some angst because you perceive that you had to massage the rules and go against "the spirit of the law." American citizens and corporations have the luxury of sidestepping this dilemma through the graces of the Treaty of Amity and Economic Relations. (See Chapter Five.)

But non-American parties can have both control and peace of mind operating a business which is listed under Category B or Category C of the Alien Business Law with Board of Investment (BOI) approval.

Saliou saw the resolution to his internal conflict in BOI promotion. For the first three years, Sofragem was so small it couldn't even manage the fairly small BOI requirement of a minimum of one million baht capitalization. But in 1988, they were able to attain

BOI promotion and Saliou was able to attain complete and legal control of the company. Thanks to the Board of Investment, Sofragem and his two other French shareholders own 84%, while Khun Sakhon owns the remaining 16%, both in name and in capital. Now Saliou has both control and peace of mind.

THE ADVANTAGES OF THE BOI

Essentially, the Board of Investment is a tool to implement the investment policy of the government. Established in 1954, the BOI is a government agency under the chairmanship of the Prime Minister which is responsible for encouraging investment activities primarily in Thailand, but also for Thai companies abroad. Overall, the Board of Investment enjoys a very good reputation among foreign investors. When compared to other departments and agencies in the Thai government, it is conspicuous in its transparency and appropriate application of rules and regulations.

Although manufacturers with an export orientation have been particularly favored by the BOI, a variety of fiscal and non-fiscal incentives and guarantees are made to any project which:

> Strengthens Thailand's industrial and technological capability;
> Uses domestic resources;
> Creates employment opportunities;
> Develops basic and support industries;
> Earns foreign exchange;
> Contributes to the economic growth of regions outside Bangkok;
> Develops infrastructure;
> Conserves natural resources; or
> Reduces environmental problems.

The incentives that are most attractive to foreign investors are the tax exemptions or reduction of import duties on imported machinery, raw materials and components, the exemption of export duties, the exemption of corporate income taxes for up to eight years, the assistance of the BOI in obtaining visas and work permits for foreign managers, technicians and experts, and permission for foreign entities to own land for use in the promoted project. And

ALTERNATIVE TO THE BOI

Businesses in Thailand that are officially controlled by foreign interests are commonly BOI-promoted as well as export-oriented. However, it is possible for a company to be foreign-controlled, and to produce products primarily for the domestic market. That's what one Singaporean did.

Chua Kim Huat developed fire safety systems for many years as a project manager for off-shore industry in his native Singapore. In 1988, he decided to strike out on his own. After analyzing the Southeast Asian region, he thought that the Thai market was big and sophisticated enough to welcome his expertise. First, he started up a consultancy called Flamtechnic, which designs and installs fire protection systems in Thailand. A few years later he started up Prostar, a manufacturer of passive fire protection materials, particularly a special cement that is applied to steel to fireproof it. The fifty-story Empire Tower on Sathorn Road, a rare example of steel I-beam architecture in Bangkok, uses materials fireproofed by Prostar. And finally, Chua has registered a third company that will specialize in manufacturing active protection products, such as fire hoses, equipment for sprinkler systems and fire alarms.

This third company is called Firepower, and it is a joint venture between Singaporean and Malaysian interests. The Malaysian company is called SRII. This company has expertise in active fire protection, so Chua thought that they would be an ideal partner. However, SRII is a publicly traded company in Malaysia, and SRII's board of directors insisted that SRII own the majority of shares and thus have some control over Firepower. As explained previously, there aren't many options for foreign shareholders who wish to have clear control of the company. In a nutshell, companies that are promoted by the BOI are often permitted the right to be exempt from the Alien Business Law's requirement to have majority Thai ownership. But BOI-promoted companies generally need to be export-oriented, and Firepower's products were destined primarily for the domestic market. Thus, Chua's only other choice was to get an Alien Business License under Category C of the ABL. In this category, foreign interests are allowed to own a majority share in certain manufacturing businesses. Approval for the license lasts up to five years, and has to be renewed every three years. However, it allows Firepower to fulfill its requirements of being 100% foreign-owned and a producer primarily for the domestic market.

of course, there is the legal right for foreigners to control a company under certain conditions.

Foreign Control: Interestingly enough, in the early 1970s, the BOI supported foreign control of a variety of manufacturing projects, particularly large ones. At the time, before the Alien Business Law was announced in 1972, there were very few Thai individuals or companies that could afford to invest 51% or more into such large scale ventures. Probably as a result of BOI's perspective, foreigners today can possess a majority shareholding in BOI-promoted businesses, especially those whose production is exported. But despite published criteria, the BOI is usually willing to negotiate on the majority percentage of alien ownership in foreign investment included in Category C of the Alien Business Law, as well as those which sell a substantial proportion of manufactured output on the local market.

Visas and Work Permits: Obtaining visas and work permits have been a chore for foreigners for decades, which is not so unusual anywhere around the world. However, foreigners working for projects promoted by the BOI have found it immensely easier to get the proper authorization to work in Thailand by virtue of the BOI's great cooperation and influence in cutting through red tape. In addition, it has gotten considerably easier for people associated with projects promoted by the BOI. In June of 1997, the BOI opened the One-Stop Service Center for Visas and Work Permits. It is what its name implies -- a place where officials from the Immigration Bureau and the Department of Employment (formerly called the Labor Department) come together to speed up a notoriously slow procedure. Getting final approval for visas and work permits from the two responsible government agencies routinely takes months and repeated trips to Immigration and Labor, departments located on seemingly opposite ends of the city. Now, the one-stop center has a mandate to complete the processing of visas and work permits in an astounding three hours, with the caveat, of course, that all necessary supporting documents are presented at the time of application. Amazingly, the one-stop center is a success.

Tax Incentives: Thailand is basically divided into three geographical zones by the BOI. Zone 1 includes Bangkok and its surrounding

provinces, and is the zone which receives the least amount of promotion by the BOI by virtue of its already established industrial and
business base. Zone 2 covers ten provinces that surround Zone 1.
Zone 3 is essentially the less economically developed regions in the
North, the Northeast and the South of Thailand. Accordingly, the
incentives offered for the location of a business in Zone 3 are the
greatest of the three. (See Appendix 3 for listing of BOI tax incentives
and Appendix 4 for map of BOI zones.)

Right to Own Land: A company called Firepower is a 100%
foreign-owned and -run manufacturer of fire protection equipment.
According to Singaporean managing director Chua Kim Huat,
Firepower owns 2,000 square meters of land in the Samut Sakhon
Industrial Estate. Although it is a bit inconvenient for Chua as he has
to drive at least three hours to get to the site, he finds owning land to
have its advantages. "Why should I lease and pay every month for
nothing," said Chua. But when I buy the land, it's mine and I can use
it to borrow money from the bank."

Both BOI and the Industrial Estate Authority of Thailand (IEAT)
allow companies to own land on which their business is conducted.
Other than foreign oil companies which can buy land if they meet
the requirements of the Petroleum Act, these are the only ways that
foreign companies can buy land. BOI-promoted companies are
often located inside IEAT industrial estates. But BOI-promoted
projects could also be, for example, hotels, hospitals, parking lots
and warehouses, which means they do not have to be located within
industrial estates. If the company decides to end its BOI-promoted
activities, it has one year to sell the land. If an IEAT promoted
company decides to end its business, it must transfer its business
and thus its land to another company, or sell the land back to the
IEAT at market price within three years. This seemingly strict law is
to emphasize that land ownership is a privilege for foreigners, and not
an opportunity to speculate or invest in property.

Of course, a Thai company, (ie: a company that is at least 51%
Thai owned), can also own land. However, any Thai company that
has 40% or more foreign ownership and wants to buy land will
probably have to undergo a thorough investigation over several
months by the Land Department. The authorities want to determine

whether a land purchase is motivated by business issues related to the specific goals in a company's Memorandum of Association, or by land speculation, and whether the company is majority Thai "owned".

THE INCONVENIENCES OF BOI

Most people who manage projects promoted by the BOI feel the advantages far outweigh the disadvantages, if disadvantages can be said to exist at all. Instead, there are inconveniences in regards to paperwork, The Customs Department, and changing business strategies, which, of course, can on the most part be avoided if the BOI is avoided.

Under BOI's Watchful Eyes: Under the BOI, promoted companies need to submit extensive amounts of information about the company during the application process and throughout the promotion. Every six months profit and loss statements have to be submitted. There's the possibility of officials from the BOI coming to inspect your premises once every year. The BOI will look at your records carefully to see if you are conforming -- whether you are using the machinery you say you are using, or importing the materials you say you are importing. According to Mr. Sylvain Bredin, the former head of CFME-ACTIM in Thailand, a French government consulting agency with the purpose of assisting French companies in setting up operations in Thailand, some foreign businesses aren't ready to make their internal operations such a public matter of record. In fact, he said there have been cases where information entrusted to the BOI is leaked to competitors of the applying company. When you apply, you submit such information as the breakdown of your costs of production, your market, your customers, your machines and your production capacity. According to Bredin, some people in the BOI have actually been fired for selling such information.

The BOI's appetite for paperwork is also seemingly insatiable, which is why it is heavily recommended that BOI-promoted companies have someone on the payroll strictly to deal with the BOI. As William Heinecke of the Minor Group noted, "BOI is a bureaucracy. There's

THE INDUSTRIAL ESTATE OF THAILAND (IEAT)

Many manufacturers, whether they are BOI-promoted or not, or whether they are export-oriented or not, commonly locate within industrial estates. If you locate your factory within an industrial estate that is managed by the IEAT, you are eligible for certain benefits, including the right to own land.

The IEAT is an independent government agency under the Ministry of Industry which coordinates and manages the activities of over 20 industrial estates. An industrial estate is like an enclosed industrial town, complete with the infrastructure necessary to handle the transportation, communications, security, electricity, water and waste disposal needs of manufacturers. Banks, schools, and shopping centers are also available for the convenience of people living and working within certain industrial estates.

There are two types of IEAT-managed industrial estate: Export Promotion zones (EPZ), and General Industrial zones (GIZ).

Export Promotion Zone: An Export Promotion Zone is, as its name suggests, an area for manufacturers that export. In order to stay in the EPZ, companies are required to make at least 80% of their annual sales overseas, including sales to companies within that or other Export Promotion zones. In many ways, the EPZ is like a foreign country with borders delineated by a fence, with a customs office at the entrance and a warehouse to expedite the process of importing raw materials. Goods manufactured in an Export Promotion Zone would be taxed if sold to companies located just outside the EPZ's fences.

Similar to BOI promotion, companies establishing a factory in an EPZ or GIZ can receive certain privileges. In addition to ease of visa and work permit processing for foreign experts, technicians and their dependents, and ease of remittance of money overseas, companies in an EPZ can usually also get exemptions from import duties for machinery, equipment and raw materials, as well as export duties. Different from companies promoted by the BOI, IEAT factories are not eligible for corporate tax holidays, unless they also apply for BOI promotion.

General Industrial Zone: A General Industrial Zone is for factories primarily set up to sell goods on the Thai market, although goods may also be exported. Many Thai manufacturers, as well as a few foreign-controlled companies that manufacture mainly for the Thai market are found in a General Industrial Zone.

Of course, it is possible to have a factory in an IEAT industrial estate and be BOI promoted. In such cases, the following privileges are added to the basic BOI privileges if a BOI promoted company chooses to establish itself in an IEAT industrial estate:

1) exemption from corporate tax for an additional three years;
2) fifty percent reduction on income tax for another five years;
3) ten percent reduction on electricity costs for five years; and
4) reduced cost on transportation from relevant authorities.[1]

---

[1] Hummel, Anita Louise and Sethsathira, Pises; *Starting & Operating a Business in Thailand*, 1991, p. 70

a lot of paperwork because they want to know if you are constantly meeting their qualifications. You got to have a fully registered, properly capitalized company with the BOI. But a lot of small companies and entrepreneurs, people who just want to figure out ways of doing business by doing all sorts of shady things, figure they don't need BOI. But BOI is like the Stamp of Good Housekeeping."

Saliou, in fact, sees some good in all this control because it forces him to focus on business basics. "We are certainly more controlled than when we weren't BOI, but in a way it's good because we need to have good management. And since from the beginning we want to be right in the eyes of the law, we like having the clear rules and regulations. We have been here eight years and in all these years, we have never had trouble with the BOI."

Customs: The Customs Department is arguably the most independent body in the Thai government. Anecdotal evidence in the newspapers about Customs ability to thwart importers, exporters and the will of other government bodies is somewhat commonplace.

(See Chapter Eight.) One of BOI's great privileges is the right to import machinery and raw materials duty free or at a considerably reduced tax. Saliou, when Sofragem was granted BOI promotion in 1988, thought he could import machinery and equipment from France free of tax. But according to Saliou, Customs blocked clearance of the shipment. BOI sent a letter to Customs at Saliou's request, but Customs did not release the shipment. Instead they demanded to know what type of alloy the machinery was composed of and told Saliou to break off a piece of the machinery and send it to their laboratory for testing. "I then said, 'OK, how much do you want?' They said they wanted the tax." Saliou paid a fee under the table to avoid the testing and to get his goods through Customs.

Another time, Saliou was requested to translate the invoice of a shipment into Thai. When he provided a translation with the original English, Customs told him that the translation wasn't very good. When Saliou again had BOI intervene, Customs reasoned that they were not against BOI's privileges, and that Sofragem didn't have to pay import duties. But according to Saliou, Customs said "we have the right to know if the material that the machine is made of is pollution free, if it is going to bring disease to the Thai people." It is certainly one of the mandates of the Customs Department to safeguard against the importation of harmful objects into Thailand. However, Saliou could not be convinced that those were the honest intentions of Customs. He had twenty people in the factory at that time. The last thing he needed was for them to sit for weeks doing nothing while his shipment sat in a Customs warehouse, for which Sofragem would be charged significantly. Customs said that if Sofragem paid the tax, which they were supposed to be exempt from, then they would get their machine. So he paid.

"The BOI privilege of import duty exemption was meaningless to us," said Saliou. "Customs really is a kingdom inside a kingdom."

However, others deal with Customs in a different manner. FEE Thai is a French company that manufactures electronic components for export. When Herve Mouly took over the company, he decided to import a great deal of new machinery. With the BOI privileges, he did not expect to pay any import tax. But Customs held the shipment -- for three months. "We waited," said Mouly. "Customs said they wanted this and they wanted that, but we waited. And we never paid. So we started using the new machinery three months late. Now we have a real reputation at Customs that we never pay."

Mouly was a bit reflective about this sort of situation, hinting that Customs isn't always in the wrong, and the BOI isn't always ineffective. "Basically, the experience I've had is that if the BOI says it's OK, Customs follows it 100%. When we pay the taxes it is because we made a mistake. If we don't prepare the documents perfectly, or we import something we're not supposed to be importing, we end up paying. Many companies try to cheat. But when you have everything correct, it goes through."

Changing Strategy: Another basic inconvenience is that BOI-promoted companies have to work hand-in-hand with the BOI in order to get approval for changes in management or strategy. This is because BOI promotes the company's project, not the company itself. Thus, for example, exporters are very often promoted because they provide Thailand with foreign currency, one of the BOI's main mandates. However, managers in companies like Sofragem sometimes feel that they are missing opportunities on the domestic front. According to Saliou, Sofragem sells nearly 100% of its jewelry overseas, and he believes he can sell up to 5% on the local market without worrying about informing the BOI. In fact, with special permission, Saliou knows that he can sell up to 20% locally. But at this stage, Saliou doesn't see the need to do so as sales overseas are still keeping his small company quite busy.

This really hasn't been a major problem for Sofragem or for FEE Thai as both companies do not really intend to sell to the domestic market in the immediate future. However, Bredin said that managers of some companies are somewhat frustrated at not having the domestic market as an option.

> Many companies set up factories in Zone 1 export processing zones in the Bangkok area several years ago, which means that they can only export. They didn't care about the domestic market. But up to the mid-1990s, there was great competition in the overseas market and potential in the domestic market, and

they couldn't take advantage. If they had a choice to set up again, they might now go to Rayong (about 220 km outside Bangkok), a Zone 3 area that would allow them to export and to sell locally. But moving a factory means great expense and loss of experienced staff and workers, so they are stuck with their original plans in changing times.

Any major changes in strategy would have to be renegotiated with the BOI. If the change in strategy is more important to a company than BOI promotion, then by all means change. Otherwise, any major changes require a reapplication process. And as Heinecke states, that's how it should be. "If you reapply, the worse thing that can happen is that you just don't get a second BOI promotion. You can't blame the BOI because quite frankly, when they encourage you to apply, they never say it's a lifetime of not paying taxes. It's supposed to be for five or six years to help get you established and to help make you money. Then you're supposed to become a good corporate tax payer."

****

When Saliou first began thinking about a move to Asia, the last place he wanted to come was Thailand. Saliou's impression of Bangkok at that time was that it was "a city of traffic and pollution, a place where the people are right even when they are wrong and are lazy, and where the government is not powerful. But today, I will forever recognize that I came here with a ridiculously small amount of money. And after a lot of hard work every day into the night, and two heart attacks, I made it. Sofragem has a good reputation and is well off. And in my opinion, this success could only have been achieved in this country."

SEVEN

WORKING WITHOUT A WORK PERMIT
It-Will-Never-Happen-To-Me Stories

Getting permission to work in Thailand can be difficult or easy, depending on who you talk to and how you go about it. For some, it's just a matter of knowing someone with the expertise in obtaining a work permit. For others, it is either too inconvenient or too difficult to secure one. For such people, working without a permit can sometimes place them in compromising positions. It is rare, but foreigners do get caught working illegally, and do get denied approval for work permits. Here is how two people dealt with such situations.

"The life of the law has not been logic: it has been experience." -- Oliver Wendell Holmes, Jr.

GETTING ARRESTED

Takashi Suzuki[1] had just finished a quick lunch and rushed back to his office to write a report for a client. His one-room office was humble, but business had been good ever since he started up his accounting consultancy three years before. Today was particularly busy because one of his assistants was on holiday and the other was at a client's company. When he got to his desk, he noticed that there was a message on his answering machine. It was his wife, Hiroko.

"I've been arrested and taken to Immigration. I will call again as soon as I can."

Shocked by the words and the tenseness in his wife's voice, Takashi sat down in his chair. After about a minute, the confusion in his brain gave way to clarity, and a sense of mission. Hiroko was working for a Japanese company called Kumaneco Tours. Kumaneco provided tours throughout Thailand for the Japanese, particularly those already living in Thailand. As many Japanese feel comfortable dealing with others in Japanese, companies like Kumaneco feel compelled to hire Japanese staff. Japanese-speaking Thais are few in number, and therefore quite expensive. More importantly, however, Kumaneco management felt that Japanese staff could deliver service with the proper touch of etiquette that only a Japanese would understand. Hiroko was hired for those reasons.

However, Hiroko was hired without a work permit. Because work permits are sometimes very difficult to get, especially if basic Labor/Immigration directives are not fulfilled, small companies will break the law by hiring non-Thais and paying them in cash under the table. The rule of thumb these days is that a company should be capitalized for at least two million baht and have four Thai employees for each foreign employee with a work permit. Of the seven Japanese employees at Kumaneco, only two had proper work permits and visas.

---

[1] All of the names in this case are aliases.

The phone rang. It was Hiroko. She explained that at around 10:30 am six plain-clothed policemen stormed the Kumaneco office. They sealed off all the possible exits and began shouting out the names of the five Japanese employees who were working illegally. One of the five was absent that day, but Hiroko was one of the four present. She was ordered to stop working. Her picture was taken at her desk. The police officers milled about, looking into files and taking pictures. And then they all waited, although Hiroko didn't know what they were waiting for. The manager of the company, Tetsuya Gotoh, did nothing but offer the officers coffee, which was refused. After about an hour, the police finally took the four Japanese without permits to the Immigration Department.

Gotoh, who was working for Kumaneco legally, went with the other four Japanese to Immigration. According to Hiroko, Gotoh said that he had informed Kumaneco's headquarters in Singapore of the situation and that a lawyer would be coming to Immigration to help. Other than that and a few phone calls here and there, he didn't really seem to be doing much. In fact, Immigration didn't seem to be doing much either. And when the clock struck twelve, Immigration staff and officers alike left for lunch. The Japanese were left waiting, without a clue as to what was going to happen next.

When Takashi got off the phone with Hiroko, he made one phone call. He called an older gentleman named Shinichi Satoh who had retired from his position as director of a large Japanese trading firm in Thailand and who had settled down in Bangkok to live out the rest of his life. Satoh was an old friend of Takashi's father. When Takashi and Hiroko first came to Thailand, Satoh very graciously helped them integrate into life in Bangkok by helping them find their first apartment, providing advice as to how to start up Takashi's consultancy, and being a sympathetic ear during frustrating times. More importantly, Satoh had lived and worked in Thailand for about twenty years and knew how to get things done. Satoh listened to Takashi's story carefully, and then told Takashi to hang up the phone and wait.

Takashi sat at his desk and waited, wondering very nervously what might happen to them. Would Hiroko be imprisoned? Would she have to pay a fine? Would she have to leave the country? Would her passport be stamped, forbidding her entry into the Kingdom again? Would their three wonderful years in Thailand come to a crashing halt?"

An hour passed before the phone rang again. It was Hiroko and she announced in a very relieved voice that all four Japanese were being released. After getting off the phone with Hiroko, Takashi called Satoh. "Oh, have they released Hiroko?" he asked. "That's good news." Takashi asked Satoh if he had played any part in her release. "Oh, I made a phone call to a friend of mine. He said he would take care of it."

However, Satoh also explained to Takashi that Kumaneco would have to pay a fine of thirty thousand baht to the authorities, ten thousand baht for each of the illegal employees, excluding Hiroko. He told Takashi to get the money from Kumaneco and then pass it on to Satoh. Satoh would then pass it on to the appropriate person.

After being released by the authorities and being warned not to work illegally again, Hiroko returned to Kumaneco's office with the others and announced that she was quitting her job. Gotoh looked surprised and asked Hiroko to reconsider. After all, no one else was quitting and Kumaneco really needed Hiroko. Hiroko packed up her things and left.

THE PATRON-CLIENT SOCIETY

When Hiroko joined Kumaneco Tours, she and the director of the company signed a contract that stated how much she would earn, what hours she would work, who she would report to, and how she could be terminated from her position. Everything in the contract was in English except for a single line in Japanese which said, "In the case of any trouble regarding visas, this company will not be liable." Since this contract was not going to be seen by anyone other than Kumaneco and the hiree, this clause in Japanese was obviously used by Kumaneco to absolve itself of any responsibility, and perhaps to make the hiree feel vulnerable. "If you get arrested, that's your fault, not ours."

It is true that the foreigner who joins a company under illegal conditions is knowingly taking a chance, but in Thailand, the odds of getting caught are quite small. The rare times one does get caught is when someone informs the authorities and tells them to raid the company. And this is what is strongly suspected as the reason for the raid of Kumaneco. More than a few Thais had quit the company previous to the raid, upset with the reportedly callous nature of certain Japanese managers. All it may have taken was one person getting upset enough to set the wheels of betrayal in motion. The authorities had the names of all the illegal Japanese employees. Only someone who had recently worked at the company would have that information. If management of the Thai staff had been more effective, perhaps Hiroko might still be working at Kumaneco. But even if Kumaneco refused to accept responsibility, they should be fully aware that the very act of hiring a person without a work permit is against the law. (Section 22 of the Act on Aliens Occupation) In fact the directors of Kumaneco could have been fined upwards of 60,000 baht, and imprisoned for up to three years.

After this incident, Takashi and Hiroko had a renewed respect for the importance of power and influence in Thailand. On the one hand, the laws seem straightforward and easy to understand. Hiroko and Kumaneco broke the law. On the other hand, so many others seemed to be breaking this same law. Hiroko's former colleagues had very little concern about resuming work that very afternoon. And in fact, anecdotal evidence indicates that the consequences for foreigners getting caught working without a permit is not all that terrible. Every so often, business centers get raided as authorities conduct sweeps in search of illegal aliens, some of whom are working for big foreign firms. Officially, the penalty for working without a permit is a maximum 5,000 baht fine and/or a maximum of three months in prison. Usually a phone call to the right person will take care of this embarrassing matter, resulting in a fine and a suspended sentence for a year. On the rare occasions when the authorities are adamant about deporting the illegal alien, the person is usually deported with an unblemished passport and is sent back to Thailand by the company on a new visa.

Sometimes you get caught, sometimes you don't. Sometimes you are given a work permit, sometimes you aren't. Sometimes you are stopped for turning left at a particular corner, and sometimes you're not. To foreigners from more industrialized nations, this seemingly arbitrary enforcement of rules and laws, and the settlement of such problems through third parties and money, smell of corruption and create a cynical impression of Thailand's officialdom. "The laws and rules exist in this country purely so that bureaucrats and lawyers can make money," said one ten-year English expat. "They don't exist for the protection of the people. The winner of any legal case will be the most powerful person, not the person who is right. In a moral or legal sense, the winner will be the person who can pay the most money to the right people. The law in Thailand is merely an excuse for bureaucrats to make money. Period. That's the way it works."

Some foreigners in Thailand find this statement to be an exaggeration, although they can understand the frustration that this particular person feels. In this case, however, the law was on the side of the authorities. Yet the influence of a long-time Japanese resident of Thailand with the authorities was able to resolve the situation in the best interests of all those involved, if not in the best interests of the law itself.

This is par for the course for patron-client societies like Thailand, a social system that has also created a people who are admired for such qualities as tolerance, kindness and good-naturedness.

> The patron-client structure exists and continues to exist because everyone concerned sees it as a good structure which brings benefits in terms of stability, order and the resolution of potentially destabilizing conflicts. The patron-client relationship continues to be important because institutions which bridge people and the state are still weak. The patron-client relationship connects officials to the people and is the most organized system to allocate social gains and interests. The patron-client relationship flourishes in a society where these is no equality in property, status and power. Little people must find a patron and offer respect, gifts and services in order to ensure favor and security. Big people try to build up their clientages in order to maximize the flow of gifts and favors. People in high office must generate

> enough money to provide resources and protection
> for their followers in order to maintain their loyalty
> in the context of keen competition among different
> factions.[2]

A disgruntled employee may have used her "Big" person to put pressure on Kumaneco. Satoh, Takashi's "Big" person, got Hiroko out of trouble with a phone call. The police looked into the matter, perhaps with the intent to do justice, perhaps to receive cash to pass on to their "Big" person, who might then filter it back down to his "Little" people.

The English expat did qualify his cynicism by stating that the system is slowly changing as more and more people in Thai society get wealthier. "And these people are going to get more and more pissed off at paying people off as time goes along."

THE LEGAL/ILLEGAL PARADOX

And yet, there remains a paradox for many foreigners living in Thailand: "I very much want to follow the letter of the law and be an upstanding citizen of Thai society, but if I somehow get in trouble with the law, I am hopeful that a way will emerge for me to get around the trouble." This is probably true of many people around the world, from shoplifters to embezzlers, from housewives to CEOs. But in a country like Thailand, foreigners, especially Westerners, may feel the paradox is more apparent here.

Why? One reason may be because Thailand is more of what can be called a particularist society, a cultural type in which people look at a situation in terms of relationships. This contrasts sharply with a universalistic society where people tend to see a situation in terms of universal standards and principles that should not be wavered from because of relationships one has with the people involved. People of 38 different nations were given a situation in which their friend is clearly responsible for hitting a pedestrian with his car.

---

[2] Phongphaichit, Pasuk and Piriyarangsan, Sungsidh, *Corruption and Democracy in Thailand,*
1994, p.4

They were then asked if a friend has a right to expect them to protect him. While only ten percent or fewer Westerners responded that the friend had the right to expect such loyalty, nearly four times as many Thais said he did.[3]

Thais are far more particularist, and therefore relationship-oriented, than many of their Western counterparts. As one well-known cross cultural management expert wrote, "A universalist will say of particularists, 'they cannot be trusted because they will always help their friends'; a particularist, conversely, will say of universalists 'you cannot trust them; they would not even help a friend.'"[4]

It could be said that there is a greater laxity in the enforcement of laws in Thailand than in universalistic nations. For example, as Chua Kim Huat of Firepower explained, the reason that fires can be so disastrous in Thailand is not because the laws don't exist, but because the government doesn't spend the money to go out and enforce the laws. "The law states that your building must have fire protection, but the fire door might be sub-standard. Maybe they put a sprinkler system in, but they installed it incorrectly. Nobody checks."

When laws are not strongly enforced, those laws are in jeopardy of being ignored. Is that good or bad? It probably depends on your perspective. If you don't think the law is a very relevant one, then you're probably interpreting the laxness in terms of an advantage. That's certainly how Happy Steiner[5] sees it. As the American said, "I find the legal system here helpful because it's so flexible." Steiner should know. He thought Thai restrictions against employment of foreigners in managerial and technical positions were a bit outdated since Thailand in the 1980s and the 1990s was undergoing a tremendous shortage of skilled human resources. When he applied for a work permit that would have legally allowed him to be the general manager of a chain of restaurants, his application was denied. But in Thailand, and other particularist nations, there is often a way around laws that are perceived to be impractical, and Steiner found one of them.

---

[3] Trompenaars, Fons, *Riding the Waves of Culture*, p. 32
[4] Ibid.
[5] Happy Steiner is an alias.

FINDING A WAY

Steiner came to Thailand because he had never been in the region before. Asia's economy was expanding while the rest of the industrial world was in decline or recovering, so he wanted to be where the action was. "Thailand was booming," he said. "So I thought, "There'll be something for me here.'" He was right.

In his first few weeks in Thailand, Steiner thought about what gap he could fill in this market, and decided to try his hand at making sausages. When he explained his plans to the foreign owners of a local chain of western-style restaurants, they thought Steiner might be the type of person they needed to manage their restaurants, which were generally losing money. The owners offered Steiner the position of general manager and assigned him the task of getting more customers to come to the restaurants.

After signing a contract to become general manager, Steiner applied for a visa and work permit. He had the company's lawyer help with the paperwork and assist with the civil servants in the appropriate bureaucracies. The process is usually several months long with repeated requests for more copies of documents, more photos or more trips to the immigration or labor departments. But with a little persistence, Steiner should have gotten his visa and work permit. Unfortunately, he didn't.

This was quite a shock to Steiner, who hadn't expected to be turned down. He was told that his application was rejected "on the grounds that my background was too general, and that a Thai could do the job." He and the company shareholders were disappointed and didn't believe that the market for skilled Thai human resources was deep enough to give them a general manager that could turn their business around. However, they tentatively accepted the decision. The ruling, although somewhat uncommon, was along the lines of how the work permit system is viewed.

The granting of a work permit is discretionary, and a number of factors designed to protect the job market for native Thais are considered in determining whether the work permit will be issued. These factors include: whether a Thai national could perform this work, whether the work meets the requirements and needs of Thailand, and whether the foreigner meets all the necessary qualifications specified under the law.[6]

For two years, Steiner worked without a work permit as unofficial general manager. Every three months he had to hop in and out of the country in order to renew his tourist visa, making visa runs to other countries. In the beginning, he was very uncomfortable defying the law.

> I was scared. I never expected to do anything illegal. But since I was rejected, I felt that I was really doing something illegal. I didn't go to the office for a long time. I worked at home. I was afraid that someone from Immigration would show up.

Tired of making visa runs, he decided to reapply for a work permit. He thought about fabricating his qualifications so that he would have the academic and professional qualifications that would impress the authorities. But he was reluctant to blatantly lie. Having changed lawyers, Steiner was asked to consider another option. Steiner could start up his own company. Thai companies can be set up with a very wide-ranging set of objectives (see Chapter One) which would allow Steiner to become a consultant to the restaurant chain, a person who would provide advice in terms of marketing and management.

And that's what Steiner did. A company was set up, very silent Thai partners were arranged, and the paperwork was properly drafted to represent a company that made a strong enough appearance of being legal. Despite the charade, the work permit was granted and Steiner now "consults" for the restaurant company.

However, as Hiroko and Takashi's story indicates, this "flexibility" of the law can lull a foreigner into a false sense of security. If you have broken the law because you have seen many people break that same law without facing any consequences, or you have skirted the law, like Steiner did, then you could be setting yourself up for

---

[6] Chandravithun, Nikom and Vause, Gary, *Thailand's Labor and Employment Law: A Practical Guide*, page 55

bigger troubles. If someone gets upset with you or your company, you could be blackmailed or visited by the police.

On the other hand, in this nation of particularists, it would then be your turn to rely upon the gracious generosity of a loyal friend to help pull you out of the legal mess you managed to get yourself into.

IS GETTING A WORK PERMIT HARD?

The answer to this question is "It depends". Those foreigners who have had to personally go through the experience of obtaining their non-immigrant visa and work permit have not necessarily had an easy time. English is not always spoken very well by the people who you deal with at the various government agencies. And the paperwork, a significant amount of which has to be in Thai, can seem excessive.

But the process can be mastered as many companies, foreign and Thai-run alike, have staff who know how to obtain and renew visas and permits. Usually it's a matter of finding the right people to give you the right information, being persistent, and facing the bureaucrats with a pleasant demeanor. "The main thing is that we wouldn't go away," said Douglas Whittaker of Guardforce Thailand. "This large, smiling farang with his little Thai wife and this young Thai lawyer. Actually they gave up pretty quickly. It took three full days, just sitting there smiling." And if you can afford to do so, there are plenty of lawyers or agents, big time and small, who have the know-how and connections to get the job done. As lawyer Harold Vickery said, "I can't imagine a client ever having a work permit application turned down."

Another long-time lawyer in Thailand, John Hancock, wants foreigners to put Thailand's work permit and visa process into perspective. "Do you know what it's like going through U.S. Immigration," asked the Australian. "I've spent hundreds of hours there. A lot of people will never know what it's like to enter their own country as an alien. They don't realize that their country can be just as bad, or even worse."

EIGHT

DELANEY'S DILEMMA
Dealing with The Customs Department

Customs can cause terrible headaches for importers and exporters anywhere in the world. Thailand is certainly no exception. Foreigners experience great frustration in getting their products, materials or possessions in and out of the country. Corruption within this particular bureaucracy is often cited as the biggest reason for these headaches. However, it is important to understand that there may be other reasons than greed why your goods are prevented from entering or leaving the country as swiftly as you would like.

> *There's nothing unusual about Thailand which would*
> *make Thailand any different from any other country.*
> *I mean if you're worried about moving goal posts and*
> *bureaucracies and regulations, the United States*
> *has got plenty of high fences for people to climb over.*
> *So what's the difference between the United States*
> *and Thailand? None. We don't find our members*
> *having any trouble with work permits, or with*
> *Immigration. <u>Customs, however, is another animal</u>.*
> -- A Governor of the American Chamber of Commerce
> in Thailand

SO LITTLE TIME, SO MUCH TO DO. . . .

Three months. That's all the time Stuart Dawson Montgomery
was given to open up Delaney's The Irish Pub, now called
Shenanigans,The Irish Pub. In August, Montgomery, the then GM of
Delaney's, was given the responsibility by the shareholders to open
its doors on Saturday, November 25, 1995. The opening date was
advertised and the shareholders had promised all their friends that
Delaney's would be the first Irish pub in Thailand with Guinness on
tap. This was a matter of face for some of these high-powered foreign
businessmen, and they hired Montgomery to open without delay.

> I didn't have time to mess about. I had a critical path
> of at least 300 operations to complete. And each day
> I had ten or twenty of those things to do: buying
> uniforms, monitoring construction work, negotiating
> insurance, talking to suppliers, sorting out advertise-
> ments, hiring and training staff.

Montgomery, who has since started up a competitor of Delaney's
called O'Reillys Irish Pub, worked at a harried pace from day one,
dealing with unsatisfactory construction work, suppliers who didn't
feel the need to give Montgomery's then unknown pub the time of
day, and a government bureaucracy with its concomitant thirst for
paperwork. A franchise of Delaney's International in Hong Kong,
Delaney's Irish Pub in Bangkok was supposed to be a turn-key
operation, according to Montgomery. In other words, Montgomery

and the shareholders of Delaney's in Bangkok thought that Delaney's International was going to come in and start up a Delaney's, train Montgomery how to operate it, and ensure a smooth opening. Unfortunately for Montgomery, he had to do a bit more than just turn the key.

Delaney's is an Irish pub and the owners wanted it to be authentic in look and feel. The Irish Pub Company, a Dublin-based design and construction company which specializes in creating authentic pub interiors in Ireland, was commissioned to produce and ship a large proportion of the furniture and decor for Delaney's in Bangkok. The furniture and bric-a-brac from the Irish Pub Company would be the key to recreating the feel of a traditional Victorian house pub with its polished dark woods and chunky, sand-blasted lighter woods, stained and polished glass, green punch-stitched leather and gun-metal iron work. It was a Friday in early October when the group general manager from Delaney's International in charge of the turn-key operation told Montgomery that a container of furniture would be arriving in Bangkok the next day. "My boss was going off to Hong Kong that evening and he said, 'Just make sure the thing's out of Customs tomorrow.'"

It took over 40 more tomorrows before the shipment was sitting in the Delaney's parking lot, arriving a little over one week before the scheduled opening.

TROUBLE CLEARING CUSTOMS

The Customs Department would not release the shipment because, it seems, the customs inspectors weren't satisfied with the paperwork provided. Exactly what they wanted was at first unclear. This was primarily due to confusion as to who was supposed to accept responsibility for clearing the shipment through Customs. Montgomery was led to believe by Delaney's International that the shipment would be a door-to-door operation, meaning that the shipping company in Dublin was responsible for dealing with Customs. The shipping company in Dublin apparently didn't think that Customs clearance would require any special effort, and thus commissioned a Bangkok company only to transport the goods from the port to Delaney's, not to clear Customs. Thus, for several weeks, no one was really interacting with Customs.

But after a great number of telephone calls and faxes between Bangkok and Hong Kong, Hong Kong and Dublin, and Dublin and Bangkok, it finally appeared that the Customs Department found the commercial invoice unacceptable. The commercial invoice is a detailed list of goods in a given container issued by the manufacturer or the company selling the goods. Apparently, the invoice was written in a way that described the contents of the container in a very general way -- certainly a reason for Customs to be suspicious.

Importers, exporters and Customs people the world round play the invoicing game. Tourists coming home from their holidays overseas very rarely declare anywhere near the full value of the goods they bring into their home countries, if they declare. And often as a matter of habit, exporters will often underinvoice (under-value the goods) a bit in order to decrease the tax burden. Or they will do so to help offset any unofficial payments commonly required to clear Customs in countries like Thailand. The Irish shipping company was actually instructed in the way to write the invoice, but for some reason, this advice was ignored. "We told them, 'please underinvoice it and please call it this, that or the other,'" said one of Delaney's shareholders. "And they just completely ignored the instructions that we gave them. We very nearly had to ship the stuff out of the country and bring it back in again under a new set of documents. Everybody knows this is a game. And if you screw up, Customs will make you pay for it."

Customs continued to hold the shipment. And Montgomery began to get worried. November 24 was rapidly approaching and there was practically no furniture in the place. "It was frightening," said Montgomery. "The furnishings were the key to the pub. If they didn't arrive, we wouldn't have a pub to open." There were repeated requests for a more thorough listing of the container contents, and repeated refusals by the Irish shipping company to admit any error by resubmitting a newly worded commercial invoice. Montgomery's worry was that if Customs decided to open up the container, Customs would take all sorts of time trying to determine the classifications of a wide variety of custom-made furniture and decorative items, and assess them at arbitrary values.

In the end, it came down to a Thai consultant, often employed by one of the shareholders, who went down and got the shipment out as a personal favor to Montgomery. The Thai hired a Customs agent who acted as a go-between, and finally worked out a negotiation that resulted in a very large payment to Customs. Call it a backhander, call it a facilitation payment, call it whatever you wish, but the shipment got cleared a week before the opening, the furniture was put in place, and Delaney's was able to open up as scheduled.

A KINGDOM INSIDE A KINGDOM

Almost everybody doing business in Thailand, Thai and non-Thai alike, has some tale of woe about the Customs Department. Whether you are importing or exporting goods or materials, there is a good chance that you will have to wait much longer and pay much more than you expect, until you've figured out how to handle the situation. As explained in Chapter Six, Customs at times can seem like "a kingdom inside a kingdom", a force so strong it can thwart the will of the most powerful people and government agencies.

One foreigner who works in the shipping business said that he once had great difficulty shipping out some outdated transportation equipment for the Thai military, traditionally the most powerful part of the Royal Thai Government. "We had the original signature of the general who headed the chief of staff on the documents," he recalled. "We had a colonel who went down to the port with us every day to try to get the documents taken care of. They would say, 'you need these documents', which we would then get from the military. We'd go back and sit down with the same guy, and then he'd say, 'Oh, didn't I tell you about this document?' And then you'd move to the next desk and he says, 'Hmmm, I need these forms filled out.' I think it took us three–and–a–half months of continuous effort to get the export permit we needed for this equipment. For the Thai military!"

An Irish company called Aer Rianta also had problems with the Customs Department, which may have resulted in their demise in

Thailand. Commissioned to operate the Thailand Duty Free Shop (TDFS) located on the seventh floor of the World Trade Center shopping mall, Aer Rianta was given the mandate to help convince shoppers going to Hong Kong and Singapore to come to Thailand for all of their high-priced shopping. Expectations were high because of this company's great successes around the world, particularly in Dubai and Moscow. But after two years of a five-year contract, the Thai government decided to end their relationship with Aer Rianta and pass the reigns of control to a Thai duty-free operator called King Power International in June of 1997. The reason given was that TDFS had had a net loss of over 200 million baht at the end of 1996, and a total loss of 367 million baht since it opened in late 1995. Its total assets of 551 million baht were dwarfed by debts of over 700 million baht. However, Aer Rianta, a division of Aer Lingus, the Irish national airline, strongly rejected claims that they were responsible for TDFS's severe financial difficulties. One of the main reasons they cited for their troubles was the Customs Department's insistence on receiving 15% of TDFS revenues. Headed by Chuan Leekpai at the time of TDFS' establishment, the government had exempted the company from the traditional Customs Department claims, but Customs simply ignored the Chuan administration directive and collected their 15%, a significant blow to Aer Rianta's bottom line.[1]

CUSTOMS AND CORRUPTION

There is absolutely no doubt that the Customs Department is a revenue-generating giant. What may be unclear is what percentage of income generated by the department actually goes into the government treasury. For example, for business people who import goods into Thailand, there is basically a two-tier payment structure: one for legitimate Customs duties payments and another for under-the-table payments. Customs knows that importers are not necessarily declaring exactly what is in their containers. If they suspect there's a significant discrepancy, they can hold up clearance of the shipment. It eventually boils down to two choices for the

---

[1] Information about TDFS was garnered from Bangkok Post articles dated March 25, April 28 and June 18, 1997.

importer. He can wait, and maybe end up paying about 30% of the goods' value in taxes, or pay a fee of only 10% of the goods' value to the Customs official to ignore the official tax. Understandably, most importers go for the smaller fee. And of course, the 30% payment would have gone into the government coffers, while the 10% payment goes into the pockets of various Customs' officials.

Inside Customs there are many steps to cover and many people to see. First you have to have all the necessary documents, e.g.: commercial invoice, business license and import cards. Then you have to get your commercial invoice approved and stamped. Then starts a series of trips to a great number of desks and officials stationed in different areas on different floors of the Customs house. And as demonstrated in the example of the Thai military's experience, you can get bogged down at any point in the process.

In fact, even if he has successfully cleared Customs, an importer's troubles don't end. Although Customs gets a bad rap, the Port Authority of Thailand is also said to be a hive of checkpoints and people to pay off in order to get a shipment from Customs to the truck that will take the shipment to your door. A foreign executive in the shipping business explained,

> Let's say I need to get this shipment to my truck. There's a system where it costs some baht to get your shipment from the boat or airplane and through the gate. You identify your container. But the port officials require fees. Whether you pay or not will depend on whether you want your container at the front of the line or the back of the line, and if you want your truck to wait fifteen minutes or three days. There are guys who operate forklifts and cranes at the Port who own BMWs and Mercedes, even though their salaries are about 8,000 baht a month.

According to a survey conducted by The Nation[2], during the period from the arrival of a ship at a Thai port to its departure, a total of 34 unofficial payments have to be made to officials of Customs, the

---

[2] The Nation, July 7, 1997

Port Authority of Thailand and Immigration. These payments range anywhere from several hundred for officials and guards escorting vessels in and out of the port, a couple of hundred baht for guards to watch your goods during the loading or unloading of cargo, upwards of 800 baht for immigration officials to visit your vessel, to 3,000 baht for a new deratting exemption certificate. As one well-known academic stated, "a corrupt bureaucracy means hidden operating costs that reduce competitiveness" for investors in Thailand.[3]

One long-time resident of Thailand who operates his own import business understands this problem all to well. He has to import his goods on practically a daily basis and has his own people handle the Customs clearance process. Every year he has to pay four to five million baht in Customs clearing, of which about half is what is often called "tea money".

> And yet, at the end of the year, none of that tea money can be claimed as a business expense. Millions of baht. That is an expense which is not an expense. It is an expense which I cannot claim. There are no receipts. So you kind of resent that. It's like one arm of the government is saying, 'You have to pay us this money under the table.' But the other arm of the government is saying, 'Well, that's not an expense.'

Like many others, this businessman sees these "expenses" as a symptom of a much bigger problem, the often-stated endemic nature of corruption in this country. "It's not just the Customs Department, "he said. "It's endemic. You are basically faced with paying tea money every day of the week, six days a week, fifty-two weeks a year. And the thing that irks me is the fact that your employees are in on it. You know that there's an arrangement between the officials and your employees who take cash to the airport. You know that your employees are putting some of that money in their pocket."

Stories abound of individuals finding ways to get a piece of the action. One small expat businessman recalls his own experience

---

[3] The Bangkok Post, June 22, 1997

100

when he was in the business of selling machines that manufactured plastic cards, much like a credit card or a membership card for a club or restaurant. He was on the verge of selling a machine to a leading hotel in Bangkok. The hotel wanted to produce cards as part of a promotion, so he suggested that the hotel buy the machine and that his company maintain it. The two parties agreed in principle, and then the expat got a phone call from the hotel's EDP manager who requested a cut for his approval of this expenditure. The deal fell through over that.

In a major reorganization effort, a foreigner was asked to take over a manufacturer that was in financial trouble. It was a company that was selling its products briskly, but at a loss. However, this was never a concern for the previous managing directors of this public company. What they did was establish their own trading companies, buy the product from the factory at very low prices, and then sell the goods to clients at a considerable markup, resulting in losses for the manufacturer and practically pure profit for the trading companies.

There may be some truth to claims that corruption, at least by Western standards, is a fairly broad-based social problem in Thailand. In a survey of staff of multi-national firms, a Berlin-based organization called Transparency International ranked Thailand as being the twenty-first most corrupt nation in the world in 1998. (See table 1.) In fact, corruption may be such a fact of life in Thailand that the Customs Department is considered a relative lightweight in bureaucratic corruption. According to a survey conducted by two Chulalongkorn University academics, the Customs Department, for all its notoriety, was ranked only tenth when a wide range of Thai citizens were asked the question "Thinking of corruption, what government offices do you think of most?"[4] (See Table 2.)

Be that as it may, except for the occasional foreigner who goes down to Customs and successfully gets his shipment without paying by raising hell, it is a state of affairs that most Thais and experienced expats accept. "Corruption is not going to go away tomorrow," said

---

[4] Phongpaichit, Pasuk and Piriyarangsan, Sungsidh, *Corruption and Democracy in Thailand*, 1994, p.144

Table 1: Least and Most Corrupt Countries in the World

Cleanest Countries (Marks out of ten)		Most Corrupt	
1	Denmark 10.0	1	Cameroon 1.4
2	Finland 9.6	2	Paraguay 1.5
3	Sweden 9.5	3	Honduras 1.7
4	New Zealand 9.4	4	Tanzania 1.9
5	Iceland 9.3	4	Nigeria 1.9
6	Canada 9.2	6	Indonesia 2.0
7	Singapore 9.1	7	Colombia 2.2
8	The Netherlands 9.0	8	Venezuela 2.3
8	Norway 9.0	8	Ecuador 2.3
10	Switzerland 8.9	10	Russia 2.4
11	Australia 8.7	11	Vietnam 2.5
11	Luxembourg 8.7	11	Kenya 2.5
11	United Kingdom 8.7	13	Uganda 2.6
14	Ireland 8.2	14	Pakistan 2.7
15	Germany 7.9	14	Latvia 2.7
16	Hong Kong 7.8	16	Ukraine 2.8
17	Austria 7.5	16	Bolivia 2.8
17	United States 7.5	18	India 2.9
19	Israel 7.1	18	Egypt 2.9
20	Chile 6.8	18	Bulgaria 2.9
21	France 6.7	21	Yugoslavia 3.0
22	Portugal 6.5	**21**	**Thailand 3.0**

Source: Transparency International, 1998

Bruce Crampton, the man who started up the first business center in Bangkok in 1986. "You and I are not going to change it. Even the Thais are not going to change it that easily. It may slowly evolve and get better, as it has in other countries. You should consider these payments as part of the expenses of the shipment. It's their way, not your way. Why don't you go down and get the best deal you can?"

Table 2:   Most Corrupt Government Offices in Thailand

Thinking of corruption, what government offices do you think of most?

		Percent
1)	Police Department	33.7%
2)	Ministry of Defense	27.0
3)	Ministry of Interior	26.0
4)	Department of Transport	22.5
5)	Land Department	10.1
6)	Ministry of Commerce	7.6
7)	Ministry of Agriculture	7.0
8)	Ministry of Industry	3.8
9)	Ministry of Finance	2.4
10)	Customs Office	1.9

Source: Phongpaichit, Pasuk and Piriyarangsan, Sungsidh,
Corruption and Democracy in Thailand, page 144

A HISTORICAL PERSPECTIVE

There is evidence that Thais and non-Thais may have varying perceptions on what is considered corruption. Although the seemingly countless fees to get goods imported or exported tend to accumulate into fairly significant amounts, Thais see these payments as part of a practice that has been as much a part of Thai culture as its food and its language. According to Pasuk Phongpaichit and Sungsidh Piriyarangsan, two Chulalongkorn University professors who have fearlessly wrote on the topic of corruption in Thailand for years, the Thai attitude toward the Thai bureaucracy has been a passive and accepting one based on centuries of conditioning.

They claim that modern-day corruption in Thailand is a natural outgrowth of the administrative structure of the nineteenth century Thai monarchy. Officials in the traditional government systems received appointments and titles from officials higher in authority but did not receive an income. The way officials made money was to collect taxes or fees for services rendered for the king, and to take a 10 to 30% cut as remuneration for themselves. Official tax farmers under the auspices of the king collected significant amounts of money for the king's treasury in such businesses as opium, lottery, liquor, gambling, tin and rubber. To pursue these ends, the kings of this period gave tax farmers a free hand in running their operations as they saw fit. Officials in general, and tax farmers in particular profited mightily from this relationship.

Even when administrative reform in the late nineteenth century created a centralized bureaucracy based on idealistic Western standards of meritocracy, and where civil servants received a salary for their services, government agencies continued the tradition of taking a percentage of the revenues they collected for their own personal use. These government agencies were filled with members of the elite families in Thai society with strong ties to the king, people who did not allow anyone of lesser rank to enter these prestigious positions. In a sense, civil servants in Thailand have traditionally been servants who owe their allegiance to the king, or at least to the bosses above them, not to the public at large. In fact, the Thai word for civil servant is *kharachakarn*, which literally means "servant of the King".

The Customs Department today may still be viewing their role in this way. As they have access to a great source of revenues in taxing exports and imports, it is safe to say that they have the money and the power to thwart the will of almost any other government agency, let alone a small business entrepreneur. Thais have grown accustomed to this exercise of power and have learned how to adapt in ways that are congruent to values Thais hold dear. As Pasuk and Sungsidh explain, what Westerners might consider bribes are seen as relationship building tools in a patron-client construct. (See Chapter Seven.)

> (People) still see bribes given to officials as *sin nam jai* or gifts of good will, which are acceptable or tolerable. At the same time, officials rationalize that since they do not request the bribes overtly, there is no moral or social wrong incurred in receiving gifts which are "willingly" presented to them. The giving and

receiving of bribes in this way is considered a "mutual transaction" between two individuals. It therefore creates no damage to any one else, or to the society   at large. In short, the transaction is acceptable as it is done in the context of *khwam mi nam jai* or generosity, which is upheld as a good thing under the social value system.[5]

NOT CORRUPT ABSOLUTELY

To say that the Customs Department isn't corrupt would probably draw more laughs than nods. However, two things about the Customs Department should be understood. First is that Customs is basically non-discriminatory. They will take anybody's money, whether   the entity is a Thai student sending her belongings back from her university in the States, a large multi-national, or the Thai military.

Second is that not everybody in Customs is on the take. Shipping agents are the people who know the ins and outs of Customs clearing. They know who to pay the unofficial fees and how much. And they make a fairly decent income helping individuals and companies move goods in and out of the country. One shipping agent was quoted in The Nation as saying, "The Customs Department has a very bad name for corruption. It's unfair for other officials in the department who do not take bribes."[6] The foreign executive in the shipping business said that there are of course many honest people in the Customs department, people who follow the Custom Department's guidelines and refuse to abuse their power. There's little incentive for them to blow any whistles because that would only jeopardize their position, but they carry out their jobs with the honest dignity and pride that the position of civil servant can embellish in certain Thais.

However, he said that a lot of problems are created by officials who have a need to feel self-important, people who will make you wait, ask for additional paperwork, or change the requirements. For

---

[5] Phongpaichit, Pasuk and Piriyarangsan, Sungsidh, *Corruption and Democracy in Thailand,* 1994, p.149

[6] The Nation, June 22, 1997

example, one time you may have been importing saucers and cups at a 5% tax rate. The second time around, you're charged 10% because your saucers and cups are no longer white, but blue. These are people who want you to know who the boss is, at least in their little crevice of the bureaucratic world.

But to be really fair, what may be interpreted by Thais and non-Thais alike as foot-dragging and veiled requests for tea money may instead be genuine confusion over how to deal with a particular shipment. This may have been partly the case with Delaney's shipment and its vague description of the furniture in the container.

The biggest problem the Customs Department faces is the task of classifying goods. Customs has an official list of goods complete with tax rates for each item. The problem is that the classifications are outdated and not entirely suitable to the millions of different items that are now routinely sent across borders throughout the world on a daily basis. For example, the foreign executive explained that if you wanted to bring your cat or dog into Thailand, you would not be able to find the classification for pets in the Customs listing of importable items. Instead, your pet is categorized as a farm animal because that's the only classification available for animals. "The whole mind set is that you're going to eat or breed any animals you bring into the country," he said. "And we had a situation where a client brought in male, neutered cats. The Customs official, however, insisted on categorizing them as farm animals as if our client were going to try to breed them."

When such liberties in interpretation can be taken, they will be taken. The executive explained that when his company had to import multimedia computer equipment, complete with cpu's, monitors and video equipment, the shipment got taxed at the rate for the cables that came with the equipment because that was the item that had the highest taxable rate in the container. "Thai customs officials have a tendency to classify a shipment by the highest valued item," he said.

Not only that, Customs at different points of entry will classify goods in different ways. David Bedford, who imports office equipment through his company Central Office Products (as featured in Chapter Twelve), once experienced a double standard between the airport and the seaport. When Bedford imports laser cartridges air freight, the tax at the airport is 5%. When he imports them by sea, Customs at the Klong Toey port demands a 20% import tax. The difference lies in the two ports' interpretations of the classifications. As far as Bedford is concerned, the airport Customs is correct in its interpretation that his laser cartridges are a powder ink product. However, the port Customs calls his laser cartridges a photographic chemical. When Bedford tries to explain to the seaport Customs officials that he is able to import his products at a 5% tax through the airport, "They just say that the people at the airport don't know what they're talking about."

The foreign shipping executive explains that Bedford's experience is a common one. "The reason this happens is because the airport is more accustomed to bringing in and clearing high value, high-tech items," he said. "Thus they are more up to date on the rules, regulations and tariffs on these items. They're usually faster too." The executive said that it is usually possible to convince the seaport Customs to change if you can show that the airport Customs have already made a determination on a product's classification. But with Customs, as Bedford found out, there are never any guarantees.

AND, AT LAST, A WONDERFUL NIGHT AT DELANEY'S

On the morning of Saturday, November 25, 1995, Montgomery told the shareholders in an emergency meeting that he was dead set against opening up Delaney's as planned. After all, the pub still hadn't installed its furniture because construction work was still going on inside. The drinks suppliers had delivered only 20% of what was planned for opening day, and the Guinness draught from Ireland, a key to distinguishing Delaney's from the rest, for some reason hadn't even made it to Bangkok yet. On top of that, the pub staff hadn't even had a dry practice run because nothing was ready. But the shareholders still decided to go ahead with the opening. In the remaining few hours, the workers furiously worked on the first floor, furniture was brought in from the parking lot, and the staff rushed to clean the pub before Delaney's first patrons walked in though the doors at 6pm. "It was sheer chaos," said Montgomery.

But in the end, opening night was a great success. Scheduled as a three-hour "soft opening", customers ended up staying until after midnight. Although there was nothing but peanuts to eat, they drank what was available and Delaney's actually ended up making a bundle on their first night. As the night progressed, Montgomery could see only glaring problems. But Delaney's first customers just didn't seem to notice.

> We knew there were problems and the pub wasn't even complete, but they thought it was finished. They thought it was a fantastic place. I was worried about the service, the control over the bar and the workers who were still putting together the closed-off second floor. But from the customers' point of view, everybody was happy. And that was the only thing that mattered.

'Tis.

NINE

GUARDFORCE'S SEARCH FOR MANAGERS
The HR Dilemma in Thailand

As foreign investment sparked and fueled a booming economy in Thailand in the late 1980s and early 1990s, there rose a tremendous demand for skilled and knowledgeable blue- and white-collar workers. Thailand's work force, although large, has been comparatively inadequate in meeting the demand. It has been said by many that Thailand's weak educational system has not worked to produce a large, educated work force, thus greatly limiting the number of Thais who can compete for management or technical positions. The smaller the HR pool, the smaller the chance of getting the human resources you need to handle the systems and technologies you may be introducing to Thailand.

> *Ironically, the biggest problem I faced in setting up
> my search company was finding the right people to
> do the work.* -- Vincent Swift, M.D. of The Wright
> Company, an executive search firm.

A BAD DREAM

"This was not a figment of my imagination. This was worse than a
very bad dream."

Doug Whittaker felt like he had entered the Twilight Zone. After
years of hard work shaping Guardforce Thailand into one of the
country's biggest security systems companies, Whittaker discovered
that chaos was reigning in his bread-and-butter business, the
Security Guarding Division. This division is divided up into eight
zones throughout the country. And for a while, unknown to Whittaker,
certain zones had somehow become independent fiefdoms, lorded
over by the operations officers. The operations officers hired security
officers whom they liked, very often friends and family members.
The security officers, unfashionably known as guards, fought
over the cushy posts in the posh hotels to avoid duty out on the streets,
and won over the operations officers with kickbacks. And on those
long nights with nothing to do, the gambling began. Then came the
gambling debts. It was as if the very worst aspects of the patron-client
culture had taken root in this division. Said Whittaker,

> You can create a very nice little way of life if you're
> an operations officer because you've got a zone
> with four or five hundred guards, a few nice looking
> ladies amongst them, a little bit of debt from gambling,
> and a little bit of income from kickbacks for
> arranging the nice spots.

Whittaker had no idea this problem was brewing in his rapidly
expanding company until he got an angry phone call from a client
who insisted that one of Guardforce's security officers had worked
36 hours straight at the client's factory. Whittaker thought that was
strange since he had implemented systems to avoid situations

110

where a guard worked too long to be effective in his duties. "To hell with your regulations. He was there 36 hours," was the angry reply.

Whittaker went straight to the Thai general manager of the company, who, as well as being second in command of the company, was in charge of the operations officers. When Whittaker asked why this environment existed in the Security Guarding Division, the general manager, according to Whittaker, hemmed and hawed a bit. What Whittaker perceived to be the problem was that in Guardforce's relatively quick jump from 700 to 2,000 security guards, the general manager had somehow lost the respect of the operations officers in the Security Guarding Division. Once matters got out of hand in certain security guarding zones, the GM had little idea how to handle the situation, other than to try to cover up the situation. In fact, he instructed the control room manager, the person who manages the information hub for all of the secured sites of Guardforce's clients as well as coordinates the movements of all security officers, to ignore the problems and to just answer the phones. She knew there was a problem, but she was too afraid to go behind the GM's back and tell Whittaker.

AN IMPOSSIBLE DREAM?

Whittaker is an ex-London policeman. He left England and worked on oil rigs throughout the world, making very good money in the process. On an impromptu vacation between jobs, Whittaker decided to take a look at Thailand. He remembers stepping off the plane at Don Muang Airport in 1977, looking around at the green lushness of the land, a welcome contrast to the barrenness of southern Iran where he had worked the oil rigs.

In his forties, Whittaker was tired of being away from family and getting covered in oil and muck, so he decided to settle down in Thailand. Always one to seek advice, Whittaker asked his friend Bryan Baldwin, the then managing director of Castrol Thailand, where he could apply for a job in the security business. Baldwin said, "Why are you looking for a job? I know you've got a little money. I've got a little money. Why don't we start our own company?" After all, at that time in the late 80's, there was a need for a reliable service. Baldwin explained that at that time, security was little more than slapping a uniform on a farmer and sending him off to take responsibility for stopping crime.

On New Year's Eve of 1988, Metropolitan Guarding Systems started operations. Castrol and the British Club were instant clients. They still are today. Metropolitan was so attractive that the Guardforce Group of Hong Kong, now a part of the First Pacific Davies Group, decided to become a major shareholder in the company about eighteen months later. Under Whittaker's leadership, Guardforce Thailand grew from four people to over three thousand, and was turning over about 25 million baht a month in 1997.

And yet, Whittaker could never really picture himself becoming a business tycoon. He instead looked forward to the day when he could relinquish control to somebody else, "work a maximum two days a week, and spend a lot more time on my bar stool or the golf course enjoying myself." And it was his genuine hope that when the time came he would be able to pass the reins of power to a Thai. Unfortunately, that hope has faded. Not only is Whittaker grooming another foreigner for the managing director position, he doesn't see himself hiring another senior Thai manager before he retires.

Whittaker had very high hopes for the general manager before his fiasco with the operations officers of the Security Guarding Division. In fact, Whittaker hoped to be replaced by this particular Thai. He felt the GM was an honest man who performed very well his first two years on the job, but somehow lost control of an admittedly "scurrilous little bunch" in that division by failing to stick to the scheduling and manpower control systems that Whittaker felt were solid in concept and practice. Whittaker gave him severance and had the GM leave the company. If it were just this person, Whittaker might still be intent on having a Thai successor. However, he said that he had been let down on three or four occasions by Thai executives in his company, too often for his liking.

Most recently, his Thai contract manager, a step below general manager, was held accountable by Whittaker for not being aware that 9 million baht in invoices had never left the third floor of the Guardforce offices. Invoices from nine months to a year back had been sitting in the desk of the contract manager's assistant, gathering dust instead of generating needed cash to pay off debts. Whittaker was wondering why his clients weren't paying, when in fact his clients were wondering why they weren't being charged. According to Whittaker, the contract manager said that he had done his job, but that his assistant hadn't.

This made Whittaker's blood boil. Although Whittaker had believed that Guardforce had a good system of checks and balances in the invoicing system, he did see that further checks had to be implemented to avoid other multi-million baht mistakes. What he couldn't see was why this contract manager not only didn't see the problem, but also why he didn't really feel personally accountable.

"This is a guy who is almost general manager," Whittaker explained with poorly concealed frustration. "This is a guy earning over 80 thousand baht a month, with a bachelor's degree from a British university. We're not talking about a dummy. We're talking about somebody with a substantial education."

As far as Whittaker is concerned, part of being accountable for a decision means checking to see if what has been delegated has been done. "Thais do not like checking on detail. Many Thai managers will delegate the authority and the task. But they also have to make sure that it has happened, and as much as I love them, their work habits are sometimes undisciplined."

This is not an uncommon observation for foreigners in Thailand. One must realize that the blame for having ineffective Thai managers could very well lie with the foreign managers themselves, for hiring unqualified people in the first place, for not placing or utilizing those people in the right places, for not giving those people the proper training or orientation to assume those responsibilities, or for having them operate within systems that aren't actually effective. However, there are two other major possible reasons why Whittaker may be having trouble finding the Thai manager of his expectations: one is cultural and the other is economic.

CULTURE AND MIDDLE MANAGEMENT WOES

One cultural explanation may be that many middle managers, and even executive level managers in Thailand are not used to such Western managerial concepts as accountability, delegation and initiative because of the hierarchal nature of the society. Ever since the Ayudhya period (1350-1767) of Thailand's history, when Brahmanist influence from India created a social structure in which the King was deified and the rest of society from the King's first son down to the lowest peasant was ranked in a somewhat rigid caste-like system, Thai people have been used to the idea that some people have a lot more power than everybody else. Although the Thais of the younger generation are more knowledgeable and understanding of Western business practices and thinking, the hierarchal tradition of Thai society has had a significant effect on basic business practices and structures within organizations in Thailand.

> Given the Thais centuries-old orientation towards deference, inequality, submission to bureaucratic rules, and highly personalized and centralized decision-making, it should come as no surprise that even today many leading local companies have tall hierarchies, autocratic leadership, top-down communication, and centralized decision-making processes. . . . For most Thais the proverb that encourages one "to walk behind a superior to avoid being bitten by dogs" still holds true.[1]

Many middle managers do what they are told, and thus, are not used to having authority. In addition, the Thai-Chinese, who have played a dominant role in Thailand's economic development, can be quite autocratic as well as discreet by nature, resulting in few chances for non-family members to maintain strong management positions within such family businesses. If the big boss is always making decisions, checking and implementing even the tasks that the middle manager is theoretically responsible for, then the middle manager never learns how to play the responsible, accountable boss. When this

---

[1] Chansuthus, Daryl and Roongrernsuke, Siriyupa, *Conflict Management in the Asia Pacific*

manager switches companies and enters an environment that asks him to take the initiative, make decisions and follow up on delegated tasks, he may feel a bit overwhelmed by his duties.

HUMAN RESOURCES STRETCHED THIN

The economic boom of the late eighties and early nineties that pushed Thailand into the business consciousness of the rest of the world may be the biggest reason why many companies, foreign and Thai alike, are having difficulty securing good managers to run their sections, divisions and companies. It is simply a numbers game. The number of Thais talented and qualified enough to work competently within international companies or firms that must perform at international standards has been far outstripped by the demand for such human resources. Vincent Swift of the Wright Company, a firm that does searches for marketing and advertising executives, agrees. "You really have to look around for talent of an international standard," said Swift. "I'm not saying it's because the workforce is stupid or untalented. It's because international quality human resources are a fairly recent arrival. That's just a market reality where everybody is stretched so thin."

Shortages of skilled labor and managers are problematic throughout the region, but arguments can be made for Thailand's shortage being the worst. The Thai economy had been the fastest growing economy in the world over a ten-year period, creating an insatiable demand for skills and talent, especially in terms of engineering and management. An educated work force is required. Unfortunately, even though Thailand possesses the third largest population in Southeast Asia, the size of its educated population when compared to its neighbors in the region is very low. The numbers are not pretty.

Thailand's government and private sector spends less than 4% of its GDP on education, the lowest in the region. Only 20% of all Thai workers have more than a primary school education. In Malaysia, it's twice that amount. Of all the Thais who could attend secondary school, only about 30% actually do. The equivalent figures for Indonesia, Malaysia and the Philippines are 43%, 60% and 73%

respectively. (See Table 1.) As for tertiary education, only about 15% of the eligible population go beyond high school. By comparison, close to 30% of all university-aged Filipinos go on to university. The director of Thailand's National Science and Technology Agency acknowledges that while 12,000 engineers and 6,000 scientists graduate from university each year, 17,000 engineers and 10,000 scientists are needed. He estimates that Thailand will need 35,000 more technicians a year.[2]

Table 1: Secondary School Enrollment Ratios For Selected Asian Nations From 1986 ~ 1992		
Nation	**Male**	**Female**
Philippines	71%	75%
Singapore	70	71
Hong Kong	70	52
Malaysia	58	62
China	59	48
Vietnam	44	57
Indonesia	47	39
Thailand	**34**	**32**
Myanmar	25	23

Source: United Nations Children's fund, 1995

Whittaker understands the basic economic principles of the situation all too well. Demand pushes up price.

> In the late 80's, you'd be paying about 4,000 baht for a security officer. At that time, because of the sizable labor pool that was here, he was probably a quality guy. He may have been able to speak a few words of English. Today, you have to pay nine or ten thousand baht or more for a man and he is not as good as the guy nearly ten years ago because the labor pool here has been sucked dry in an enormous way.

---

[2] The Economist, August 16th, 1997

With so few qualified people for so many skilled positions, simple economic theory will tell you that salaries will climb. All firms in Thailand spend a lot of time and money looking for good people. Tired of searching for just the right person, some companies get desperate enough to accept anyone who has seemingly good qualifications. During the boom years, secretaries, MBA graduates, and department heads alike got what many feel were astronomically high compensation packages. For the budget-conscious entrepreneur starting up a small to medium sized firm, the pickings can still be extremely slim as the skilled work force exercises their advantage.

Trevor Allen, the Scottish general manager who started up the Pacific City Club, had great difficulty recruiting people before the club opened in February of 1995. First people may have somehow assumed the club to be a place where rich gentlemen could relax with women and drink. In fact, the Pacific City Club is a very exclusive place for executives of big business to hob nob over drinks or meals with politicians, celebrities and high society, a place for them to feel at home away from home and away from the occasional media   glare. Secondly, people who have worked in the hotel business would rather work for the Hiltons, Four Seasons and Orientals of the world, not a new, unknown club.

> We had to educate people about our concept. But people didn't feel comfortable because we were a small operation. If they were coming from a 800-room hotel, they had a staff medical room, staff laundry room and staff canteen. When they came here for an interview, that's what they looked for. They didn't feel secure because of the size and because we didn't have an international name. On top of that, when the young ladies went home and told their daddies that they'd been offered a job in a club made up of all these prestigious businessmen, Dad would say, stay with the Dusit Thani.

That's the reality for smaller companies. William Heinecke, the CEO of the Minor Group and starter-upper of many a company, said that you have to deal with that reality. "Very often the smaller company has to pay more because it has no credibility. Nobody wants to work for the small company unless there's some unusual circumstance. Perhaps you're giving someone a chance to do a bigger job than they would normally be getting. If you are, you're taking a chance and you've got to be very lucky."

Up until mid-1997, the pool for Thai human resources was so shallow that it was sometimes cheaper for a company to hire a foreigner than a Thai in certain fields. And if a foreign-managed company could convince the government to grant more work permits, they would have. But when the Thai economy slowed to a crawl in late 1997, the cost of hiring foreigners skyrocketed and general demand for new hirees plummeted. As many Thais lost their jobs or scrambled to find better opportunities outside such floundering fields as finance and property, personnel people of big and small companies alike began to have greater choice in their selection of new people. And yet, the highly skilled and well-educated class of engineers and managers are and will still be greatly sought after. Now, more than ever before, the very best talent that Thailand has to offer will be called on to help nurse Thailand's fragile business environment back to health.

TEN

DISTRI-THAI MANAGES ITS WAY TO THE TOP
Creating Motivated and Loyal Staff in Thailand

Hiring the right person for the job is difficult enough with Thailand's rather limited skilled labor pool. Keeping that person once you've hired her is even more difficult. To successfully manage people in Thailand, a good understanding of the culture can help the expat entrepreneur create a "family-like" atmosphere which satisfies and motivates Thais. At the same time, an unbiased, professional approach to human resource management can provide the promising career path that talented Thais have difficulty finding in traditional Thai companies.

119

The ultimate Thai workplace (according to many Thais) is where he or she feels at home. After all, she's going to see more of her boss and co-workers in a given week than she is her own family and friends . In fact, she may spurn higher-paying offers from other companies if she considers the people she works with as " family" or friends. They are people she enjoys chatting with, having meals with, taking trips with, and working hard with. -- Henry Holmes and Suchada Tangtongtavy from Working with the Thais[1]

If you have someone good, the only way to keep them is to convince them that they're getting something out of you, because as soon as they think they're not getting anymore, they're out. And that's not just about money. That's about wanting to learn and grow. -- David Cohen of Malcolm Bruce Ltd.

THE BENEVOLENT DESPOT

"I am a benevolent despot," said Richard Murray rather provocatively. "I tend to be paternalistic and look after my people. But I don't like to be taken advantage of either."

Murray is the managing director of Distri-Thai Ltd., a distributor of foreign periodicals in Thailand. Although Murray's staff would probably only jokingly agree with his self-imposed title, the description does hint at a desire to build up loyalty by building on relationships, and an insistence that standards for performance are met.

Some will say good management is finding the right balance between managing relationships and increasing performance. Overemphasizing one may create a country club-like atmosphere where people are so comfortable with their work situation that they begin to take advantage of the company. Or it could create a military-like atmosphere where the emotional needs of people are rarely taken into account by management, resulting in demotivation and a long-

---

[1] Holmes, Henry, Tangtongtavy, Suchada, *Working with the Thais*, page 76

term decrease in performance. Both scenarios are just as common in Thailand as they are anywhere else in the world. However, knowing how to facilitate relationships and motivate employees to increase performance in Thailand may be the difference between a short-lived venture and a long-lasting one.

Murray seems to understand this balance. Through the nineties, he struggled to build up a reputation for on-time deliveries to his buyers and accurate sales tracking reports for his suppliers, while creating an environment that encourages people with ability to take initiative and be accountable for their decisions. By late 1997, Distri-Thai was firmly established as the largest distributor of foreign periodicals in Thailand and was the sole distributor in Thailand for over 20 of the top foreign publications in the world, including Time, Forbes, The Economist, Fortune, Cosmopolitan, USA Today and The Financial Times. His company also re-exports its magazines to Cambodia, Laos and Vietnam, publishes books under the brand name "bookSiam", and has successfully opened up a chain of bookstores in Thailand called Bookazine. Commuting from his beachside home in the resort town of Hua Hin[2], Murray is finally enjoying life as a successful entrepreneur after years of profitless publishing ventures in his native Canada.

Murray is feeling particularly confident about the future because he believes he finally has the staff with the right skills and expertise to let him step back so that they can run with the ball. Those who have stayed with Murray over the years have come to appreciate his style, and in turn have given him the dependability and loyalty that Murray needs to perpetuate the company's success. Said Distri-Thai's general manager, Chokchai Worachatrawanich, "We love him. He's very kind and he works hard. He supports us and gives us opportunity. So everybody wants to work as hard as he does."

CARING BY EXAMPLE

These are the type of words any boss wouldn't mind hearing. They are also words that may reflect the caring side of Murray's managerial

---

[2]   Hua Hin is about 230 kms south of Bangkok.

style. At Distri-Thai, hospital bills of employees are taken care of by the company. Cash bonuses are given at the birth of children. Depending on the employee's years of service and need, the education of his children may be paid for. Employees' weddings or the funerals of close relatives of employees are attended by Murray. According to Chokchai, when some of Distri-Thai's delivery people lost their homes in a fire, they were given significant cash gifts on the spot and relocated until new homes were found. "If you're willing to give me an honest day's work, you can stay here until you die," explained Murray. "I'll take care of you."

Murray has adopted a management philosophy that focuses on the positive aspects of Thai-style patron-client relationships. In chapters seven, eight and nine, the more negative aspects of the patron-client society are discussed -- interdependent relationships between seniors and juniors based on fear and favors. But there is a positive side to patron-client relationships as well, one based on kindness and gratitude. Murray understands that acts of kindness can create strong feelings of indebtedness in others, which encourages them to perform acts of kindness in return. People of all cultures desire to be the recipient of kindness, but many non-Thais who come here to do business may be surprised by how much is expected of the boss in Thailand. Dr. Henry Holmes wrote, "If the Thai manager holds considerable power, he also feels that he must carry a greater degree of responsibility for the personal lives of his constituents than do his western counterparts."[3]

This sense of responsibility arises from a value deeply rooted in Thai culture -- a value known as *bunkhun*. Dr. Suntaree Komin, an authority on Thai values, explains *bunkhun* as "a psychological bond between someone who, out of sheer kindness and sincerity, renders another person the needed help and favors, and the latter's remembering of the goodness done and his ever-readiness to reciprocate the kindness."[4]

A long-time observer of Thai culture, Niels Mulder, further explains that this value evolves from early childhood as the mother-child

---

[3] Holmes, Henry, Tangtongtavy, Suchada, *Working with the Thais*, page 63, 64
[4] Komin, Suntaree, *Psychology of the Thai People*, page 168

relationship commonly develops into a life-long interdependence. According to Mulder, the child is taught that the mother loves the child more than anybody else, that she has sacrificed her own health to provide as much sustenance and love as she can, and that the child "will never be able to repay her for the overflowing goodness she has done" for him. And it is often the unspoken hope of the mother and father that they will be taken care of when they get old.

The feelings and beliefs gradually extend to other members of the family as well as to friends and acquaintances, and they are at the center of what many Thais desire in their relationships. Mulder summarized this point by writing:

> Respect and obedience to elders, trust in their wisdom and protection, the need to return favors received, all these are strong themes in Thai culture. The underlying idea is the principle of mutual dependence and reciprocity, and the principle of being practically and morally indebted. It is the recognition that people need each other if they want to go on with the business of living, formulated in a system of mutual but unequal moral obligations, with due respect for tradition and the wisdom of elders.[5]

The interdependent relationships that Murray has fostered serve as the catalyst for the fullest positive expression of *bunkhun* in patron-client relationships. Now he has the trust, respect and gratitude of the 100 or so employees of Distri-Thai. They look up to him as the founder of the firm, the main source of expertise as well as the problem solver of last resort. They also have the confidence that Murray intends to be around to help and guide them for many years to come. In October of 1997, Murray received permanent resident status. Legally, Murray no longer needs to worry about his own yearly visa extension process, or about whether he will be granted a work permit.

Murray feels that there is a great advantage to having permanent resident status. One is that a competitor who might have an axe to

---

[5] Mulder, Niels, *Inside Thai Society*, page 58

grind against Murray would not be able to put pressure on Immigration or the Labor Department to discourage them from extending Murray's work permit. Murray believes that "it's a lot harder to get rid of me because my work permit is virtually automatic due to the permanent resident status." But even more than that, permanent resident status sends a signal to the employees of Distri-Thai that their big boss isn't going anywhere. "Thais will think, 'This company is you,'" said Murray. "'If you aren't here, we don't have a job'. But with permanent resident status I'm here in Thailand forever. I feel it demonstrates to my employees a sense of commitment." Remarked Chokchai about his boss, with some amusement, "I'm pretty sure he's not going anywhere. He seems to want to be Thai."

THE SIGNIFICANCE OF SPEAKING THAI

Murray, in fact, does not consider it farfetched for him to become a Thai citizen. He may consider it in the future. But from the very beginning, when he first arrived in Thailand in 1989, it was his plan to establish a company and attain permanent resident status. And even before that, he knew he had to master the Thai language. Now fluent in Thai, he communicates with his entire staff in their native language. "It was never a question of whether to learn or not," said Murray. "I had to assimilate myself into the culture, and I had to become as much a part of the culture as I could in order to succeed."

In contrast, a vast majority of foreign expats and entrepreneurs do not learn the language. Perhaps they feel they are not linguistically capable or they do not have the time. Perhaps they feel that hiring the right Thais with passable to strong linguistic skills can more than make up for their own inability to communicate in the local tongue.

However, Murray knows there are significant advantages to being able to speak Thai. Knowing Thai increases the size of the talent pool available to you as so few Thais, especially at the worker and clerical level, can speak foreign languages. It puts your staff at tremendous ease as they are free to express their thoughts in a way that will allow them to sound more intelligent, confident and dignified, which of course only increases their motivation to work with you. And finally, knowing the language will better ensure that you, the foreign

Learning Thai the Natural Way

There are many good Thai language schools which can meet the wide variety of needs of expats determined to learn the language. The Thai language program at American University Alumni (AUA), however, deserves special mention because of its unique and effective approach to teaching languages. Most other Thai language schools tend to teach the major disciplines of listening, speaking, reading and writing in a coordinated effort to help the student attain fluency and literacy within a year, if the student has the patience and will to memorize. A well-regarded school in this traditional approach would be the Union Language School. However, AUA's Thai program teaches students in a manner that simulates the way children learn a language -- by observing and listening to people and events around them. In this manner, children assimilate vocabulary, pronunciation and grammar without ever consciously attempting to do so, and end up speaking their language fluently. The basic AUA assumption is that adults can learn languages in the same, natural manner, and at an even faster rate than children do.

Under that assumption, AUA emphasizes the ability to listen and understand as the paramount language skill, long before reading, writing or even speaking are encouraged. The Thai instructors, usually in pairs, will sit at the front of the classroom, and in essence, have a conversation with each other. The instructors talk and the students listen. In fact, students are basically discouraged from speaking any Thai. But subliminally, vocabulary and sense of pronunciation are being developed at a surprisingly fast rate. This may sound like an ordeal, especially for people who find it urgently necessary to communicate in Thai. But the success behind the school's unique methodology are the instructors. They appear to be hired based on charisma, intelligence, energy level and openness, and thus are able to employ a variety of engaging techniques to get the "audience" to understand much of a particular topic at hand. And very often, what is being learned by students, even more forcefully than language, is the multi-faceted and fascinating aspects of Thai culture that simply cannot be understood by reading the current literature available. But of equal importance to the instructors' teaching ability, the rapport among AUA's instructors, staff and students is unparalleled, creating a school environment of caring and encouragement, qualities that further motivate students to continue their studies.

entrepreneur, will know what is happening around you. In a foreign land, where the cultural cues differ, guessing what others are thinking and doing can become a hazardous adventure. Murray explains:

> I see this all the time. An expat opens up a small company. He hires people who can speak very good English. By doing this he thinks, 'OK, now I don't have to learn Thai.' But you know, not everybody is a saint. Sooner or later, certain people are going to figure out that they can bleed you white if they want to. You can be sitting right there and not know what's going on. And yet you are so dependent on them that you become less cautious. You begin to think that just because you can communicate with them in English, you can be more trusting than you ordinarily would be in your home country. You say, 'I'm going to Europe for two weeks. Here's the checkbook.' Well, they can steal you blind. When I started my business, I decided that I never wanted to be taken advantage of.

Understanding the language can protect you from potential trouble. But it can also reveal levels of the culture previously hidden to the foreigner. And better understanding the culture allows the foreigner to better relate to the Thais around him, and they to him. Peter Williams, managing director of ISP Thailand, knew that learning Thai would be important to his success in Thailand, but he also found speaking Thai to be a socially liberating act, one that allows him to communicate more effectively across the social strata than even a Thai can.

> I made an effort. I wanted to learn Thai and learn about Thailand. I can sleep on floors, eat cheroots and drink lao khaao.[6] I gave it all a try. I spent Songkran in Mae Sai. I took motorbike trips to Burma. I camped out on beaches of Pattaya and lived in Thai households. I went to funerals and weddings. As a foreign resident I have a fantastic opportunity. I don't have to worry

---

[6] a strong alcoholic drink made from rice.

about social class, as the Thais do. I can go and speak to an old lady in a rice paddy, or I can go and meet with the royal family, as long as I know how to act. Thais can't do that as easily.

PRIORITIZING RELATIONSHIP OVER TASK

Knowing Thai, showing commitment to the company and the country, attending weddings and funerals, helping staff with financial matters and generally creating an atmosphere where people feel they are part of a family -- these are examples of integral leadership behaviors in successful small to medium sized ventures in Thailand. It is true that Thailand has undergone great social change due to tremendous economic growth. And according to a prominent expert in the field of individualist and collectivist cultures, cultures that become more modern, complex and dynamic become more individualistic.[7] However, Thailand is only a generation removed from a predominantly agricultural style of life, and is often still considered a collectivist culture. In other words, compared with people in more advanced industrial economies, the people of Thailand tend to place higher priority on such concepts as face, social status, and patron-client relationships.

Thus Thais will tend to be more self-effacing, more deferent, more indirect and more likely to avoid conflict in their interactions with others. Thais tend to emphasize the importance of the relationship over the task at hand. A typical example of culture clash is when a western boss offers a solution to a problem which the Thai subordinate believes will not be effective. Quite often, the Thai will say nothing, desiring to save the face of the boss. The solution is implemented and found ineffective. When the boss realizes through debriefings afterwards that the Thai indeed had another, better solution, the boss wonders why the Thai did not offer his idea earlier. An expert on organizational culture, Edgar Schein, analyzed this particular problem that Asian subordinates and Western bosses sometimes have, revealing the different assumptions

---

[7] Triandis, Harry C., *Individualism and Collectivism*, page 16

each party may hold in regard to relationships and task, and how this difference causes confusion and diametrically opposed inferences about the other.

> From the point of view of the subordinate, the boss's behavior is incomprehensible because it shows lack of self-pride, possibly causing the subordinate to lose respect for that boss. To the boss the subordinate's behavior is equally incomprehensible. The boss cannot develop any sensible explanation of the subordinate's behavior that is not cynically colored by the assumption that the subordinate at some level just does not care about effective performance and therefore must be gotten rid of. It never occurs to the boss that another assumption such as "one never embarrasses a superior" is operating and that to the subordinate that assumption is even more powerful than "one gets the job done."[8]

Both sides need to check their assumptions. However, there are arguments to be made that the greater responsibility lies with the boss, who officially wields greater power. Non-Thais need to be aware of this Thai prioritization of values, and perhaps examine the advantages of toning down their own MBO-modeled, get-the-job-done, gung-ho attitude. Understanding the culture, the psychology and the language of the Thais is not imperative to conducting business in Thailand, but it can be the key to developing long-term relationships with and instilling loyalty in Thais, inside and outside the company.

PRIORITIZING TASK OVER RELATIONSHIP

Understanding that Thais tend to value relationships over task in the workplace does not mean that they do not wish to take the initiative, be assertive, be accountable or "get the job done". Certainly, if the leader of the company exhibits behavior that makes people

---

[8] Schein, Edgar, *Organizational Culture and Leadership*, page 26

128

feel their health and well being are high priorities, Thais will more often than not be grateful and motivated to do what they can for the leader, and thus for the company. Under the right conditions, they can be as effective and efficient in accomplishing personal and company goals as anybody else.

But a warm, family-like atmosphere can go only so far without a conscious effort by the head of the company to maintain a policy of fairness. Employees are often asking themselves, "Are my salary, benefits, hours, title, work space and training opportunities on an equal par with my colleagues? Do my colleagues have the same level of ability and knowledge that I do?" Thus, Murray believes that one important facet of fairness is advancing people who work hard and have ability.

> I recognize that there are cultural differences but I think the cultural differences can be overemphasized. We take the staff out every year. We have parties. We get involved in weddings and funerals. And that creates a bit of loyalty. But I think by far the most important element to good management is a sense of fairness. The employee asks, "Am I going to be treated fairly?" If he feels he has a decent shot at advancement based on his diligence and ability, then he'll probably stay. I don't think that's much different from how you should operate in Canada or the United States.

Murray explained that very often a westerner has a perceived advantage in the eyes of Thai employees who have worked for more traditional Chinese-style family businesses, a management style that is common in Thai corporations, big and small. Thais in such businesses run into a ceiling to advancement fairly quickly as family members, close and extended, fill most or all of the positions of responsibility. He said that a lot of bright Thais get frustrated with nepotism and the inability to make almost any decision without having to consult someone in the family circle of power. "Companies managed by foreigners are seen as running a bit more on management principles as opposed to emotion," said Murray. " 'We're not doing this because my daughter wants to do this. We're doing it because it's a decision with a sound business basis.' Here, I believe people are treated fairly. Maybe it's not quite as easygoing as they would like, but there are more opportunities in the long run. And that's important for a lot of Thais."

Murray believes in the western ideal of delegation, letting his people make the decisions within the area of their responsibilities. Like many other managers, he wants people who will take the initiative in solving problems and advancing the productivity of the company, people who will accept responsibility for their tasks and do what is necessary, within ethical boundaries, to get the tasks done. Fairness is about setting clear standards and evaluating people's performance based on those standards.

However, as explained in Chapter Nine, it is not easy finding people who do not require training in these concepts. Some people need time to develop, and patience is often required. But there is also a need to deal with people who do not make the effort, who merely do the minimum in order to get their monthly paycheck. Murray calls such people "civil servants", evoking the negative stereotype of the pencil-pushing bureaucrat. "They look at their watch, and they ask themselves what they're going to have for lunch." According to Murray, such people, ultimately, have to go. In a company that claims to be fair, nothing is more unfair than the perception that one is working hard to achieve company goals while others are not.

THE DESPOT OF FAIRNESS

To create an environment where effort and ability are rewarded, incompetence has to be eliminated. As one means to that end, Murray has fired, in his words, "a lot of people". He takes no pride in this fact for he feels it is an admission of failure, of selecting the wrong people for the jobs. He knows that the labor pool in Thailand for educated and skilled people is very small. He knows that those with talent aren't going to beat his doors down asking for jobs. And yet this insight doesn't make the frustration of finding people who meet his standards any less.

Murray admits that he is not so patient in dealing with what he perceives to be incompetence or dishonesty. "I'm pretty demanding in terms of work ethic as well as moral ethics. You can close your eyes and put up with it. But to me, that's admitting defeat. That's saying, 'Okay, I know there's a cancer in my body, but maybe it'll go away."

Several years ago, Murray broke up a strike in his company. There was a delivery boy who had the job of picking up the daily newspapers at the airport and delivering them to the various retail outlets by motorcycle so that they were on sale within an hour after arriving in Thailand. According to Murray, the newspaper was routinely late to the outlets as the delivery boy was busy playing cards with his friends. Another delivery boy would wait until Wednesday to deliver weekly magazines that should have been on sale on Monday. Murray wasn't so much upset with them as with their boss, the distribution manager. "This manager basically covered for everybody, even though I had evidence that certain messengers were doing their jobs poorly. He felt that I had no right to go in and deal with the delivery boys." Murray, fed up, called in the Distribution Manager and fired him. The delivery boys all went on strike. Murray brought in other delivery boys to do the job. And by the third day, the striking delivery boys saw, in Murray's words, how "nonchalant" he was about the strikers. With a better understanding of what kind of performance was expected of them, they decided to stay with Distri-Thai and ended their strike. Murray took a chance because challenging a strike in Thailand can have violent ramifications. But he got away with it. And in his mind, business basics won out over the dark side of patron-client relationships.

BUILDING A REPUTATION

Distri-Thai is growing. In addition to expanding its wholesale business by distributing books, re-organizing its retail outlets for greater efficiency, and publishing more book titles locally, Distri-Thai still looks to expand its bread-and-butter magazine wholesale division. In late 1997, Murray signed an agreement to form a joint venture with a German individual who owns the rights to distribute German publications outside of Germany. Murray immediately hired the Thai operations manager who was working for the German businessman before the joint venture was formed. And quite fortunately, a woman who left Distri-Thai to study in Australia had just returned to Thailand. Murray rehired her immediately as the office manager of the new joint venture because he knew she was "good and trustworthy."

Nowadays, hiring good people has become significantly easier. Murray has always paid salaries over the market rate so that people will take notice of his firm. But, according to Murray, successful recruiting is often a function of size. If the basis of fairness is to give people opportunity for learning and advancement, how can one really be fair with a small operation. "You have to reach a certain size," said Murray. "With one bookstore what can you do in terms of management? But with six, you can offer a greater variety of opportunities and attract good people."

Before, Distri-Thai was small and unattractive, which Murray believes led to a cycle of mistaken hirings and eventual firings. Now he feels he has developed a reputation for providing opportunities to talented people. In the latter half of 1997, after years of searching, he hired a sales and marketing manager. He added a good accounting supervisor and promoted his operations manager of the wholesale division, Khun Chokchai, to general manager of the entire company.

Once Murray hires the good ones, he has confidence they will stay. "A lot of people have been pushed out, but I haven't experienced much job-hopping," said Murray. He believes that the average Thai, not necessarily the MBA-touting, multi-lingual, well-connected variety that has been known to job hop, is actually looking for stability by their mid-twenties. "Generally speaking, by the time a Thai is 25 years old, he, or she, believes that he had better have his act together. Before then, they would have worked for two or three companies. But when they're 25 or 26 they ask themselves, 'Am I going to stay here?' If the answer is yes, then very often they'll stay as long as the company will have them."

Murray has worked hard to create a stable environment built on the premise of fairness and on providing opportunity to the talented and hardworking. And he has become a father figure to a company that responds appreciatively to his willingness to adapt to Thai ways. "I consider myself Asian," said the tall Caucasian from Canada. "Some people feel they were born in the wrong skin. I probably was, because I feel very much at home here in Thailand."

Three Views on Firing Employees

Finding the right person for the job is difficult. Many feel that firing a person is even more difficult. According to a lawyer, the Labor Department will interpret the Thai labor laws in such a way that a company can fire anybody for almost any reason as long as the fired employee is given the legally prescribed severance pay.[9] There are only certain cases in which severance pay is not required by law: If the employee "is discharged for dishonesty, intentionally causing damage to the employer, violating rules or regulations after a written warning has been given, being absent from work for three consecutive days without prior notice, negligently causing serious damage to the employer, or being convicted of a felony."[10]

One American entrepreneur desperately wanted to fire someone whom he felt was clearly unable to do the job she said she could when she was hired. Unfortunately, the American didn't want to give her severance pay, and the woman's case didn't seem to fit any of those legal conditions. The American, based on advice of a Thai friend, decided to get the woman to quit by making her lose face in a meeting.

> In the middle of a meeting, I told her, politely, that she wasn't doing her job. I told her that if she needed some help, then I thought that she should ask the rest of us. And of course she said, "I don't need any help." Then I explained to her, "Why don't you tell me what you know about this particular application. "And then all of a sudden, she didn't know English very well.

---

[9] New labor laws which change the amounts employers have to pay when firing or laying off employees went into effect in August, 1998. Workers who worked for four months to one year are eligible for one month's compensation. Those who have worked more than one year but less than three are eligible for three months' compensation. Employers must pay six months compensation for those with three years of service but less than six. Eight months of severance is to be paid in the case the worker has been employed for more than six years but less than ten years. Those with over ten years of service are to receive ten months of severance pay.

[10] Chandravithum, Nikom and Vause, Gary, *Thailand's Labor and Employment Law: A Practical Guide*, p 42

He eventually got the woman to quit the company, and was thus not required to pay severance pay. Another face-losing tactic is isolating the employee from all meetings. Most Thais in management positions who are so isolated usually quit, making direct confrontation unnecessary.

Another expat feels that firing people is a necessary part of running an effective and efficient organization. And this Swiss manager believes that saving the face of an incompetent employee is not as important as eliminating waste. But different from the American, he believes that managers should not be overly concerned about the cost of paying severance.

> If somebody doesn't care about his job or whether he is helping put the company and other employees' jobs at risk, then I don't care about him. I will make that person's life impossible. I will put pressure on him and make him lose face. They quit and I don't have to pay severance. But in most cases, if you are not productive anymore for what I need, I will usually be the nicest, fairest guy. I can pay seven months. I can pay twelve months. I will look for someone who can do the job and who will help me gain back in one month all the money I lost in paying severance.

Distri-Thai's Murray believes that the only way to fire anybody is in private and with severance pay to cushion the blow. He believes that as much as possible should be done to deter the fired employee from causing problems for you or your company in the future.

> If I was going to chew someone out in Canada, the first thing I would do is to bring them into the office and close the door and talk to them one on one. In Thailand I do exactly the same. If I wanted someone to leave, making him lose face is just stupid anywhere. I think it's very dangerous to make someone lose face. If we're making someone redundant, we pay according to law. And if we're firing someone for incompetence, then I will still pay severance.

ELEVEN

METRO IS THE MESSAGE
Changing the Perceptions of the Thai Market

In any rapidly developing economy, local business people are exposed to a multitude of new business practices often introduced by foreign investors. Shifts in emphasis from price to quality, short-term to long-term goals, and local to global markets are taking place in board rooms and meeting rooms all over the world. However, while the local business community and work force seek to digest this sudden influx of new ideas, there is often resistance to change. Successfully bringing new ideas to the Thai market often means having the skill to convey your message convincingly as well as the patience to allow your ideas to gain acceptance.

135

Are you getting it at home? Or do you still have to go out and buy it. -- an early ad for Metro magazine subscriptions

A MINI-MEDIA EMPIRE

John Twigg, founder of Metro Magazine, got a phone call one day telling him that one of his own messengers was selling current issues of his magazine on the street for 60 baht, a 20-baht discount off the newsstand price, and pocketing the cash. This is the type of incident that incites some foreigners to hop on the soapbox to preach the evils of Thailand's "endemic corruption". Twigg, however, was philosophical. "I actually admired the fact that this guy was working hard selling my magazine." He never punished the guilty messenger, but told his messengers if they would sell Metro on the street at the cover price, he'd gladly supply them at wholesale rates.

After all, the name of the game for Twigg is getting the name out. Metro Magazine was launched in August of 1994 as an under capitalized publication, written in a foreign language into a frag-mented and subsequently depressed market. By July of 1997, Metro Magazine has managed not only to stay alive but grow to almost cult status. And the more popular the magazine is and the more well known the name Metro becomes, the more advertisements Twigg can sell. The more ad revenue comes in, the more ways City Media, Twigg's company which publishes Metro, can sell itself. Slowly but surely, City Media is pushing into radio, the Internet, and sponsorship of events, and maybe one day, the mother of all media, television. To Twigg, Metro Magazine isn't just a popular Bangkok city listings magazine. It is the start of a mini-media empire.

However, 1997 was not a year for media moguls in Thailand.

UP AND DOWN INDUSTRY

When Metro began in 1994, the English publishing business in Thailand was considered a strong one with a good future. The Wattachuk Group had just started up Bangkok's third English daily newspaper. This was particularly impressive since Thailand has one of the worst records in education in the region, and already possessed two popular and prestigious English newspapers, The Bangkok Post and The Nation. A year later, the aggressive Manager Group launched The Asia Times, a business daily to compete with the Asian Wall Street Journal within the region. Many people had high hopes for the English publishing industry in Thailand because they saw that with the turnover of Hong Kong to the Chinese in 1997, and with censorship commonplace in the more authoritarian governments of Indonesia, Singapore and Malaysia, Thailand had the potential of being the freest, and perhaps busiest press in Southeast Asia. If the tariffs for importing newsprint were cut, some believed that Thailand's publishing business would boom.

In the early morning of July 2, 1997, the Bank of Thailand announced that it was placing the Thai Baht on a "managed float," which resulted in a de facto devaluation. In the months preceding the managed float, checks were bouncing all over town, salaries weren't being fully paid, or paid at all, blue collar and white collar employees alike were being laid off, and what was once a go-go, giddy atmosphere of healthy greed was now gloom and doom.

It was practically the same period when two publications in English -- Manager Magazine and The Asia Times -- stopped printing. Wattachuk's Thailand Times followed in August. Although it is doubtful whether there was a direct relationship between the end of those two publications and the devaluation of the baht, it was clear that the Manager Group and the Wattachuk Group were in trouble. The English publishing business in Thailand was standing on very fragile ground. As advertising budgets were being slashed left and right by previously free-spending corporations, fewer and fewer scraps were left for the English publications after the best Thai newspapers and magazines got the shrinking lion's share.

METRO TAKING OFF

And yet, on that day of doom and gloom, Twigg was feeling confident in the tumbling English language publishing industry. The New Zealander felt he had established one of the highest quality magazines published in Thailand. To get an up-to-date and entertaining overview of events, eateries, nightspots and trends in Bangkok, The Tourism Authority of Thailand, the Lonely Planet Guide and the Rough Guide all enthusiastically recommend Metro. One of the largest distributors of magazines in English once wrote, "I can categorically state that in all the years I've been in the publishing business in Thailand, there has never been a magazine this successful on a newsstand as Metro. No other locally-published English language magazine even comes close to Metro in terms of single copy sales."

This is not to say that Twigg's City Media is immune to financial difficulties. In his case, however, difficulties were more related to the average difficulties suffered by any start up. When Twigg launched Metro, costs were five times what he had budgeted. When his brother, an attorney, came to visit a month later and saw that revenue was 140,000 baht and costs were 800,000 baht, he said, "How long are you going to do this?"

Up till recently, Twigg had to routinely scramble to make payroll. In bad months, he would follow the policy of paying the lowest paid people first, which usually left him and his seconds-in-command without a paycheck. Even those who got paid received checks in installments, with a plea not to cash them until the following week. Collecting money is the biggest headache, as wrestling a check for 100,000 baht from a delinquent client is sometimes the difference between making payroll or not.

But financial matters seem to have finally made the turn for the better. Sales for advertisements were steadily increasing in the first half of 1997, certainly an anomaly in these tough economic times. In fact, since the end of 1995, ad space in Metro Magazine had increased 100%. The percentage of ad space in a single issue had actually crept up from about 18% of print space in the magazine to over 20% of print space over the first six months of 1997. And completely bucking the trend, ads made up 26% of the magazine in the July, 1997 issue, a time when the economy was arguably at an all-time low.

CHANGING PERCEPTIONS

Twigg's team developed Metro from the ground up -- they looked at similar city magazines from around the world and chose what they judged were the best elements from each for the Thai market. Although originally aimed at the Expat market it became apparent that Metro might also appeal to Thais also, and has aggressively pushed into that market. "These days, we just say it's for locals -- race is unimportant." In fact, if you want to see Twigg blow steam, then compliment him on what a nice tourist magazine he's producing. That's when he'll probably shout the mantra of his nightmares, "We're not a tourist magazine!"

At first glance though, you would think that Metro Magazine is a farang magazine. After all, it's in English and frankly, Bangkok has never been confused with Singapore. And even if the average well-educated Thai were to pick up an issue of Metro, she might not be comfortable with the colloquial style, the flashy and sometimes wild layouts, or the occasional racy story. And indeed, Metro Magazine's market is strongly supported by TOSSers and FLITs, Metro marketing shorthand for Tourists on Short Stays and Foreigners Living in Thailand. Twigg claims that about fifty percent of his readership is TOSSers and FLITS. The flip-side of that claim is that basically the remaining readers are Thai. And for Twigg, these are not your ordinary Thais -- these are the elite EARNers, a.k.a. Educated Abroad Rich Nationals.

> These are people who are fluent in both languages -- English and Thai, although probably more in English than in Thai for the pure reason that they have probably been in America or Australia since they were twelve, went to college overseas, and at the age of 20 came back to Thailand. In comparison, someone who went to university here, she might speak fluent English as well as read and write well in English. But chances are, she would probably rather read a Thai magazine. The market I'm looking at are the people who, when they talk on the phone, speak half in English and half in Thai.

Although this may seem to be a very small market to be chasing, it is in fact demographically very appealing to anyone selling high quality products and services. And yet, is Metro really reaching this audience? Twigg admits that he's barely scratching the surface of this market, but he really believes that many of these EARNers are not going to stop with the Bangkok Post, that they will also pick up Metro and become regular readers. At least this is the perception that Twigg is trying to sell. And this has been a very difficult sell to the advertisers.

"During the first year, nobody was going to come near us," said Twigg. "We were too new. And that's a problem for any publication starting up, particularly one without a credible foundation." On top of that, marketers and advertisers immediately associated Metro with a non-Thai audience, not the obviously larger Thai audience.

As a result, the first-year issues had very few ads. Even when Metro succeeded in finding a big client to place an ad, advertising for Metro would often come out of a client's market development budget, and not the client's advertisement budget. "Let's say they're going to spend 15 million baht on advertising and one million baht on market development. What that says to me is that as a media they don't take us seriously."

Another reason why Twigg had difficulty selling ad space was that in the beginning, he charged very high advertising rates and was loathe to discount. The idea was to differentiate Metro from the fragmented magazine market. He explained, "We had a superior product and we didn't want people saying, 'I'll take Metro but it's a bit more expensive than I can afford,' which would then open the way for us to negotiate them to buy a smaller size at the listed rate. It was a tough policy to follow, but my feeling is that it has worked -- we're now perceived to be a much better product than most others, which puts us in a strong bargaining position." Twigg insists to clients that Metro is offering greater value for their baht. He would personally go to potential clients again and again, explaining that an ad in Metro is more effective in reaching their audience than an ad in most other Thai magazines. Why? Twigg has a theory.

THE "BEFORE-CONTENTS" RULE

According to Twigg, every advertising text states that the first right-hand page is the best position for an advertisement, and that a place before contents is great if you can get it. However, Twigg believes that this has been overdone in most local magazines. The result is an overloading of advertisements in the first twenty pages of the average Thai magazine. In certain magazines you can flip through as many as 20 pages before you even get to the table of contents.

> You look at most local magazines and you have page after page of ads. Not only that, you'll have a beer ad followed by a toilet bowl ad. There's no rhyme nor reason for that. I tell them, 'Why do you want to be opposite another ad?' With all these ads up front, people just flip ahead to look at the contents. Nobody's bothered to educate people about this. What tends to happen is that a whole bunch of ads are crammed in the front of the magazine while the back half is black and white pages with no ads.

In a sampling of magazines sold in Thailand in June, 1997, Twigg's "Before-Contents" theory seems to hold water. As can be seen in Table 1, four magazines (Money & Banking, Phujadkarn, Thailand Tattler and Elle) are dominated by full-page ads in their first twenty pages. In fact, in Thailand's most popular and successful business magazine, Phujadkarn, eighteen of the first twenty pages are ads. And Money & Banking's June issue is a quintessential representation of top-heavy advertising as it contains streaks of 60 and 40 straight pages of black-and-white text.

Now a case could be made that Twigg is jealous because he can't sell as many ads as Phujadkarn, Elle or even Thailand Tattler. Nevertheless, even with ad space in Metro increasing over the first half of 1997, text and text-related graphics still dominate Metro, especially in the first half of the magazine. You just won't find more than three full pages of ads in a row in Metro, let alone ten.

Table 1: Number of Ads in the First 20 Pages of Selected June, 1997 Magazines Published in Thailand		
Magazine	**# Of Ads First 20 Pages**	**% Of Ads In Magazine**
Metro Magazine (English)	4	21
Money & Banking (Thai)	13	22
Dichan (Thai)	13	28
Elle (Thai)	13.3	33
Thailand Tattler (English)	16.5	33.5
Phujadkarn (Thai)	18	37

Source: Author

So Twigg tries to sell clients on the placement of their ad. He tells them that they don't have to be on page three and that they certainly don't want to be between ads. If the magazine has interesting articles, why not put the ad where the reader will see it. If you're a restaurant, why not put the ad in the restaurant listings section? And why does the ad have to be an expensive full-page one? A quarter-page or eighth-of-a-page ad, selected in a section that is relevant to the ad will definitely be seen by motivated readers, no matter what the size is. In fact, most of Metro's ads are 1/16 to 1/2 page in size, very much at odds with other local magazines, and also more profitable as revenue yield per page increases.

In the days of the economic boom, advertisers never really had to consider these types of factors. Companies were able to make a lot of money regardless of the quality of their marketing strategies. Thus, for smaller magazines like Metro, price was often the only selling point Metro's clients considered.

> The whole reason it's so difficult to get the rack (list) rate is because the market is so conditioned to cheap page rates, as well as conditioned to buying full page ads. It took me two years to sell ad space to a leading

hotel. The woman I dealt with originally said, 'I never pay full price and I only do full page advertising.' Finally, she took out a black-and-white, eighth-of-a-page ad at full price, which was appropriate for what she was trying to promote. It's just a matter of knocking on doors and constant headbashing, convincing people that we're offering value for money.

Twigg suggests that the economic downturn has in a way helped him because now advertisers and marketers are having to be more accountable for their placement of ads. With Metro, Twigg feels his clients can justify their choice of media.

GROWING MINI-EMPIRE

Simply put, if Twigg can find a way to promote and sell the name and style of Metro, he will. Twigg has dabbled in radio and has plans for producing programming for television as well. However, it is on the Internet that Twigg has established a fairly solid presence.

Since August of 1995, Metro has been on the Internet with its own website. City Media hasn't really publicized it because Twigg and his people have been tweaking it, trying to work out the kinks and get the right feel for the saaviest net surfers. Experienced internet users are getting tired of too much flash -- they want more and better content. Twigg feels he has the content to make his website a popular one for those who wish to come to Bangkok. Although Metro Magazine is only partially reproduced on this electronic medium, web surfers have access to a considerable number of back-issue articles with a few clicks of the mouse.

The world wide web on the Internet is a medium, and it is a potentially massive one. Few people in the world are currently making money directly from their presence on the web, but most believe that it is a matter of time. At this stage, Twigg has sold a limited amount of ad space on the website, and hopes to generate a bit more income by allowing other publishers from around the world to simply download a Metro article for a fee. Even though the website was a bit costly to start up, he feels in the long run it will pay off.

Getting on the Internet is something that we had to do because the web is changing the whole media industry. And you had better be familiar with its working ways or else you're going to be in trouble. Now we're just spending a little money maintaining the site. And we're learning new tricks to keep up to date. Eventually we'll have something that works great, generates money, and ties the whole thing together. If you like, this is a movement into multimedia, where everybody in publishing is going to have to go.

Promote and sell. Sell and promote. That's what the business is all about. And to be honest, if the price were right, Twigg would sell the entire mini-empire tomorrow. "We're for sale. After all, isn't everything in Thailand for sale?"

TWELVE

CENTRAL OFFICE CALLING
Having a Good Idea is One Thing, Keeping it is Another

New ideas are introduced to Thailand all the time, very often by foreigners who have had success with such ideas in other countries. And in Thailand's competitive, entrepreneurial business environment, good ideas are bought, improvised upon or copied by people all the time. Laws exist to prevent blatant copying of intellectual property, but laws and enforcement may not be as strong as many non-Thais may want. And yet, in the long run, skilled imitators may become skilled innovators, and the new ideas introduced today may be the seeds for greater creativity in the Kingdom tomorrow.

> *All too often, the capacity to assimilate technology is called "copying," and dismissed. Yet economic progress by definition involves copying, in the sense of moving into industries and products that have been pioneered by others. In the high-growth U.S. economy of the late nineteenth and early twentieth centuries, Americans took pride in what was termed "Yankee ingenuity." By this was generally meant the taking in of European discoveries and developments, adapting and commercializing them, and building on these imported technologies.* -- James C. Abegglen and George Stalk, authors of *Kaisha - The Japanese Corporation*

NO IDEA IS A SAFE BET

In the late 1980s, when making money in Thailand seemed to be as easy as starting up a company, David Bedford cut out his own slice of the expanding pie. While Thailand's GDP growth rate was cracking double digits and new hotels were sprouting up all over Thailand to keep up with the tourism boom, Bedford thought that hotel safes would be a fairly easy sell. Foreign tourists in particular would be familiar with safes made available in their rooms for their private use, and would probably like to have such a service available here. He was right.

After securing a licensing agreement with a Brazilian company, Bedford quickly saw that demand for the room safes was strong. Although the first 200 were imported, he realized that it would be more advantageous for him to manufacture in Thailand and sell the safe throughout the region. In six years of business, Bedford's company sold about 20,000 units. Unfortunately for Bedford, but inevitably, other people began to think that this was a good business as well. Other companies began to enter the market, some of them simply figuring out how to make a reasonable copy. According to Bedford, six copies of his safe's design, as well as other designs from outside the region flooded the market, and profits began to drop. So while the number of new hotels was decreasing in the early 1990s, the number of companies selling hotel safes increased. On top of that, Bedford was finding it tiring and expensive flying all over Asia supporting his sales agents. In 1994, Bedford no longer felt safe in the safe business, so he got out.

BORING BUT PROFITABLE

Unsure of what to do next, Bedford thought about going back home to Australia. He had sold office supplies via telemarketing before moving to Thailand, so he thought he might go back to that line of business. When his friend suggested that he try telemarketing in Thailand, Bedford reconsidered his repatriation. In January, 1995, Bedford established Central Office Products (COP). The philosophy behind his company is staying focused. COP sells typewriter ribbons, laser printer cartridges and bubble jet ink cartridges. These products are not only consumable, but they also have fairly high gross profit margins, especially typewriter ribbons. "You'd be surprised how many companies here still use a lot of ribbons," said Bedford.

Bedford has also introduced computer screens and recycled laser cartridges, two more hot sellers. But generally, he is very cautious about expanding his product line. "Basically we want to stick to the same old boring products," said Bedford, "because these are the products that every office needs." There are many other types of products that you might think would be common sense for COP to offer, fax paper for instance. But if the product isn't small or light, he doesn't want to make it available. All COP products are delivered by motorcycle. If COP were to sell fax paper at a bulk rate of at least 12 per order, he said COP would have to start considering the use of cars or small trucks, a major expense and the kiss of death for fast deliveries in the clogged arteries of Bangkok's road infrastructure.

The competition to sell these particular office products is intense as department stores, office equipment stores and computer stores square off with the "mom and pop" stationery stores located on every little corner. But Bedford says that he has the edge over the retail stores in terms of service, as he can deliver right to the customers' door, and in terms of price, since he buys from the manufacturer and sells directly to the end-user. Without the middle man, he can afford to sell at a lower price and gain a higher profit margin than his competition. In 1998, when most companies were scrambling to survive, COP's sales were up 50%. Bedford's edge is telemarketing.

TELEMARKETING BEATS THE TRAFFIC

Telemarketing is the selling of products or services over the telephone. Although common, and sometimes notorious in the West for its annoying 24-hour prevalence, telemarketing has become recognized as one of the more effective and efficient methods of selling in recent years. But good telemarketing is more than just a matter of smooth-talking someone over the phone; it is a sophisticated series of scripted responses and questions that appear to be very potent in getting a total stranger to buy a product sight unseen. Explained Bedford,

> This system works. We have an answer for every question or response. "I don't want any." "I've got too much stock." "I can buy cheaper elsewhere." "My brother's in the business and I buy from him." Responses to all these comments are scripted, which our sales people basically read. Of course, after a while they become skilled enough to smoothly engage the customer and they don't have to read it anymore. I'd say this method works on probably half the buyers we talk to.

COP's phone bills are high, but other than rent, salaries and bonuses, expenses are relatively low. COP doesn't have to advertise and doesn't have to waste the time of sales people by having them fight their way through traffic just to meet two or three people a day. According to Bedford, COP telemarketers instead make 30 to 40 phone calls a day, of which about half result in sales. COP has sold to 5,000 companies in two years, of which over 70% are repeat customers. Through telemarketing, around 200 new customers are added every month. Bonuses are quite healthy for COP's saleswomen.

There are bonuses for making the first sale of the day and bonuses for producing a repeat sale. At the end of the day, the sales room takes on a buzz as the sales staff gets closer to its daily goal. At the end of the month, attaining targets also translates into higher incomes. Every few months, the incentive targets are mixed up and changed around to keep the challenge stimulating. As a result, COP telemarketers, whose base salaries are about 8 to 12 thousand baht a month, earn some 30 or 40 thousand baht in commissions. The better ones make close to 100 thousand a month in total income.

IMITATED BUT NOT FLATTERED

Central Office Products and its sales staff make good money using a good idea. And good ideas sometimes make people think that they can do it on their own. A year after Bedford started COP, his sales manager, whom he had sent to Australia several times for training and who was with the company from the very beginning, was apparently planning to quit and secretly start up her own business modeled on COP. It was a secret because she was hoping to take a chunk of the sales staff with her. But as she began to surreptitiously recruit her sales team to join her future company, sales noticeably dropped. "In this business the sales manager has to keep everybody's morale up and keep their mind clear and concentrating on what they're doing," said Bedford. "But when she started saying 'Come and work for me,' the girls didn't know what they were doing." When it became clear to Bedford what was going on, he fired the sales manager and her assistant.

Bedford suspects that the sales manager copied the company manual, complete with all of the scripts and explanations of what should be done in certain situations of a telephone interaction. He also believes that she photocopied all of the company's client lists, hoping to sway them away from COP. "She would ring up our clients and say that we were out of business, and that she was the new company that had taken over," said Bedford. When some customers called COP to see if it was out of business, Bedford's sales people, all of whom stayed, reassured customers that they were indeed still in business.

Bedford understands why his sales manager did what she did, but he was disturbed by her actions. "I expect it to happen because when people see such a big gross margin, they think, 'Wow, this is great!' I even told her when she started that one day she might want to leave and do this herself. I have no problem with anybody wanting to leave and start their own business, but she stole a lot of stuff from us."

It is painful at times to invest time, money and effort into a new business only to see others take your ideas, skip much of the experimentation and uncertainty that went into building a business, and go on to become a competitor. Although Bedford was quite low-key about all the problems he faced, Frank Crocker was incensed.

Crocker, the man who started up The Document Storage Company (featured in Chapter Two), was upset to see his former employees form companies and directly compete with his company. He was upset when they gave their companies names like "Document Storage Company" and "Document Storage Services". Crocker claims that his one-piece storage box for documents, which he personally designed, was copied. And he was really surprised when he saw the brochure of a newly formed company which used pictures cut and pasted from Crocker's brochure. But it was the copying of the contract that he used with his customers that caused him the most pain.

> As you operate a business over a period of years, there are many opportunities for you to get into conflict with a client. If you're sensitive to client needs and sensitive to changing trading environments, you can accumulate an awful lot of sensible, well-defined legal positions on a contract that helps the client see their obligations and helps you to see their obligations. And once you put all these things together, you have to send them to lawyers to get their interpretation and let them re-write and re-draft it. It's very, very time-consuming and very, very expensive if you've got a drawn-up contract. You're talking many, many thousands of US dollars for a small contract. Unfortunately, the industry at large seems to be using my contract.

COPYRIGHT, PATENT AND TRADEMARK PROTECTION IN THAILAND

Is there legal recourse for businesses who have had ideas "stolen" or "copied"? Crocker and Bedford weren't sure whether there was or not. But even if laws designed to protect their interests did exist, they didn't believe that it would be worth the time and expense to fight a Thai competitor in a Thai court. And in fact, their understanding of the situation may not be far from the truth for people running small - to medium-sized businesses.

There are laws to prevent violations in copyright, patent and trademark. As pressure from the West to protect intellectual property rights grows in Thailand, the laws have changed and become clearer and tougher. It is actually possible for Central Office Products to take the former sales manager to court for copyright[1] infringement. As Bedford has permission to translate and use the telemarketing scripts and manual from the Australian author, a friend of Bedford's and a partner in COP, Bedford has three legal options. He can take his former sales manager to criminal court, which, if successful, could result in imprisonment of six months to four years, or a fine of 100 to 800 thousand baht, half of which would go to the court.[2] He can also take her to civil court, which would give Bedford the possibility of getting an injunction to stop her business at least temporarily and maybe permanently, as well as unlimited compensation in damages. The third option would be to take her to both criminal and civil court. These same options would be available to Crocker as well in regards to his contract.

Crocker may have a chance to fight off competitors who try to give their companies similar names to his own company. For example, a company named SP Microsoft was brought to court by Microsoft, the famous American computer software company, under a law called "company name infringement", which is under the civil and commercial code. The name of the company does not have to be trademarked in this case.

---

[1] Copyright protection is available to such areas as literary works, including telemarketing scripts, computer programs, dramatic works, artistic works, musical works, audio-visual materials, cinematographic works, and sound recordings.

[2] Copyright Act, 1994, Chapter 8, Section 69

But that is as far as the law will allow Bedford or Crocker to go. Crocker never had a patent for the design of his document storage box. Bedford also never had his Brazilian supplier get a patent on its design in Thailand. If they had, they might have stronger cases to stop imitators. But according to a lawyer who specializes in intellectual property rights, these type of court cases can typically take a year to settle, and the Thai courts tend not to be as strict as the plaintiffs would like them to be. "The client often wants the infringer in jail, but normally the Thai courts are not quite ready to put these people in jail because they see things like trademark counterfeiting as a business crime, not like killing someone," said Rutorn Nopakun.

Rutorn went on to say that generally copyright cases are very hard to prove while patent and trademark cases are easier if the trademark and patent are registered with the Thai government. He suggested that all companies, big and small, consider registering their trademarks and patents. However, he did admit that proving such cases, even when the case is fairly clear, may take a not-so-small amount of money. "It all depends on how much your property is worth," he said. "If your company's future depends on it, then it's worth it."

COPYING AND LEARNING

When you walk around a tourist area, you can easily buy fake watches that claim to be manufactured by Tag Heuer and Rolex, or unlicensed T-shirts with Walt Disney characters or brand names like Gucci and Chanel printed on them. Pirated CD-Roms of Sony PlayStation games and the latest software for computers are sold for a fraction of the original product's price. When the newest Apple operating system, MAC OS 8, hit the Thai market in 1997 at about 3,500 baht, pirated versions were quickly available for 800 baht or less. The big law firms in Thailand are constantly organizing police raids to prevent these types of infringements.

Bedford, who has had over a decade to adapt to Thailand, is a realist who accepts that people will go down the path of least resistance, in this case, "borrowing" or "adapting" good, fresh ideas. But a few others will look at a country like Thailand and express themselves more vindictively, labeling it a country that condones counterfeiters and copycatters and that is unable to learn how to produce original ideas on its own. Living in a foreign environment, especially for the first time, can encourage a foreigner to exaggerate the differences he sees between his culture and the new one he has entered. Some people go overboard in singing the praises of a new environment while others complain bitterly and continuously about its apparent defects. Many will switch back and forth in a cycle of positive and negative attitudes towards the host country, especially in the early stages of one's cross cultural adventure. There is an intenseness in peoples emotions when placed in new environments where expectations just aren't as reliable as they were back home.

This discomfort can result in strong, negative attitudes toward the new culture whether it is towards the local people, the host country's handling of the environment, the effectiveness and efficiency of the state bureaucracy, or the copying of intellectual property. It is true that a company should be concerned about protecting its ideas in Thailand, as well as most of the rest of the world. But as any lawyer will tell you, if it's important enough, then money and patience are needed to insist on the exclusiveness of a company's ideas.

But it may also help to understand that copying, or stealing ideas, is a part of the creative process, anywhere in the world. Apple until recently had Microsoft locked up in a court case over Microsoft's Windows operating system. Apple claims Microsoft stole the look and feel of Apple's graphical interface, but in fact Apple got their look and feel from Xerox's research on computers in the early 1970s.

According to Dr. Henry Holmes, a leading authority on Thailand, Thais are doing what comes normal to humans everywhere. "It may be that along the path to industrial leadership, the first stage is to get it right -- i.e., get the basics down properly and copy correctly what's already known -- before having enough confidence to venture into the new and the untested."[3]

---

[3] Holmes, Henry and Tangtongtavy, Suchada, *Working with the Thais*, page 125

THIRTEEN

HANAKO SELLS DIRECT
Marketing Up-Scale Up-Country

Many say that Thailand is a tale of two countries: Bangkok and the rest of the nation. Despite having only 10% of the country's population and 0.3% of its total area, Bangkok accounts for 35% of Thailand's gross regional product, has 60% of its commercial bank deposits, and 70% of its cars. Bangkok certainly is the starting point for most foreigners wishing to start up in Thailand. And for most products and services, if you don't succeed in Bangkok, then chances are you won't succeed anywhere else. Despite all that, a good business person must consider that 90% of the nation is not in Bangkok, and that some of that 90% have the money and desire to buy what their cousins in the big city are buying. In the case of one high-end cosmetics company, direct sales was found to be a very effective way to penetrate the up-country markets.

Everybody says, "OK, we accept that the Thais in Bangkok are very savvy. They like pizzas, hamburgers, and all that. But people in Chiang Mai, they aren't the same as people in Bangkok." I say, "What the heck are you talking about! Do you think they come from another planet? People up-country are exactly the same. They just haven't been exposed yet to the opportunities. But it's coming. It's only a question of when. -- William Heinecke, Chairman of the Minor Group

BUILDING A HIGH-CLASS, HIGH-QUALITY IMAGE

Members of Thai royalty rarely appear in television advertisements. But there she was, elegantly maneuvering through sun-filled land and seascapes, flowing white scarves revealing a shy, but winning smile. The woman in this 1994 sixty-second commercial was M. L. Saralee Chirathiwat. The M.L. before the name of this prestigious presenter stands for Mom Luang, a title automatically conferred to the great-great-great-grandchild of a king of Thailand. (M.L. Saralee is a direct descendant of King Rama V and a niece of H.R.H. the Queen of Thailand.) It is a fact that the royal family in Thailand, much more than in most other monarchies around the world, is highly respected and genuinely loved by its people. For a virtually unknown company called Hanako Cosmetics, less than a year old in a very competitive, high-priced cosmetics market, gaining the assistance of a close relative of the immediate Royal family was a tremendous image boost. In a 20-million baht commercial, one of the most expensive ever filmed, M.L. Saralee made an unprecedented inference to women watching TV all over Thailand: Royalty use Hanako cosmetics.

M.L. Saralee was quoted as saying that she indeed did use Hanako Cosmetics.[1] But securing the services of a person of such stature was still quite an accomplishment, particularly since Hanako Cosmetics didn't even exist before November, 1993. Hanako was started up by an ex-professional photographer-turned-businessman

---

[1] Bangkok Post, July 2, 1994

named Sobun Tsukikawa. After working in Thailand at businesses in travel and jewelry export, Tsukikawa felt he wanted to be involved in a business that was less dependent on fluctuating seasonal and global demand. Tsukikawa knew that the consumers of Southeast Asia were experiencing a tremendous growth in purchasing power. Thailand's capita GNP has more than doubled since 1985. As a result, more women, especially in Thailand, were finding work in offices than ever before, and so more and more women felt the need to buy cosmetics.

In 1996, the estimated size of the Southeast Asian market for cosmetics was US$4 billion, and up till then had had an average growth rate of about 18% per year. Thailand and Indonesia alone accounted for half of that market. Previous to 1994, Thai import duties on foreign cosmetics were as high as 100%, but were lowered to 40% in 1995 and then 20% in 1997,[2] making high quality goods more affordable for Thai women. In addition, sales volume of cosmetics in the Southeast Asian markets of over 400 million is dwarfed by sales in Japan and China, leading some to believe that the best is yet to come.

Hanako opened the doors to 11 beauty centers across Thailand in late 1993, offering a brand new line of cosmetics created and manufactured completely in Japan. Tsukikawa sparked awareness for Hanako by broadcasting a sixty-second commercial starring Michael Wong, a Hong Kong-based actor very well known in Thailand. Hanako quickly built up a reputation for quality and an understanding of the specific dermatological needs of Thai women, people who believe their skin to be more delicate than the skin of Western women. At special promotions in such leading department stores as Sogo and Central, Hanako repeatedly broke single-day counter sales for those retailers.[3] It is Hanako's hopes that they are giving cosmetic giants like Shiseido, Estee Lauder and Lancome a run for their money in the Thai market.

---

[2] Sourced from a speech by Mr. Surapat Krisadapong, director of the Thailand Cosmetic Manufacturers Association, on emerging markets in ASEAN, presented at the 5th Annual Conference on Cosmetic Regulation in Washington, D.C. in April, 1996

[3] Bangkok Post, February 11 and May 30, 1994

HIGH-END DIRECT SALES

In Japan, the chief channel for cosmetics is the million or so pharmaceutical retail outlets that seemingly dot every block across the country. In comparison, prestigious international brands in Thailand are available in only a little over 30 major department stores, and in a small but growing number of chain drug stores, the bulk of which are located in Bangkok. The more economically priced brands like Avon are sold nationally, quite successfully, via direct sales. Hanako management pictured Hanako becoming the luxury brand of choice for all Thais. This required a strategy that would create awareness and availability throughout Thailand, so they carved a unique niche for themselves as a high-priced brand distributed primarily through direct sales based in beauty centers located in all parts of the country.

Hanako created a network of sales people who fan out and sell directly to the customer. Avon, with an estimated 70,000 sales people, and Mistine, a Thai firm that has an estimated 90,000 sales people, dominate the direct sales cosmetics market.[4] But their niche is low-end cosmetics, while Hanako's is high end. An example of the difference in target markets is in the pricing of skin whitener, a product that has seen tremendous growth due to the Thai perception that light-colored skin is a quality of beauty. In mid-1997, Avon was selling a 50-gram tube of whitener for approximately 140 baht. Hanako was selling 30 grams of its whitener for 2,550 baht.

One way to develop a nationwide network of sales people is by recruiting people who have experience in direct sales, and who have their own network of sales people beneath them. A national sales manager was hired to create that network, which grew to about 14,000 after three years. In 1997, although Hanako sold its cosmetics through department stores and its own beauty centers, about 70% of sales were through direct sales.

But this method was not without its problems. A majority of the sales people recruited into the Hanako sales family were people who formerly had sold cosmetics. This might sound like a common

---

[4] Sourced from a 1996 report released by Advanced Research Group. These estimates, however, may be somewhat exaggerate.

157

sense recruitment strategy, but unfortunately the people who joined the Hanako network were used to selling low-end cosmetics, which often meant selling on price.

Yugo Tsukikawa is the son of Hanako's chairman, Sobun, and the director in charge of business development. When Yugo joined Hanako in 1993, he remembered how frustrating it was to get sales to change their sales approach.

> Our sales people were used to saying, "This is a 100 baht item. I'm going to give it to you, my friend, for 50 baht." That's not how you sell a high-end cosmetics product. You can give your friends a certain discount, a 10% discount, but that's not your catch. The main point is high quality. And it's high quality because of this ingredient. It's important to have this ingredient in your skin because it promotes so and so. You have to sit them down and explain the science of it. They said they understood, but I don't think they really believed it. Some of these people had been programmed for years to sell on price.

Sumit Champrasit was brought in as managing director in 1996 to make sure that Hanako sales representatives better understood how to sell high-priced items. Sumit was the former general manager at Electrolux, a Swedish line of consumer goods that enjoys a high-end reputation in Thailand. One of his mandates was to make sure that the training in Hanako created a sales force that could sell on quality. He understood that many of his sales people had previously sold Avon and Mistene. And as a result, he knew that sales people for low-end cosmetic companies did not really have to sell. All they had to do was show their clients thousands of items inexpensively priced in very detailed catalogs. "I don't really call them direct sales," said Sumit. "I call them mobile retails. I mean, how can a sales lady know everything about all these products?"

According to Sumit, these sales people received little training because their catalogs and special promotions made it easy for their clients to buy based on price. But Sumit said that Hanako sales people needed to be trained thoroughly and constantly in understanding such areas as facial structure, skin qualities and the needs of high-income clientele. Hanako Beauty Consultants, as they are called, train initially for three days in the office, and then for a week in the field. After that, they are called in for six more one- or two-day sessions before their first year is over.

A database monitors the performance of Hanako beauty consultants. When a beauty consultant's sales drop below a certain level over a period of time, they are warned and then asked to stop selling if the trend continues. On the other hand, the system is performance-based in the sense that the more one sells, the further one advances in the company. A beauty consultant who consistently sells well can move up to the salaried position of district sales manager, and still retain   the commission she got as a beauty consultant. She also has the understanding that she can move up the ladder to Regional Sales Manager, or even National Sales Manager, as well as move back down if her numbers fall. A person who is responsible for the training of another who advances up the ladder also receives a bonus, hopefully creating incentive for the advancement of all involved in sales.

MARKETING UP-COUNTRY

Training doesn't just take place in Bangkok. Training takes place all over Thailand, in beauty centers from Hat Yai in the south to Chiang Mai in the north. In fact, when Hanako started operations, only one was located in Bangkok. The rest were in such towns as Phitsanulok, Khon Kaen, Kamphaengphet, Rachaburi and Nakon Sawan, places that most foreign business people never visit. Before anybody had ever even heard of the name Hanako, Sobun Tsukikawa and his management team decided to invest in a nationwide infrastructure that cost from 4 to 14 million baht per beauty center. The beauty centers offer personal facial treatments and provide a physical up-scale presence in a particular town's business or shopping district. But in addition to providing facials and product awareness, these beauty centers serve as storage for supplies and training centers for beauty consultants in those areas.

But the thing many foreign business people might want to know is, "Is there any money in selling high-priced cosmetics up-country where a significant part of the population still work on the farms? Can these people afford 450-baht lipstick and one-thousand baht facials?" The answers to these questions are: "not yet" and "yes".

The Japanese, rightly or wrongly, have developed a reputation for long-term thinking. Hanako seems to be another example of this perceived cultural trait. As far as Hanako management is concerned, Hanako is here for the long haul, and Yugo Tsukikawa fully expects Thais living up-country to eventually have the buying power of their brethren in Bangkok. "Everybody who produces high-end products focuses in Bangkok because that's where the market is today," explained Tsukikawa. "But they're forgetting that in another five years or so up-country areas will start to get developed." Hanako wants people up-country to start believing that Hanako is the high-class brand of choice, just as many Thais aspire to the Mercedes Benz brand. If they aspire to Hanako, chances are that they will buy it when they can afford to. Thus, Tsukikawa believes that the awareness built up over a period of years will be a tremendous advantage if any other big-named cosmetic firm really tries to assert itself into a lucrative up-country market.

But Hanako isn't just looking long-term. Sales up-country are already good! According to Sumit, 70% of Hanako's direct sales is from up-country, while Bangkok has 30%. Part of the reason Hanako may have such a high percentage of sales up-country is because until the end of 1997, its Siam Square beauty center was the only direct sales center in Bangkok. But another reason for the high percentage is that there simply is a market up-country for the same type of goods and services provided in Bangkok. "The amazing thing is that up-country, rural areas are very strong, more than people think," said Tsukikawa. "You think they don't have money. But they're hungry for new products, good products, and they'll spend for them."

Sumit explains that the relatively fast shift in Thailand's economy from one based on agriculture to one based on manufacturing has changed the needs of people up-country. "Before women in rural areas worked in the rice fields, but they work in the factories now," said Sumit, "which means that their lifestyles have changed. They socialize more and have more opportunities to dress up and go to parties. This has helped the cosmetics market grow up-country."

160

Naturally, wealthier Thais, people earning 50 thousand a month and up, are buying Hanako cosmetics. The middle class, those making 20 to 30 thousand a month, are also buying Hanako. But surprisingly, even people who are earning around 10 to 15 thousand a month or less are buying. "In the States, the people who purchase high image brands are at the high income end," said Tsukikawa. "In Thailand, the same is true. But there are also a lot of middle income people who buy high. And even people at the low income level are tiptoeing and buying these products."

Sumit said that in Thailand and other parts of Asia, these "high image/ low income" tastes are quite common. "Thais want to look good. Even if they can't afford a good car, they'll try to buy it. I think that, especially in Thailand, they have traditionally had a low cost of living. Many live with their parents. So many of them don't worry about the future so much, and spend more than they should." Sumit said that such spending habits aren't good for the country. But he knows that these consumers may become loyal Hanako customers in the long run.

In the end, marketers have to come to grips with the fact that Bangkok makes up only one-tenth of the country's entire population, and that it is a matter of time before it will become necessary to market goods or services nationwide. William Heinecke, whose Pizza Hut chain is profiled in Chapter Fifteen, explains.

> It has been like marketing to two cities. For the most part 50% of your sales was in Bangkok and 50% was in the rest of the country. Well, now up-country sales for Pizza Hut are up to 60%. Soon it may be 70%, and finally it'll be 80% as the affluence grows in those markets. After all, there's over 50 million people out there.

EXPANSION THROUGH FRANCHISING

Little by little, Hanako has been opening up counters in the limited number of department stores and drug stores available in Thailand. But retail sales account for less than 10% of Hanako revenues. Hanako management decided that the best way to increase sales is to simply increase the number of people selling the product. They believe that the major vehicle for this expansion will be franchising.

In 1996 Hanako sold its first franchise. Just as a member of the royal family was asked to lend her image to Hanako, so was a famous actress Chadaporn Rattanakorn. A popular television actress in the early 1990s, Chadaporn was asked to be a presenter for Hanako products. When asked to become Hanako's first franchise owner, she jumped at the chance. "As a presenter I had used Hanako cosmetics and liked it," said Chadaporn. "Other actresses also liked Hanako so I was confident that it would be a good business."[5]

It was good enough to convince another famous actress, Chanana Nutakom to start up her own franchise. A third well-known actress has also bought a franchise for Chiang Mai. As Yugo Tsukikawa explained, building on a celebrity image is nothing new around the world, but it has been very effective in bringing other celebrities into Hanako's franchising fold. "Prominent people have a face, and when they succeed, others follow. In fact, it has become known that actresses show up at Hanako showrooms and Hanako's image gets stronger."

In mid-1998, Hanako had nine franchises, all owned by actresses and prominent members of their communities. Hanako no longer intends to open up their own beauty centers because they believe they can find eager franchisees. These new partners will take care of the 4 to 10 million baht in start up costs and provide tremendous marketing advantages by virtue of who they are and who they know. And if Hanako selects the right people, these franchise owners should be motivated enough to run a tight ship and maintain a high level of service.

Although Tsukikawa recognizes that owning and operating its own beauty centers could theoretically result in higher profits, he feels that this strategy would be too slow and costly in the end. Hanako wants franchisees to take care of the "hardware", in other

---

[5] Quote from a 1996 Japanese television program called "Asia o Kakeru" profiling Hanako in its series about Japanese investors in Asia

words, the building of the beauty center and the running of it, while Hanako supports them. Tsukikawa said that Hanako wants to be the McDonalds of up-scale cosmetics, a reference to McDonalds incredible global growth through franchising.

> "Hardware", in terms of owning and maintaining Hanako beauty centers, is advantageous. But when you have an annual budget, you have to ask yourself where do you want to spend the money? Our policy is to concentrate on "software". We can expand very quickly and effectively if we focus just on assisting them with the IT systems, management systems, inventory control, marketing, and training. Eventually, we would like to own 15% of the beauty centers while the remaining 85% is owned by franchisees.

But these initial franchises are, in a sense, a prelude to Hanako's true intention for franchises. Hanako's first four franchises are labeled Type-A, places in which one can get a facial or buy the product. But a type-B franchise will also be set up for direct sales. For Hanako, direct sales is where the money is, and the more beauty centers around the country that have their own sales networks, the higher the expected revenue. Hanako has a full-time franchise manager who goes out and scouts potential owners. And in the course of setting up the first four Type-A franchises, Hanako has gotten invaluable insight in working with franchise owners, and so has had time to develop the software necessary to help a franchise owner manage their own sales network. Despite the economic downturn in 1997, Sumit is optimistic about the popularity of Hanako franchises and sees them as a major engine for growth in the years to come.

Direct sales, particularly in a country like Thailand that is relatively short on retail shelf space, is the wave of the present that seems to have a strong future. With the success of such companies as Avon and Amway, and the arrival of Nu-Skin, a tremendous number of people are joining a direct sales network. This in turn creates even more sales as the success grows. Is Thailand far from a future where everybody is selling something to someone? Hanako wouldn't mind.

FOURTEEN

PIZZA HUT DELIVERS
Finding Your Niche in a Land of Opportunity

Thailand went from an agricultural economy to a booming industrial nation in a very short period. As good entrepreneurs know, change means opportunity. Economic change has created greater wealth and influenced the buying behaviors of all Thais. The young and old, male and female, wealthy and poor alike have been exposed to greater choice, and their raised expectations for greater choice will continue to spark a demand for higher quality, lower prices and better service. Business people in Thailand, both Thais and foreigners, have often been able to achieve competitive advantage by introducing products or services that proved successful in other countries.

"Whenever you see a successful business, someone once made a courageous decision." -- Peter Drucker

SAY CHEESE!

All human beings produce an enzyme in their system called lypase when they are born. It is an enzyme that breaks down milk and other dairy products. Those who drink milk from childhood will continue to produce lypase into adulthood. Those who stop drinking milk, or never start, cease to produce the enzyme. However, if you drink milk or eat a milk-based product without the lypase enzyme in the body's system you may experience varying degrees of discomfort, even nausea.

As milk has traditionally not been a part of many Asians' diets, some Asians, particularly older ones, do not drink milk, eat cheese or enjoy ice cream. Westerners drink milk and eat butter, but it has not been an Asian custom to do so. The Japanese used to have an insulting expression for Westerners whose body odors were disagreeable to them. They would call Westerners "bataa-kusai", which could loosely be translated as "My God, you reek of butter!"

So what was William Heinecke thinking in 1979 when he introduced fast-food pizza, with its healthy toppings of cheese, to Thailand? This was before the economic boom had suddenly swelled the purchasing power of Thai consumers. And before large air-conditioned shopping centers, kids with money, and fast food Americana. Thai food is a culinary delight to Thais and non-Thais alike. Trading tasty rice-based dishes for heavy bread smothered with the gooey, smelly white stuff was probably not what most Thais, nor savvy marketers of the time, had in mind.

And yet, the Pizza Hut chain in Thailand is a success today. In the 1990s, pizza sales have more than tripled from a little over 400 million baht in 1992 to 1.4 billion baht in 1996. What was once a whim, a restaurant that Heinecke thought might only appeal to foreigners, is now a symbol of the incredible growth of Thai purchasing power and the rapidly changing patterns of Thai consumer behavior. Starting up businesses on gut instinct is not something you necessarily learn in business school. Which is just as well because Heinecke never even bothered to go to college.

A MINOR TAKES A MAJOR STEP

In 1966, William Heinecke had just graduated from the International School of Bangkok. He had been living in Thailand for four years as his father was working for the American military based in Thailand. And at the age of 17, the younger Heinecke was looking for a challenge. He decided to decline his acceptance to Georgetown University in the United States, instead opting to stay in Bangkok to be an entrepreneur. After borrowing US$1,200 from a local moneylender, Heinecke started up a professional cleaning service because he had heard people complaining about how dirty their offices were. At the same time he started up an ad agency that specialized in creating and placing ads for foreign companies.

Success came relatively easy to Heinecke. In 1974, at the age of 24, he sold his office cleaning company to Jardine Matheson for US$ 200,000, and sold the ad agency to Oglivy & Mather for US$300,000. He ran Oglivy & Mather (Thailand) for two years, more than doubling the company's billings to US$6 billion, but decided that he had had enough of politics in a big international firm and wanted to be his own boss again. He still is his own boss.

Today, Heinecke is the head of Minor Group, a business empire founded primarily on three public companies. The Minor Corporation PCL markets a variety of brand-name goods, including Esprit fashion, Sheaffer pens, Titleist golf wear and products and Lancome cosmetics. The Royal Garden Resorts PCL owns and/or operates several luxury hotels, malls and condominiums. The third company, called The Pizza PCL, is responsible, as of 1997, for operating over 100 Pizza Huts, over 50 Swenson ice cream parlors, 8 Sizzler restaurants as well as a few Dairy Queens. In 1994, The Pizza PCL also established the Minor Cheese Co., Thailand's first cheese manufacturing plant, so that it could supply the Pizza Hut chain, the largest buyer of mozzarella cheese in Thailand. When Heinecke opened up his first Pizza Hut it probably never crossed his mind that he would eventually have to start up a factory that would produce hundreds of tons of cheese for a population of young, lypase-producing Thais.

IN SEARCH OF GOOD PIZZA

It was the late 1970s and Heinecke simply wanted a pizza. Oh, there was the odd place or hotel coffee shop that had pizza on the menu. Heinecke recalls one place in particular on Sukhumvit soi 49 where foreigners would often gather on the weekends. But good, American-style pizza just wasn't around the corner as it would be in New York or Chicago. In fact, he had to go all the way to the Philippines for that. In a nation heavily influenced by milk-drinking Spaniards and Americans, Heinecke was able to find a Shakey's restaurant in Manila one day and have his long-desired American pizza.

At the back of his mind, Heinecke realized that American-style fast food businesses were beginning to make a dent in the Asian consciousness. Although McDonalds wouldn't open their first restaurant in Thailand until 1985, the Golden Arches were becoming popular in places like Japan and Hong Kong. Why not take a chance in bringing fast food pizza here, he thought. Unfortunately, a large Filipino firm had the Asian rights to Shakey's, and they told Heinecke that they would do it themselves. So, by default, Heinecke called up Pizza Hut headquarters in the States. Pizza Hut had just been acquired by PepsiCo. Encouraged by the international nature of their parent company, the management at Pizza Hut thought that Heinecke's ideas for a Thai presence could work. When it was clear that PepsiCo's Thai agent didn't want to get involved in restaurants, Heinecke got the rights to Pizza Hut.

Since Heinecke wasn't sure that Thais would go for pizza, he decided in 1980 to open up a restaurant in Pattaya, a popular vacation spot for foreigners, as well as a regular stopover for the United States Navy. Heinecke figured that even if Thais didn't walk in, at least he'd have a steady flow of foreigners who could keep the place going. "It was a test," said Heinecke. "Even if it flopped with the Thais, it would be fun to do. And I'd get to eat a good pizza."

He wasn't making a lot of money, in that first restaurant, but he wasn't losing money either. And one statistic was particularly encouraging that first year. About half of the clientele at Pizza Hut were Thai. About a year later, Heinecke opened a second restaurant on Surawong Road in Bangkok. The following year he opened another one in Siam Square. Slowly but surely in the 1980s, Pizza Hut was establishing a presence. After ten years, there were ten Pizza Huts, prompting the Pizza Hut executives in America to label the Minor Group Chairman "One-Store-A-Year Heinecke". "I'm a practical person," he said. "When we started things, I just wanted to do one good one. And then if it works, do a second, and a third." As of mid-1997, there were 102 around the country, and Pizza Hut dominates the fast food pizza industry.

CHANGING CONSUMER BEHAVIOR

When the Thai economy went into overdrive in the late 1980s and early 1990s, The Pizza PCL started cranking out six or seven restaurants a year. The middle class was expanding and children were getting very used to milk, ice cream and fast food. Not only that, Thais wanted better food served quickly and at their convenience. Pizza Hut was one of the first companies to create a free delivery service for pizza almost anywhere in the city, helping Thais to avoid the infamous Bangkok traffic. Pizza Hut also created small "counter" outlets for people who wanted a quick slice or to take away a pie to eat at home.

In 1994, while 58% of sales were generated by sit-down customers, 25% took out their pizza and 17% had their pizza delivered. "There is a noticeable change in consumer behavior related to food consumption," wrote Heinecke in The Pizza Company's 1994 annual report. "Their demands for food have become more sophisticated, with emphasis on convenience, quality and service. And the trend is that this degree of sophistication will increase further, as a greater variety of services continue to be made available to consumers."

Change came quickly to Thailand as capita GNP doubled from 22,731 baht in 1985 to approximately 48,000 in 1995.[1] What took

---

[1] Phongpaichit, Pasuk and Baker, Chris, *Thailand's Boom*, p.31

the Western world and Japan a good part of a century to do, Thailand did in some twenty years, transforming itself from an agriculturally-based economy into a vibrant industrial nation. With such sudden changes, opportunities blossomed. In the 1970s and 1980s it was fairly easy to come into Thailand and provide a basic service or product that had succeeded elsewhere.

That was certainly Heinecke's thinking. He figured that if a business succeeded in one market, then it probably would in another, if done well enough. He had heard that one famous fast food chicken chain had failed in Thailand in the early seventies because their chicken "tasted like fish". On the other hand, he points to Reader's Digest as being the most popular magazine in the world, and McDonalds as being the most popular restaurant in the world. In addition to Pizza Hut, Minor Group has successfully introduced to Thailand a wide mix of international brand names from Mister Donut to Piper aircrafts. "It's my theory that people are more similar than dissimilar," said Heinecke. "If a business has worked in America, chances are it's going to work in Thailand, assuming the Thais can afford it."

As the economic landscape transforms, laws change, tariffs are lowered, competition increases and people's attitudes and values undergo adjustment. And now, in the late 1990s, even though entrepreneurs have to look a little harder, there are still market niches to be found whether it is in providing more value for a product or service that already exists, or starting a business that has yet to be exploited. Even Heinecke, the man who got Thais to eat cheese, has been surprised by the degree to which the Thai market has been open to new ideas.

Although Heinecke likes to scuba dive, drive fast cars and fly planes, he was never really into doing the things that people in the West were doing to keep fit. As a result, he feels he missed out on the business of running shoes. "I didn't see it," he said. "I thought that Thailand was too hot and had too much pollution. Can you even imagine Thais jogging for pleasure?" Another time he had some executives from America come to see him about the possibility of opening up a chain of convenience stores, but he thought they were nuts. "'You can't compete with all those mom and pop stores,' I said. I drove them out of my office." Of course, one of Thailand's

169

biggest companies, CP Group, went on to open up hundreds of 7-11 convenience stores soon after that.

Change can be very good for entrepreneurs, at least those who can see the trends and have the will to seize the opportunities. The following are sketches of four other people who saw their niche and seized.

NOT JUST FOR BOYS ANYMORE

Joy Menzies was brought in to run the Angus Steak House. This was a chain of five restaurants started up in the late 1970s to cater to foreigners who wanted a good t-bone. Catering to the foreign market, Angus Steak House eventually had five restaurants, two in Bangkok and one each in Hua Hin, Pattaya and Chiang Mai. The original owners were a group of foreign men who wanted a restaurant that they could call their own, a place where they could unwind with a big, juicy steak and some cold beers.

Menzies didn't really have any experience in food and beverage operations. But she was a marketer and she could clearly read the writing on the wall. First, she knew that Westerners were eating less and less red meat. Second, Menzies felt that in order to survive in Thailand she couldn't depend only on the foreign market. And third, not only was Angus Steak House's market catering primarily to foreigners, it was catering primarily to foreign men.

> The Angus Steak House was mainly a boy's kind of place, much like many of the drinking places in Bangkok. So I wanted to introduce a place which was for both girls and guys. When I first came to Bangkok, there was no place for somebody like myself to go for a drink and have a calm meal in a relaxed pub atmosphere. Hotel bars are just too expensive and you have to dress up a bit. So there was no real place for women or couples to stop by for a couple of drinks.

After managing the chain for a few years, Menzies felt that the Angus Steak House had to adapt to the times. First she changed the name to The Great British Pub Company, to emphasize a switch in focus from restaurants to pubs. Second, she convinced the shareholders to allow her to close the Chiang Mai and Hua Hin restaurants, two money-losing operations. Then she embarked on transforming a couple of foreign haunts that may have outlasted their culinary welcome.

The old Angus Steak House on Sukhumvit Road was given a complete face lift. What was once a dark, forbidding place to which foreign men brought their girlfriends has turned into a pub called The Bull's Head, a clean establishment with an inviting, light atmosphere where women don't feel the least bit threatened. In Thaniya Plaza off of Silom Road, another Angus Steak House was converted into a wine bar called the Barbican. Designed for the Thai market, the Barbican is slightly upscale, a place where couples as well as business people can stop by for a snack and a drink. Menzies believes that Thais, especially female Thais, feel comfortable walking into this bright, clean and not terribly noisy wine bar that they could probably bring their mother to.

There is a quickly rising Thai middle class, both male and female, looking for reasonably-priced places that offer relaxed, trendy atmospheres, wines and cocktails, as well as good food. Menzies feels that the Bulls Head and the Barbican are two steps in that direction. "I've pulled this company out of the Seventies," she said. "Now I'm trying to bring it into the Nineties."

THE TECHNOLOGICAL EDGE

When you start up a business you have to identify a need in the market place. What's the biggest need in Asia? According to Vincent Swift, it's human resources. "The biggest shortage in Asia is not capital, it's people," said Swift. "This problem is not going to be solved. In fact, it's going to get worse. Now, if you approach it professionally, you can make money in this situation."

After 15 years in the international marketing business, and ten years with Leo Burnett running their operations in China, Hong Kong and Thailand, Swift finally felt the need to strike out on his own. In 1993, Swift started up The Wright Company, an executive search company specializing in the area of multinational consumer marketing. As country manager for Leo Burnett in Hong Kong, he had a payroll of US$6 million and twenty different nationalities working under him. After his responsibilities for developing strategy, Swift found that his other major responsibility was finding the people to implement his strategy. "I spent half my time head-hunting for people," he said. "I was very used to doing high level recruitment so I felt I should start up in an area I fully understood."

Forming the Wright Company was not a snap decision. Contrary to many of the entrepreneurs profiled in this book, Swift's business niche was carefully thought out. First, he knew there was a critical need for executives who specialized in marketing because demand had completely outstripped supply. Second, he believed there was a lack of competent competition in his area of executive search in the market place. Third, he felt it would be fruitless to compete with companies placing executives in Thai firms, so he decided to concentrate on multi-nationals, or Thai firms "looking to beef up to international standards". And fourth, he felt he could create a technological advantage by utilizing sophisticated database expertise.

Swift feels that one of the competitive advantages his firm of 16 people has is its database of marketing and advertising executives in Thailand. According to Swift, "headhunters have traditionally not used databases. They used word-of-mouth and contacts. That is the intuitive way of doing the business, not systematic. I thought, 'Look, it's going to be expensive, but let's just blanket the market and map it with a database.'" Now, at the touch of a few keys, he has access to detailed information from about 6,000 executives. In addition to basic information about the person's current position and contact number, this database also contains the candidate's professional and educational backgrounds as well as evaluations on a variety of job dimensions. These evaluations are conducted in interviews by The Wright Company's consultants, who rate job candidate's abilities on a scale of one to ten. Swift feels that the database gives his consultants an edge in efficiency and accuracy over other search firms.

Of course it's impossible to have access to all possible candidates because databases get out of date every second. People are getting hired and fired all the time, changing careers. We have five consultants and two researchers who make twenty phone calls every day -- a hundred forty phone calls a day. And they all have on-line access and update capability. If we're looking for an executive marketing manager, our competition might take three phone calls to find a candidate, but we can do it in two. If they can do it in two, we can do it in one. Now you say, does that make a difference? Yes it does. It makes us thirty to fifty percent more efficient than our competition. It means more calls for our clients. That's what it's all about.

This database didn't come out of thin air. Swift hired an independent consultant to put it together for The Wright Company. This consultant was so good that Swift worried about losing him to another company, so he suggested that they set up a new company, take on clients and take advantage of this man's abilities. Swift's Thai private limited company then became the Thai shareholder in Business Address Databases Co. Ltd., and Swift had what he claimed was "the best MIS department of any human resource operation in Asia, without the overhead."

QUALITY SELLS

Finding diamonds in the rough is literally Roberto Cacciola's job as he imports rough diamonds to Thailand. But in his ten years of bringing these most precious stones to Thailand, finding a good cup of coffee in Thailand has been a much greater challenge. "As an Italian, I was always looking to get a decent espresso in Thailand, which had been almost impossible," said Cacciola. A true entrepreneur, Cacciola decided to stop looking and to introduce to Thailand what he believes is the very best in Italian-style coffee -- Illy Caffe.

"It takes approximately fifty beans to make a cup of coffee, but it takes only one defective bean to spoil the flavor." So claims world-renowned Illy Caffe, a leading manufacturer of espresso coffee, which uses advanced technology and decades of experience to make sure that only the best Arabica beans are selected, and the most advanced processes are employed to create a cup of consistently good espresso or cappuccino. In fact, according to Illy Caffe, it is the only coffee company in the world to have achieved ISO-9001 certification, the most stringent of the ISO quality assurance standards. With confidence in the product, Cacciola formed his second company in Thailand, Thai Ultimate Espresso, and attained the right to be Illy's sole agent and distributor.

There's one problem with selling one of the best brands in the world. The best tends to be very expensive. Not only is Illy Caffe one of the most expensive espresso brands in the world, tariffs and taxes combine to seemingly price Illy out of the market. As a result of an extraordinary 99% import duty, plus another 20% in various taxes, a kilo of Illy Caffe was sold for 1,350 baht in 1997. In contrast, a kilo of the local coffee roast went for 350 baht.

In other words, some clients would have to pay, say, 400,000 baht for their coffee bill as opposed to the 100,000 baht they were used to paying. In addition, a restaurant would have to buy an expensive, industrial use machine if they wanted to serve Illy coffee. But as Gianmaria Zanotti, Ultimate Espresso's former sales manager explained, it wouldn't be a loss of several hundred thousand baht. It would merely be a loss of several baht per cup of coffee. When compared to the 50 or 60 baht a restaurant sells a cup of cappuccino for, it is a small sacrifice, he tells them. The extra cost, he says, is more than made up for in increased volume. "In Italy, people drink four to five cups of coffee a day." Zanotti explained. "If a European is sitting at a dinner table with friends, and he has a mediocre cup of coffee, he won't have another. But if it's good, and he still wants to sit and talk, he'll certainly order another. And he'll recommend the good coffee to others."

Could Cacciola sell a product that is four times more expensive than the locally-produced java? Would restaurant and hotel owners or managers want to spend so much more for coffee, no matter how good it tasted? Westerners have been drinking coffee for centuries and they might see the reasoning in paying a little extra for good coffee, but would the Thais? Cacciola looked for market data on how much and what kind of coffee is consumed in Thailand, but he just couldn't find that sort of information. As David Cohen of Malcolm Bruce Ltd, a consultancy that specializes in helping start ups in Thailand, said, "Thailand is not like the West where marketing managers can get supermarket withdrawal data, and would know exactly how much share his product has. For example, if you want market data on shampoos, your data won't include the many mom and pop stores all over Thailand." Definitive answers are unclear because market statistics on most industries in Thailand are often vague or unreliable. But Cacciola took a chance and believed that Thais would like Illy Caffe despite the price.

Cacciola put his money where his mouth is, guaranteeing customers a 30% increase in coffee sales in six months, or their money back. Cacciola claimed that not one has asked for a refund. Cacciola has had to battle through a few price-conscious local hotel owners to convince them to try Illy Caffe, but he's won more battles than he's lost. In fact, Illy Caffe can be found in close to 300 hotels, restaurants, coffee shops and bars around the country, and he feels that he and his national network of sales agents have only scratched the surface. In this fast-changing Thai market, quality is a value rapidly rising in importance.

SCRATCHING OUT A NICHE

If you want to know how far people will go to find a niche here in Thailand, then talk to Claes Ostrom. Since the age of ten when he received a commission for arranging the sale of a friend's house in his home country of Sweden, Ostrom has done deals in a wide variety of businesses including art galleries, music promotion, discotheques, leather goods and handbags. When he came to Thailand, he was an agent for clothing companies in Sweden. For several years, Ostrom rode the wave of cheap labor to respectable profits exporting mainly upscale men's shirts. But when the Swedish kronar was suddenly devalued by 30% in the early 1990s his shirts were no longer cheap in Sweden, and he lost a lot of business.

Instead of getting discouraged, Ostrom looked at his options. With a devalued kronar, he figured that now might be the time to import something from Sweden. And coincidentally, the Thai government had just reduced the import duties for fiberglass from 100% to 45%. After looking at a variety of building products, Ostrom chose to become the exclusive Thai agent for the biggest manufacturer of flagpoles in the world, Tida Flag. Although Ostrom's main business is still textiles, he changed his company name to Poliville, and pioneered a niche. As far as Ostrom knew, he had no competition.

Ostrom said that flags had always had a special meaning to him and his father as they believed they symbolized something transcendent in the lives of humans, the pride one has in one's nation or company. And he felt that it was a shame that so many people in Thailand were placing the nation's flag on make-shift flagpoles, wooden sticks or drain pipes welded together. On top of that, they would have to maintain these flagpoles by painting them every so often. But Ostrom thinks that he has a great product. This fiberglass product is light, strong, requires no maintenance and will last a very long time. With the kronar devaluation and the lower import duties, "Suddenly I could offer a quality eight-meter-tall flagpole at a reasonable price of 25,000 baht, instead of the 100,000 baht it would have cost a few months before." But as one can imagine for such a unique product, it was a struggle to sell in the beginning .

> How do you open a market with a new product that nobody has seen before? I pushed a lot. I brought around small pieces as samples. I got a few people who liked it, and finally I sold two. On that basis, I decided to bring in my first container of 99 poles. Then I had to figure out how to sell the rest. I printed a catalog and I did blind mail outs. I spent one-and-a-half million baht in marketing the flagpoles at fairs and exhibitions. I thought that if they didn't sell well I was going to walk up and down Sukhumvit Road and sell them one by one. Everyone said I was crazy. Some people finally bought from me just to get rid of me.

Today, the flagpoles sell themselves as customers recommend Ostrom's flagpoles to others. He has sold over 500 flagpoles to factories, hotels, schools and showrooms in three years of business.

And he and his partner, Tida Flag, are committed to a long-term business relationship. If all goes well, then Ostrom may even set up a flagpole manufacturing operation in Thailand to supply the region. It is a business that he feels will be viable for many years to come, a company he can pass down to his three sons. After a lifetime practicing entrepreneurship, it seems as if Ostrom's marketing and sales abilities haven't flagged a bit.

FIFTEEN

INTEGRA'S SHIFT FROM LOW TO HI-TECH
Who's Missing the Boat to Vietnam?

Thailand was the darling of the international business community for a good part of the 1980s and 1990s. Thailand's large market, flexible and friendly business environment and its central location within southeast Asia are common reasons given for investing here. But competition for investment dollars continues to get keener. China, Indonesia, India and Eastern Europe are just a few of Thailand's bigger rivals. Vietnam in particular has been viewed as a potential threat to Thailand's economic supremacy in the Indochina region. And yet, Thailand is far from ceding its position. More and more people are realizing that economies like the one in Vietnam are still many years from having the means to support fruitful investment ventures, while Thailand still has one of the most open, most entrepreneurial economies in the region.

Opportunities are like buses. There's always another one coming along. There are still such great opportunities here in Thailand so I'm in no hurry to go to Vietnam. It's still a long way from being where Thailand was 20 years ago. -- William Heinecke, CEO of the Minor Group

THE THREAT FROM VIETNAM

In the early 1990s, many people believed that Vietnam was the next land of opportunity in Asia. Despite a decade of delirious growth in Thailand, more than a few business people thought that Thailand should be looking over its shoulder for a Vietnamese tiger. Vietnam not only had the second largest population in Southeast Asia (70 million), one of the better educated workforces in the region, and bountiful natural resources, but it also had a reputation for being vibrant and hungry.

The "Vietnam War", as Americans call it, devastated the country. An economic trade embargo led by the Americans helped keep the Vietnamese economy on its knees. In 1993, the per capita GNP was a mere US$200, a figure that made Vietnam one of the poorest countries in the world. But foreshadowing the fall of the Berlin Wall and communism in Europe, and concessions by communist governments that a certain degree of capitalism was necessary for their economies to improve, Vietnam implemented an economic reform policy in 1986 known as Doi Moi, which promised greater transparency of business laws and practices as well as smoother foreign access to seemingly boundless opportunities.

One of the men who truly believed in the potential of Vietnam was Raymond Eaton, an Australian businessman who has lived and done business in Thailand for over 20 years. He is the chairman of the Integra Group, the umbrella company for the companies he has started up in Thailand. Eaton has conducted business in Vietnam since the late 1980s and is considered to be an expert on the business environment of the country. In his many speeches on Vietnam in the early 1990s, he strongly spoke out against the American government's economic embargo, making such statements as,

> Never in the history of the world has any nation ever been forced by another nation to undertake such an accounting as has been imposed by the USA against Vietnam. The virtual revenge by what is today the world's superpower against a small, impoverished nation has resulted in suffering and degradation for the population of Vietnam - of whom 53% or 40 million were not even born when the American military were in Vietnam.[1]

President Bill Clinton finally lifted the embargo in 1994, allowing World Bank, International Monetary Fund and Asian Development Bank funds to flow into the country. Industrial output in the first quarter of 1994 rose by 11.4% over the previous year, while foreign investment grew nearly 300% from US$278 million for the first quarter of 1993 to US$1 billion for the first quarter of 1994. Vietnam, a nation that had fought and struggled for so long, was finally allowing itself to be optimistic about the future.

A SUNSET IN THAILAND?

Eaton decided to do business in Vietnam in 1988, long before it was fashionable for foreigners to even consider it. He sold Thai-made office furniture in Vietnam and exported clothing out of Vietnam through representative offices in Hanoi and Ho Chi Minh. He also formed a joint venture with Vietnam's National Centre for Science and Technology in 1992 to process and sell gems overseas.

Over the years, Eaton's main company, Export Development Trading Corporation (EDTC), has enjoyed profitable times as an exporter of garments, furniture, footwear, jewelry and handicrafts manufactured in Thailand. But in the late eighties, Eaton noticed that his bread-and-butter businesses, which at one time had brought in as much as US$70 million in revenue a year, were beginning to lose steam. He began to wonder how long the Thai economic engine could continue to maintain near double-digit growth. In the 1990s, EDTC saw a

---

[1] Eaton, Raymond, Speech to the Europe/East Asia Economic Forum and World Economic Forum in Hong Kong, October 13-15, 1993.

significant drop off in high volume budget-priced garments and footwear as companies moved their production to such areas as Indonesia, China, Bangladesh, India and Eastern Europe.

In a speech to Thai and Vietnamese businessmen and government officials in August, 1993, Eaton strongly suggested that Thai exporters prepare for the worst. He told them to "face reality", to recognize that Thailand was bound to lose the basic labor intensive industries, and that "the trend was irreversible". He said that Thai industry had to upgrade its technological manufacturing base to increase efficiency and improve quality, or begin to transfer their high-volume, low budget factories to Vietnam so that they wouldn't lose competitiveness.[2]

But not even a year and a half later, in a speech at a Bangkok symposium sponsored by the Ministry of Commerce in January of 1995, Eaton reflected the frustration of many exporters in Thailand.

> Unfortunately, there were important changes that should have taken place in Thailand, but did not -- in many factories there was only minimal upgrading of operations instead of investment that would have resulted in the introduction of more sophisticated technology; there continued to be a scarcity of quality staff in almost every sector of the industry; there was only a nominal improvement in the overall quality of garments being produced; little innovation of new fabrics and yarns emerged; and strict adherence to contracted shipment dates often did not receive sufficiently serious attention.

Due in good part to the above reasons, total exports from Thailand declined in 1996 after ten straight years of at least 13% growth.[3] Textile exports in particular fell 15% in 1996 to 137.2 billion baht ($5.7 billion), down from 160.8 billion baht in 1995.[4] Eaton has tried

---

[2] Eaton, Raymond, Speech to the State Planning Committee of of the Socialist Republic of Vietnam in Bangkok on a market economy training and study tour on August 8, 1993.
[3] The Nikkei Weekly, March 24, 1997
[4] Asian Wall Street Journal, June 17, 1997, as sourced from the Ministry of Commerce

to compensate for the decreasing competitiveness of Thai products by building up his businesses in Laos and Vietnam, and looking into opportunities in Burma and Cambodia. The grass certainly seemed greener on the other side. That is, until he took a closer look. . . .

RETREAT FROM VIETNAM

Eaton has always been an outspoken supporter of Vietnam and its chances of becoming a strong, industrialized nation if given the chance. He still is. But he's also a realist, and since his early years of doing business in Vietnam, he has been fairly quick to point out the challenges that foreign investors face.

First, Vietnam is a poor nation. Even though the size of the educated workforce in Vietnam compares very favorably to Thailand's, Eaton said that the 90% literacy rate may be exaggerated, and that a lack of money has resulted in a shortage of schools. In addition, businesses are very low on working capital, and can't afford to buy the materials needed to manufacture basic goods. Eaton wanted to increase his export garment business in Vietnam but found that local factories requested potential buyers to supply the fabric, the labels, the thread, the buttons and all the packing materials. Many foreign buyers didn't want to go through all the trouble just to have them cut and sew the garments.

Although Vietnam is a very poor nation, the cost of doing business can be quite high. Labor costs are the same as in China and just a little less than Indonesia even though those economies are far stronger. In addition, international joint venture companies are required to pay wages at a higher rate than local Vietnamese companies. This two-tier cost structure extends to other fundamental operation costs, and according to Eaton, compares very unfavorably with Thailand. "I believe that the Thai's fairness in the treatment of foreigners was a key factor in that country's development," said Eaton. "There is no gouging on rents, wages, or installation of telephones. A foreigner is charged exactly the same as a Thai. Why can't this apply in Vietnam?"

Smuggling is rampant in Vietnam. In 1993, it was estimated that the black market accounted for 40% of Vietnam's total economy, and that 60% of all goods imported into Vietnam was smuggled.[5] These figures are obviously not very attractive to international firms that wish to export to Vietnam or start up local import substitution factories. Although the government has made attempts to clamp down on smuggling by issuing decrees that carry heavy punishments, even capital punishment, it is the government that is also heavily involved in the smuggling. An investigation by the Vietnamese Ministry of Trade revealed that over 70% of state-run organizations in 14 provinces have cooperated with the private sector to smuggle goods into the country.[6]

The biggest problems that foreign investors face in Vietnam is in fact the government. For all the complaints that foreigners have about the bureaucracy and corruption in Thailand, it seems as if the state of affairs is worse in Vietnam.

> The underlying problem (in Vietnam) is a chaotic government structure. Foreign investment laws are flawed and incomplete. Decisions made by the central government are undermined by power-hungry local bureaucrats. Decrees and ordinances are churned out by ministries, commissions, and other departments alike -- often with little regard for whether or not they overlap. And while foreign investors are officially welcomed, ideologues and party hacks swipe at them through the state-controlled media, blaming foreigners for inhumane working conditions and other social evils as well as accusing them of being spies bent on overthrowing the government.[7]

This type of governance is fertile ground for corruption. According to Eaton, the joint venture in which he invested US$1 million to process and export gems failed because his government partners

---

[5] Eaton, Raymond, Speech to the Foreign Correspondents Club of Thailand, on July 14, 1993.

[6] Ibid.

[7] Far Eastern Economic Review, October 6, 1997

saw the job as a great opportunity to enrich themselves. Eaton said that the Vietnamese managing director of the business was using company funds to buy raw materials for himself, processing the gems through the factory, and then selling the gems on his own. Formal complaints to the Economic Crime Division and the State Committee for Promotion Investment fell on deaf ears. Frustrated and sickened, Eaton simply shut down the factory and locked it up. He assumes it still sits idle.

In Eaton's opinion, Thailand has a very friendly environment for foreign business people compared to Vietnam, a place he considers a bit xenophobic. He doesn't like the situation, but he thinks he understands why. "The Vietnamese have been fighting foreigners for thousands of years. They had to fight off the Chinese, then the French, then the Americans, and the Chinese again. And so I think this nationalistic spirit is greatly embedded in every part of their thinking. They just don't seem to be able to comprehend that they can open up their country and welcome people."

As a result of these problems, and despite the country's competitive advantages and still impressive growth rate of a little under 7% in 1997, direct foreign investment was going down, not up. Approved foreign investment for the first eight months of 1997 was down 20% from 1996, and 35% from 1995. Hundreds of projects had failed and foreign investors were displeased with business conditions in Vietnam.[8] "What's the best way to become a millionaire in Vietnam?' the joke goes. The answer: "Start out as a billionaire."

THE SUN RISES AGAIN

The year 1996 was a busy year for Eaton and his Integra Group, but it was not a profitable one. The export businesses were flat, just breaking even. Eaton had invested 20 million baht in a venture in 1995 that was designed to increase the efficiency of trucks for transportation businesses and the drivers of those trucks, but sales were slow. An idea to open up a chain of gourmet ice cream parlors

---

[8] Far Eastern Economic Review, October 6, 1997

never materialized. In the first half of 1997, the economy was appearing to worsen and companies all over Thailand had difficulty paying their bills. When the government placed the Thai baht on a managed float, and the baht devalued from approximately 25 baht to 55 baht to the US dollar within six months, people were forced to realize that the Thai economy had passed its peak and was tumbling downwards.

But strangely enough, Eaton didn't mind. His garment export business, an operation he said the year before he wouldn't mind dropping, was picking up considerably. He conceded that there may have been a five to ten percent price decrease due to the baht devaluation, but he believes that efforts to upgrade production methods and machinery in his suppliers' factories were finally paying dividends in very competitively priced, high-end garments. Lead times were down and quality was up. His Japanese client, a mail order catalog marketer of garments called Otto Sumisho, were so pleased that they decided to decrease its purchasing from other markets to increase their purchasing from Thailand, an amount that accounts for 25% of their inventory. As an executive in Otto Sumisho wrote to Eaton, "the quality of garments that we are buying today from Thailand is definitely the best in Asia, and in some cases equal to Japanese domestic production." A company called Poliville, which, among other products, exports high-end shirts to Europe, also experienced markedly improved sales during these rough economic times. According to M.D. Claes Ostrom, one of the main reasons for this is because his suppliers in Thailand had made major improvements to their production operations, and now "make the best shirts in the world."

GOING HI-TECH

As Eaton discovered, and continued to understand, out of crisis comes opportunity. Introduction of technology, whether it is state-of-the-art textile manufacturing machinery, advanced management processes or sophisticated computer software, can have a stirring effect on the market place. In the mid-1990s, Eaton thought that information technology in its various shapes and forms could be a lucrative field in Thailand. And when he read about a product called Turbolog in a magazine, he contacted the manufacturer and secured an agreement to license its products and services in Thailand. Turbolog is an on-board computer for trucks which monitors every moment the truck is operating, providing data that can assist a company in terms of fuel consumption, safety and the maintenance of a truck.

The Turbolog can also monitor a driver's performance. Some long-distance truckers have been known to drive at high speeds for two or three hours, stop and sleep in the truck for a while, and then drive "like a crazy man" again, racing through the gears, breaking and accelerating. Every time he goes over a certain speed, or he decelerates, it is recorded in the onboard computer. One of the purposes of the data gathered is to mold the behavior of the truck driver so that he drives at a more consistent and reasonable speed. According to Eaton, this will decrease the number of accidents, save up to 30% on fuel consumption, extend the lifespan of tires up to 25%, as well as decrease the wear and tear on the truck's gear box and brakes. In monthly reports prepared by specially-trained Turbolog analysts, one major oil multi-national was very happy to see that none of its trucks were going beyond 100 kilometers per hour, certainly a key to avoiding traffic accidents on the sometimes poor infrastructure that connects the country.

In the first two years of Turbolog in Thailand, sales were disappointing. But after the economy took a nosedive, sales of Turbolog took off. "When the economy was good and companies were making easy profits, people weren't really cost-conscious," said Eaton. "With the rapid decline in the economic situation, company profits fell and they were forced to look for every baht. Quite a number of companies that had previously shown only marginal interest, have suddenly become very interested." Since the baht devaluation, sales have increased by several hundred percent as the big firms in the oil, petrochemical, transportation and cement industries are buying hundreds of Turbologs for their truck fleets. At 40,000 baht a machine, plus 400 baht per truck per month, Eaton is optimistic about Turbolog's future.

****

The entire Southeast Asian region is a fascinating and vast ocean of opportunity. And as the Thai economy matures, some people are tempted to say, "Don't miss the boat! Get in Vietnam, China and Burma while you can!" But Eaton, and many other experienced entrepreneurs living in Thailand don't see it that way, at least not yet. In the yin-yang world of business, bad economic times can also mean opportunity for the efficient, the creative and the fortunate. And as far as Eaton is concerned, the boat's still docked off the shores of Thailand, and won't be leaving for a while.

SIXTEEN

IN SUMMARY . . . .

Thailand is a wonderful place to live and work, especially when one possesses the patience and curiosity to learn how the country and its people operate, the friends who will guide one towards such wisdom, and the entrepreneurial spirit to see Thailand for what it is -- a land of opportunities.

"In the long term, Thailand will be one of the strongest markets in Asia. It's a growing country and Bangkok in particular has an expanding population. Its commerce will grow stronger." -- Mr. John Power of Air France in explaining the rationale for moving Air France's Asian regional office from Hong Kong to Bangkok in early 1998, despite the poor economy[1]

GETTING STARTED

As one successful foreign businessman in Thailand said, a company is the tool of an entrepreneur. Just as a carpenter can't work without a good strong hammer, an entrepreneur cannot excel without the right corporate structure.

Foreign business people who want to start up a company in Thailand commonly choose one of three routes. They can:

1) form a Thai private limited company;
2) form a foreign-controlled company with Board of Investment (BOI) approval; or
3) form an American-controlled company with protection under the Treaty of Amity and Economic Relations between Thailand and the United States.

By far the most common structure for foreigners is the Thai private limited company, a venture where at least 51% of the shares are owned by Thais. Despite the Alien Business Law, which bans or restricts foreigners from entering a large variety of businesses, non-Thais are able to engage in almost any business they wish by establishing a Thai private limited company.

If you have plans to open up a factory that produces goods primarily for export, then the BOI may be an excellent option for you. In addition to the possibility of being granted tax breaks on profits, imported materials and machinery, as well as exported products,

---

[1] Bangkok Post, February, 26, 1998

the BOI allows for foreign ownership and control of your enterprise. Applying for BOI promotion requires a considerable amount of paperwork about your intended venture, an uncomfortable prospect for the impatient and discreet.

A final option is available to Americans or American entities. Thanks to The Treaty of Amity and Economic Relations between Thailand and the United States, Americans are given a distinct advantage over other non-Thais. With the exception of a few business areas, any company in Thailand which can prove that a majority of its shareholders and directors are American citizens can become a 100% owned and operated American company.

FINDING PARTNERS

Many people are entrepreneurs because they enjoy realizing their vision of creating and running a business on their own. If in their home countries they are reluctant to take on partners, then they will probably be even more reluctant to take on Thai partners here. Such independent tendencies lead some to form a Thai company with nominee shareholders. This is an illegal but common maneuver designed to create the appearance that the enterprise is at least 51% Thai owned when, in fact, the company is controlled by the foreign shareholder or shareholders.

Although many foreigners, especially those whose businesses deal primarily with advanced technology or systems, export markets or international clients, feel little need to have involved Thai partners, there are obvious advantages to such a partnership. Thai partners can help you understand Thai laws and customs, which should decrease the stress built up when your rational mind requires rational explanations for procedures and requests that don't make sense to you. Thai partners can interface with government agencies with much greater efficiency and effectiveness than you may ever hope to achieve. They can also assist you in administering, or finding people to administer your Thai staff. In short, a good Thai partner could be one of your company's most important assets.

The question, of course, is where such an effective and trustworthy partner is going to be found. For many, finding a partner is often a matter of hit or miss. Common sense probably tells you that it would take a few years to get a feel for whether a person, of any nationality, is the right partner for you. Unfortunately, common sense often takes backstage to expediency as the non-Thai entrepreneur seeks to get his enterprise up and running. After that, it's like a marriage. You either work at it or you get divorced.

MANAGING PEOPLE

Finding a good partner would be your most difficult personnel task. But finding employees for your company would probably be your second most difficult task. The skill and knowledge level required to handle the new ideas, systems, products and services coming to Thailand is high, and increasing steadily. And yet, the number of people available in the Thai work force who have the skills and knowledge to cope with the new standards is small, the direct result of one of the weakest educational systems in the region. Although the economic slowdown following a ten-year boom has resulted in a lower demand for skilled labor, the demand for highly skilled managers and engineers in particular is still significant.

Once you find people to handle your books, answer your telephones, manage your staff, manufacture your products, sell them, deliver them around the country, and do whatever else is required, you want to try to keep the people you feel are doing a good job. Compared to people in more industrialized economies, Thais tend to favor a work place which has a family-like environment. The head of the company is often seen as a person who is expected to have the answers to problems, to make most of the decisions, and generally shoulder more responsibility than a western company head is used to. He is is also expected to be more involved in the personal lives of his people -- knowing what is happening in their personal lives, presiding over weddings and funerals, paying hospital bills, taking them out for meals, and showing flexibility, understanding and responsiveness in extraordinary situations.

But in the attempt to ensure the emotional satisfaction of your employees, the ultimate goal of creating a profitable company that rewards competence and performance cannot be lost. Thais are looking for organizations that have clear opportunities for learning new skills and advancement up the hierarchy. And again, like anybody else, Thais want to be treated fairly. They want to work in an environment where compensation and advancement are based on ability and performance, which is not necessarily the case in many traditional family businesses that dominate the local business landscape.

In contrast, companies that foster warm ties with their employees, and treat the employees fairly as well, will be rewarded with staff loyalty.

DEALING WITH THE GOVERNMENT

Like anywhere else, laws in Thailand are written in lawyer-speak, a language that can defy the no-nonsense entrepreneur's ability to understand exactly what is required of him and what is allowed to him. In addition to linguistic problems, western legal concepts exist but are relatively new to the collective consciousness of Thai society. Thus, the degree to which the law is uniformly enforced is probably less than many non-Thais are used to, while the range of its interpretation is probably greater.

For some people, this sort of legal system is a flexible and advantageous one. It can provide a great deal of leeway to one's business interests, particularly when interpreted by people who know the ins and outs of the law. For others, the law may at times seem confusing in its application, a maze of shifting goal posts manipulated by people more obligated to serving patrons and clients than the spirit of the law. Getting shipments cleared, choosing the right corporate structure, making sure you have all the paperwork that is required, convincing the immigration and labor departments that you deserve to be granted a visa and work permit -- these are all common situations in which the Thai law can seem either flexible and accommodating or hypocritical and unfair.

In order to negotiate the sometimes confusing and lengthy procedures required by government offices and officers, it is probably very wise to find a person who knows the ropes. For example, you could probably personally raise a storm and get your shipment out of Customs without paying any "fees", but you won't have the time or patience to do that every month. Hire someone who knows how to do it. The same goes for permit applications, visa applications and communications with the BOI. Get a lawyer, a consultant, anybody who understands how to get things done. There are affordable ones out there. You or someone on your staff can learn how to interact with government civil servants and eventually develop relationships with people who can be very helpful to you in the future, but it can be a long and frustrating educational process.

SEIZING OPPORTUNITIES

It's a common story. A foreigner comes to Thailand on vacation, drinks in the warm weather, enjoys the company of a friendly people, and is energized by the hustle and bustle of the capitalistic capitol. Soon, he's set up base in Bangkok, started up a company and knows the beaches of Thailand like the back of his hand. In short, what many non-Thais see in Thailand is opportunity -- opportunity to provide a service or product that has succeeded elsewhere but hasn't been introduced here yet, opportunity to lead the independent life of the entrepreneur, and opportunity to create a lifestyle of relative comfort and ease amidst tropical surroundings. Many of those who have made it in Thailand couldn't imagine trying to start up anywhere else.

Many entrepreneurs came to Thailand during the 1980s, a period of great economic development. Economic development means social change. As more Thais saw their purchasing power grow, their needs evolved. Thais of all economic levels wanted greater convenience, higher quality, faster service, finer luxuries, higher status and the latest technologies. Much of this need for rising aspirations was fulfilled by foreigners and foreign companies who brought new ways and ideas to the kingdom.

Although it may seem easy to some to start up a business and succeed in Thailand, most entrepreneurs will tell you that the risk is as great here as it is anywhere else. A great deal of patience is required to adjust to the Thai business environment, and perseverance is required to convince a skeptical Thai market that you or your concept is here to stay. However, once you begin to change minds, you have a wide open niche before you, an opportunity to have a market all to yourself. But for how long? If it's a good idea, and a fairly easy one to duplicate, it **will** be duplicated, and competition will be breathing down your neck, through your shirt and into your socks if you're not fast or smart enough.

Still, opportunities abound. For many of these entrepreneurs, opportunities in Thailand are so great that if one is driven beneath the bottom line by the competition, there are always other products and services to introduce, other market segments to attack. Even in the late 1990s, as the economic boom slowed to a crawl, many business people express confidence that Thailand will continue to be a land of opportunity again. They believe much of the country will still need to be developed, a middle class will continue to emerge, and recent local and global political changes will encourage the government to be more open to foreigners and foreign ideas.

And in fact, the sudden economic slump has created opportunities for people with ideas to cut costs and increase productivity. The faster, better and cheaper your company is, the more successful your business will be. This is common sense for many non-Thais who have experienced economic recessions in North America, Europe or Japan, but not so for businesses in Thailand, a relative newcomer to global economic strife. Many ideas to help companies through tough economic times will come from outside Thai borders.

Thailand's honeymoon with the rest of the world's investors is over. Competition for capital and technology is fierce as Thailand tries to divert the attention of investors away from China, Eastern Europe, Latin America and other nations in ASEAN. And yet, Thailand is still a formidable contender in the fight for foreign investment. Thailand has a large market of 60 million, with considerably less social conflict than might be found in countries like Indonesia, Malaysia and the Philippines. It is centrally located within the region, entertaining hopes of becoming an economic hub that unites Indochina with Thailand's southern neighbors. Corruption is a problem in

Thailand, but compared to many of its neighbors, Thailand is far from being the worst. Despite its relative political instability, Thai governments over the past few decades have been consistently pro-business, which has not been the case in socialist nations as Vietnam and China. And in Indonesia and Malaysia, some believe Islamic influences have had a restrictive effect on foreign investors.

Beauty is in the eye of the beholder, and arguments can be made for starting up businesses in any of the nations mentioned above. And yet, Thailand does indeed have an inviting nature. This can be seen in the laissez-faire style in which the government tends to run its economy, in the business community's thirst for new ideas and technologies, in the beauty of its varied sea and landscapes, in the generally friendly and non-confrontational way that Thais interact with other Thais and non-Thais alike, and in the optimism these qualities tend to encourage.

Perhaps this is the way it has always been in Thailand. Proud of their historical past, Thais will often look to the Sukhothai Period of King Ramkhamhaeng some 700 years ago as a validation of the goodness and good fortune of their race, a collective memory that makes one proud to be a Thai. On a stone in the ruins of Sukhothai, the ancient capital of Thailand, are the following words that for many still ring true:

> In the water there are fish, in the fields there is rice.
> Whosoever wants to trade in elephants, so trades.
> Whosoever wants to trade in silver and gold, so trades.
> The faces of the citizens are happy.

Acknowledgements

When 76-year-old Dr. Alex Comfort was interviewed for the 25th anniversary of his internationally renown book, *The Joy of Sex*, he admitted that he was hardly an authority on the topic before he started writing the book. "I wrote the sex book before I knew very much about it," said Dr. Comfort. "If you wait that long (to become an authority), you wait forever. That's the way to find out about anything. Write a book on it."

And with that advice in mind, I set off to write a book on a topic I knew very little about: doing business in Thailand. It started merely as a need to write a more stimulating alternative to the fairly dry books catering to foreign entrepreneurs available in bookstores, and ended in a volume filled with the stories, insights, worries, delights, recommendations and facts, I believe, most practical business people crave. This book was possible due to over forty people who gave of their free time to openly talk about their experiences in Thailand, and to others who assisted in connecting me with such people, or provided advice to me on the content, style and grammar of my drafts.

First and foremost, I would like to extend my deepest gratitude to Dr. Henry Holmes, a gentleman who gave me my first opportunity to write books. Assisting Dr. Holmes in the writing of the book, *Working with the Thais*, was a stimulating exercise that has made me a better writer and us closer friends. His input into this book has also been invaluable, as he provided questions and comments that required me to probe deeper into the less obvious points of Thai culture. And without his kindness, my family and I might not be in Thailand at all.

Many of the interviews conducted for this book would not have happened without the tremendous assistance of Stuart Dawson Montgomery. Mr. Montgomery, whose experiences are also related in this book, was responsible for introducing me to eight fascinating people, all of whom are quoted in the book, and five of whom ended up being featured in their own chapters. His introductions led fortuitously to other introductions, and got my book project off to a flying start. I am eternally grateful.

Two of my colleagues at Sasin in particular helped me on a regular basis throughout this project. Daryl Chansuthus, who possesses one of the sharpest of Ockham's razors, improved my drafts by slicing away weak arguments and uncovering subjective and judgmental prose. She, more than anyone else, pushed me to maintain balance in my reporting of the entrepreneurs and their stories. Rochelle Powtong also found time to read and edit my entire draft. I always appreciated her speedy responses as I constantly thirsted for feedback. Thanks to her, there are far fewer examples of verbosity, awkwardness and grammatical error.

Because of the many legal concerns in this book, I have needed the assistance of experts in Thai business law. I am grateful to all of the lawyers who graciously spent their time with me so that I could present the Thai legal aspects of starting up a business in the most accurate way possible. All were very open in discussing any point of law I brought up, sometimes going out of their way to clarify my understanding of legally sensitive areas. Two lawyers in particular were extremely helpful. David Lyman of Tilleke and Gibbins not only gave me an hour of his time, he opened up his firm's library to me, affording me the great opportunity of examining documents that were vital to providing me with a historical perspective on the Alien Business Law and the Treaty of Amity and Economic Relations between the United States and America. Mr. Harold Vickery of Vickery and Worachai also gave me an hour of his time, providing me with great insight into the Treaty. But even more significantly, he repeatedly took the time to examine final drafts of certain chapters for legal accuracy, providing me with lengthy detailed explanations and responses.

Again, many people have helped me in the creation of this book. Listed below are the names of other people who were interviewed for the book, who introduced people who were interviewed for the book, or who assisted me by providing information or giving feedback on drafts. Thank you all so very much.

Trevor Allen, Bryan Baldwin, David Bedford, Patrick Blot, Verneita Boonlom, Sylvain Bredin, Pramut Butra-Pinyo, Roberto Cacciola, Alvin Carley, Sumit Champrasit, Nangnoi Charoenthaveesub, Piyanut Charoonpongsak, Kharisorn Chaturachinda, Kwek Loong Cheng,

Adith Cheosakul, Andrew Clark, David Cohen, Bruce Crampton, Frank Crocker, Allan Davidson, Winston Doong, Raymond Eaton, Domnern Garden, Elizabeth George, Jon George, Robbie Gilchrist, Mark Greenwood, Philippe Guenat, William Heinecke, John Hancock, Tony Hoolahan, Chua Kim Huat, Graham Jeffery, Chanya Kamolchaikaimoog, Chaisit Kupwiwat, Joy Menzies, Herve Mouly, Richard Murray, Rutorn Nopakun, Ken Pas, David Quine, Claes Ostrom, Sarote Phornprapha, Sebastien Raynal, Bennett Robinson, George Romanyk, Siriyupa Roongrernsuke, Patrick Saliou, Tom Seale, Siripong Silpakul, Kiat Sittheeamorn, Vincent Swift, Maddi Thurston, Yugo Tsukikawa, John Twigg, Michael Vatikiotis, Joseph Webber, Dana Whorton, William Whorton, Gary White, Douglas Whittaker, Peter Williams, and Gianmaria Zanotti.

APPENDIX 1:
Routinely Listed Objectives Of Thai Companies

1. To buy, procure, obtain, lease, hire-purchase, own, occupy, develop, use and otherwise manage any property including fruits thereof.
2. To sell, transfer, mortgage, pledge, exchange, and otherwise dispose of property.
3. To be a broker, agent, commission agent for all types of transactions and business except for insurance business, solicitation of membership for associations, and securities trading.
4. To borrow money, overdraw money from banks, juristic persons, or any other financial institutions, and to lend money or extend credit by any other means, with or without security, including to accept, issue, assign and endorse bills of exchange or any other negotiable instruments.
5. To establish branch offices or appoint agents within and outside the country.
6. To be a partner with limited liability of any partnership and to be a shareholder of any company.
7. To engage in the business of trading in rice, rice products, tapioca, tapioca products, maize, sesame, beans, peppers, jute, kapok, cotton, lac, castor beans, wood, rubber, vegetables, fruits, forest produces, herbs, animal skin, horse, living animal, meat, sugar, animal feeds, and all kinds of agricultural produces.
8. To engage in the business of trading in machinery, engines, tools, labour-saving devices, vehicles, electricity generators and electrical appliances, refrigerators, air-conditioners, fan, electric cookers, irons, water pumps, heaters, coolers, kitchenware, hardwares, copperwares, brasswares, sanitary wares, household utensils, furniture, electrical accessories,

pipe-water accessories, including parts and accessories thereof.

9. To engage in the business of trading in fresh foods dry-foods, finished foods, canned foods, food seasoning, beverages, liquors, beer, cigarettes, and other consumer products.

10. To engage in the business of trading in fabric, thread, clothing, ready-made clothes, garments, ornaments, cosmetics, beautifying appliances and equipment, and other consumer products.

11. To engage in the business of trading in drugs for curing and preventing diseases for man and animals, medical supplies, chemicals, medical and pharmaceutical tools, fertilizers, pesticides, nutriments for plants and animals, scientific tools and instruments.

12. To engage in the business to trading in gold, copper alloy, silver, diamond, saffire, and other other precious stones, including artificial materials thereof.

13. To engage in the business of trading in paper, stationery, textbooks, printing forms, books, studying accessories, calculating machines, printing machines, printing accessories, printed materials, newspapers, document-storing cabinets, and all kinds of office supplies.

14. To engage in the business of trading in construction materials, construction equipment and tools, all kinds of mechanical tools, paints, painting equipment, and all kinds of decorating materials for buildings.

15. To engage in the business of trading in plastics or any other similar materials, either in raw or furnished nature.

16. To engage in the business of trading in raw rubber, rubber sheets, or other kinds of rubber or other kinds of rubber produced or derived from any part of para rubber plants, including synthetic rubber, and artificial facsimiles thereof produced by scientific process.

17. To engage in the business of rice growing, gardening, farming, salt farming, forestry, rubber plantation, animal raising and livestock.

18. To engage in the business of rice mills, sawmills, factories and plants for wood planing and drying, automobile-body assembly, ceramic and porcelain manufacturing, pottery

manufacturing, jute compressing, vegetable oil extracting, paper manufacturing, gunny bag manufacturing, textile, thread spinning, fabric dyeing and printing, tyre manufacturing and tyre-tread casting, ironworks, metal casting and lathing, corrugated iron manufacturing, finished food processing, liquor distilling, gas, cigarette producing, sugar mill, plastic utensil manufacturing, metal pressing and casting, door and window manufacturing, glass, beverage, rubber casting, automobile assembly.

19. To engage in the business of printing, book printing, book printing for sale, and newspapers publishing.
20. To engage in the business of ice producing plant.
21. To engage in the business of fishery, fish raft, fish jetty.
22. To engage in the business of rock exploding and milling.
23. To engage in the business of construction of buildings, commercial buildings, residential buildings, offices, roads, bridges, dams, tunnels, and all kinds of construction, including civil works.
24. To engage in the business of mining, smelting, separating, transforming, casting, dressing, exploring, analyzing and testing, grinding and transporting ore.
25. To engage in the business of hotels, restaurants, bars, night clubs, bowling alleys, massage parlors, cinemas and other entertainment establishments, resorts for recreation, sporting fields, swimming pools.
26. To engage in the business of cargo and passenger transport and transit facilities by air, on water and land, both domestic and international, including the services of cargo clearance at sea ports in accordance with customs procedures, and all kinds of freight forwarding services.
27. To engage in the business of tourism and other business in connection therewith.
28. To engage in the business of foreign currency exchange (subject to permission of the Ministry of Finance).
29. To engage in the business of importing and exporting items of goods as stipulated herein.
30. To engage in the business of barbering, hairdressing, beauty salons, tailoring and laundry.

31. To render the services of photography, photographic film developing and printing, photograph enlarging, including photocopying.
32. To engage in the business of making and distributing motion pictures.
33. To engage in the business of petrol filling station and such services as car repairs, maintenances, inspections, car washing and greasing services, application of rust resisting agent for motor vehicles of all types including such other services as installation, inspection and fixing of all kind of safety devices.
34. To engage in the business of providing legal, accounting, engineering, architectural, and advertising services.
35. To engage in the business of providing guarantees of debts, liabilities and contractual performance of any other persons, including to provide guarantees for individuals who travel into or out of the Kingdom in compliance with the law of immigration, taxation, and others.
36. To engage in the business of providing consultancy and advisory services pertaining to administration, commerce, industry and also production, marketing and distribution.
37. To engage in the business of providing services of data collecting, collating, editing, publishing and publicizing of statistics and information on agriculture, industry, commerce finance, marketing, including analyses and evaluations of business enterprises.
38. To engage in the business of private hospitals, clinics, curing and caring for patients and sick people, and provision of medical and health care teaching and training.
39. To engage in the business of executorship and trusteeship in fiduciary capacity, of the properties and interests of other individuals.
40. To engage in the business of tendering and bidding for the sales of goods and hire-of-works, in accordance with the objective of individuals, corporate bodies, juristic persons, government authorities and organizations.

APPENDIX 2:

The Alien Business Law NEC 281

Category A

Chapter 1 Agricultural Businesses
- i) Rice farming
- ii) Salt farming, including salt mining except rock salt

Chapter 2 Commercial Business
- i) Internal trade in local agricultural products
- ii) Land trade

Chapter 3 Service Businesses
- i) Accounting
- ii) Law
- iii) Architecture
- iv) Advertising
- v) Brokerage or agency
- vi) Auctioning
- vii) Barbering, hair dressing and beauty shop ownership

Chapter 4 Other Businesses
- i) Construction

Category B

Chapter 1 Agricultural Businesses
- i) Cultivation
- ii) Orchard farming
- iii) Animal husbandry, including silk worm raising
- iv) Timber
- v) Fishing

Chapter 2 Industrial and Handicraft Businesses
- i) Rice Milling
- ii) Flour making from rice and other cash crops
- iii) Sugar Milling

iv) Manufacturing of alcoholic and non-alcoholic drinks
v) Ice making
vi) Manufacturing of pharmaceuticals
vii) Cold storage0
viii) Timber processing
ix) Manufacturing of gold, silver, nielloware and stone inlaid products
x) Manufacturing of casting of Buddha images and bowls
xi) Wood carving
xii) Lacquer-ware making
xiii) Match manufacturing
xiv) Manufacturing of white cement, portland cement and cement finished products
xv) Dynamiting or quarrying of rocks
xvi) Manufacturing of plywood, veneer wood, chipboard or hardboard
xvii) Manufacturing of garments or footware except for export
xviii) Printing
xix) Newspaper publishing
xx) Silk spinning, or weaving of silk fabric
xxi) Manufacturing of finished products from silk fabric, silk yarn or silk cocoons

Chapter 3 Commercial Businesses
i) All retailing except for items included in Category "C"
ii) Ore trading except for items included in Category "C"
iii) Selling of food and drinks except for items included in Category "C"
iv) Trading of antique, heirloom or fine arts objects

Chapter 4 Service Businesses
i) Tour Agency
ii) Hotel, except for hotel management
iii) All businesses under the law governing places of service
iv) Photography, photographic processing and printing
v) Laundering
vi) Dressmaking

Chapter 5 Other Businesses
i) Land, water, and air transportation in Thailand

Category C

Chapter 1 Commercial Businesses
    i) All wholesale trade except in items included in Category "A"
    ii) All exporting
    iii) Retailing of machinery, equipment and tools
    iv) Selling of food or beverages for promotion of tourism

Chapter 2 Industrial and Handicraft Businesses
    i) Manufacturing of animal feeds
    ii) Vegetable oil refining
    iii) Textile manufacturing including yarn spinning, dyeing and fabric printing
    iv) Manufacturing of glassware including light bulbs
    v) Manufacturing of food bowls and plates
    vi) Manufacturing of stationery and printing paper
    vii) Rock salt mining
    viii) Mining

Chapter 3 Service Businesses
    i) Service businesses not included in Category "A" or Category "B"

Chapter 4 Other Businesses
    i) Other construction not included in Category "A"

APPENDIX 3:
BOI Tax Incentives

Zone 1	Zone 2	Zone 3
1. 50 % import duty reduction on machinery which is not included in the tariff reduction nonification of the ministry of Finance	1. 50 % import duty reduction on machinery which is not included in the tariff reduction notification of the ministry of Finance	1. Exemption of import duty on machinery.
IF at least 80% of total sales are exported, OR IF the project is located in an industrial estate or a promoted industrial zone.	2. Three-year corporate income tax exemption extendible up to seven years	2. Eight-year corporate income tax exemption
2. Three-year corporate tax exemption	IF the project is located in an industrial estate or a promoted industrial zone.	3. Exemption of import duty on raw or essential materials used in export products for a period of five years
IF at least 80% of total sales are exported, OR IF the project is located in an industrial estate or a promoted industrial zone.	3. Exemption of import duty on raw or essential materials used in export products for a period of one year	IF at least 30% of total sales are exported.
3. Exemption of import duty on raw or essential materials used in export products for a period of one year	IF at least 30% of total sales are exported.	4. 75% reduction of import duty on raw and essential materials used in production for domestic sales for five years, renewable on an annual basis
IF at least 30% of total sales are exported.		IF that raw or essential materials comparable in quality are not being produced or are not originating within the Kingdom in sufficient quantity, not including projects or factories in Laem Chabang Industrial Estates.
		5. Other Potential Privileges; a) Reduction of corporate income tax by 50% for five years after the exemption period; b) Double deduction from taxable income of water, electricity, and transport costs for 10 years from the date of first sales; c) Deduction from net profit of 25% of the costs of installation or construction of the projects' infrastructure facilities.

APPENDIX 4:
Map

BOI Zone
Zone 1
Bangkok, SamutPrakan, Pathum Thani.
Nonthaburi, Nakhon Pathom and Samut Sakhon
Zone 2
Samut Songkhram, Ratchaburi, Nakhon Nayok
Angthong, Ayuthaya, Kanchanaburi, Saburi
Chachoengsao, Chonburi and Suphan Buri
Zone 3
Remaining provinces outside Zone 1 and Zone 2

APPENDIX 5:
The Proposed Foreign Business Law[1]

Category One
Businesses Related to National Safety or Security or Affecting Culture, Arts, Traditional Customs, Folk Handicrafts or Natural Resources and the Environment

Chapter 1: Businesses related to national safety or security
1. Manufacture, disposal or maintenance of firearms, ammunition, gunpowder, explosives, components of firearms, ammunitions and explosives, including armaments, military ships, aircraft or vehicles, or accessories or components of war equipment of all kinds
2. Advertising business; publishing or newspaper business, radio or television business
3. Domestic land, water or air transport, including domestic airline business
4. Trade in land

Chapter 2: Businesses affecting cultural arts, traditional customs and folk handicrafts
1. Rice, field crop or orchard farming
2. Trade in old objects, antiques or art objects, being Thai artwork, handicrafts or ancient objects or objects of historical value to the country
3. Manufacture of wood carvings
5. Silkworm raising, Thai silk production, Thai silk weaving or Thai silk pattern printing
6. Production of Thai musical instruments
7. Manufacture of products from gold, silver, niello, bronze or lacquer
8. Manufacture of crockery of Thai cultural arts

---

[1] This information is based on the draft version of the law available as of October, 1998.

Chapter 3: Businesses affecting natural resources or the environment

1. Production of sugar from sugarcane
2. Salt farming, including subsurface salt production
3. Rock salt production
4. Mining, including stone blasting and quarrying
5. Forestry from natural forests
6. Wood processing
7. Fishery, exclusively aquatic animals in Thai territorial waters

Category Two

Businesses in Which Thai People Are Not Yet Ready to Compete with Aliens

1. Animal raising
2. Rice milling and production of flour from rice and field crops
3. Fishery, exclusively aquatic animal cultivation
4. Forestry from man-made forests
5. Manufacture of plywood, wood veneer, chip board or hard board
6. Manufacture of lime
7. Accounting service business
8. Legal service business
9. Architectural service business
10. Engineering service business
11. Construction, except
    a) construction of things providing fundamental services to the general public in the field of utilities or communications requiring special equipment, machinery, technology or expertise, with an alien minimal capital of 50,000,000 baht or more.
    b) construction prescribed in ministerial regulations
12. Brokerage or agency business, except
    a) brokerage or agency in buying and selling securities or services related to futures trading in agricultural commodities, financial instruments or securities

b) brokerage or agency in the sale of procurements of goods or services necessary for production or the provision of services by an enterprise

c) brokerages or agency, in the nature of international business, in the sale, purchase, distribution or acquisition of markets, both domestic and foreign for the distribution of domestically manufactured or imported goods, with an alien minimal capital or 50,000,000 baht or more

d) brokerage or agency of other kinds as prescribed in ministerial regulations

13. Public auction, except
   a) public auction in the nature of international bidding which is not a bid for old objects, antiques or art objects being Thai art work, handicrafts or ancient objects or of historical value to the country
   b) public auction of the kinds prescribed in ministerial regulations
14. Domestic trade in indigenous agricultural products not yet barred by law
15. Retail or wholesale of goods of all kinds with an 8. Manufacture of crockery of Thai cultural arts

Bibliography

Abegglen, James and Stalk, George, *Kaisha, The Japanese Corporation* (Charles E. Tuttle, 1988)

Bangkok Legal Consultant Ltd., *Doing Business In Thailand* (Bangkok Legal Consultant, 1995)

Bhongbhibhat, Vimol, Reynolds, Bruce, Polpatpicharn, Vimol and Camp, Beatrice, *The Eagle and the Elephant* (United Production, 1987)

Brislin, Richard, Cushner, Kenneth, et al, *Intercultural Interactions -- A Practical Guide* (Sage Publications, 1986)

Butra-pinyo, Pramut, *Pocket Thailand in Figures 1994* (Alpha Research Co., Ltd.)

Chandravithum, Nikom and Vause, Gary, *Thailand's Labor and Employment Law: A Practical Guide* (Manager Publishing, 1993)

Chansuthus, Daryl and Roongrernsuke, Siriyupa, *Conflict Management in Thailand: The Land of Smiles*, a chapter from a book called *Conflict Management in the Asia Pacific* (John Wiley & Sons, 1998)

Cooper, Robert, *Thais Mean Business* (Times Books International)

Holmes, Henry and Tangtongtavy, Suchada with Tomizawa, Roy, *Working with the Thais* (White Lotus, 1995)

Hummel, Anita Louise and Sethsathira, Pises, *Starting & Operating a Business in Thailand* (McGraw Hill Book, 1991)

Indorf, Hans, *Thai-American Relations in Contemporary Affairs* (Executive Publications, 1982)

Klausner, William J., *Reflections on Thai Culture* (The Siam Society, 1993)

Komin, Suntaree, *Psychology of the Thai People -- Values and Behavioral Patterns* (NIDA, 1990)

Laothamatas, Anek, *Business Associations and the New Political Economy of Thailand* (Westview Press, 1992)

Mulder, Niels, *Inside Thai Society -- An Interpretation of Everyday Life* (DK Books, 1994)

Osland, Joyce, *The Adventure of Working Abroad* (Jossey-Bass Publishers, 1995)

Phongpaichit, Pasuk and Piriyarangsan, Sungsidh, *Corruption & Democracy in Thailand* (Chulalongkorn University, 1994)

Phongpaichit, Pasuk and Baker, Chris, *Thailand Economy and Politics* (Oxford University Press Books, 1995)
_____*Thailand's Boom* (Silkworm Books, 1996)

Schein, Edgar, *Organizational Culture and Leadership* (Jossey-Bass Inc., 1992)

Tilleke & Gibbins, Standard Chartered Bank, *Thailand Business Basics* (Tilleke & Gibbins and Standard Chartered Bank, 1993)

Trompenaars, Fons, *Riding the Waves of Culture* (The Economist Books, 1993)

Triandis, Harry C., *Individualism and Collectivism* (Westview Press, Inc., 1995)

Vatikiotis, Michael, *Political Change in Southeast Asia* (Routledge, 1996)

Wyatt, David, *Thailand A Short History* (Silkworm Books, 1984)

Author's Information

Roy Tomizawa is a lecturer of management communications at the Sasin Graduate Institute of Business Administration of Chulalongkorn University in Bangkok, Thailand. A native New Yorker, he was an award-winning reporter for a Gannett newspaper in the Philadelphia area, as well as a consultant in cross cultural management in Tokyo where he developed, sold and conducted training seminars for overseas-bound Japanese managers. He also collaborated in the writing of *Working with the Thais,* authored by Dr. Henry Holmes and Suchada Tangtongtavy.

He welcomes any comments or questions in regards to this book and can be contacted by email at :

<tomizawa@netserv.chula.ac.th>.

Working with the Thais
A Guide to Managing in Thailand

Working with the Thais is the culmination of 20 years' work by Dr. Henry Holmes and Suchada Tangtongtavy, cross cultural consultants to many of the best organizations, large and small, here in Thailand. Filled with examples, anecdotes and plain common sense, **Working with the Thais** will help you anticipate the common problems between Thais and Non-Thais -- and lots of opportunities --, as well: how the problems can be dealt with, and best of all, how pitfalls can be avoided in the first place!

> *"There is more to working in a foreign country than increasing market share and other measurements of business success.* **Working With the Thais** *deciphers the essential elements for managerial and business success, and helps the Expatriate manager to appreciate that there are more ways than his own to achieve business success in Thailand."*
> **Beau Wilson, Country Manager, Citibank**

> *"Excellent reading material for businessmen, trainees, students and professionals working with the Thais, regardless of their nationalities. The book captures the very essence of the Thai value system and provides a relevant guide to successful, workable relationships with the Thais. Flops and cultural mistakes can be sealed off.* **Working With the Thais** *is a must read for anyone planning to spend time in Thailand."*
> **Kazunori Somaya, Managing Director, Sony Thai**

> *"A must for everyone who has business responsibility in Thailand. You will enjoy it after the first reading, but it will be your reference throughout your stay in the Kingdom."*
> **Don Carkeek, Country Manager, Digital Equipment Corporation**

Working with the Thais. 146 pages, 395 baht
Call or fax your order to : **Alpha Research Co., Ltd.**
289/8 Lad Prao 35 Rd., Jatujak, Bangkok 10900
Tel. 02-939-0764, 02-939-0765 Fax: 02-939-0763

Alpha Research's publications, April 2003

Thailand in Figures
Current edition : 2002-2003 8th edition
Reference book on Thailand's socio-economic statistics and information on each of 76 provinces

Price:	Thailand	2,000	baht
	ASEAN	120	US$
	Rest of the world	150	US$

Thailand Food Exporters
Current edition : 2002-2003 1st edition
Reference book on Thailand's food and beverage export statistics and directory of food and veberage exporters

Price:	Thailand	1,800	baht
	ASEAN	100	US$
	Rest of the world	140	US$

Thailand Public Health
Current edition : 2002 4th edition
Reference book on Thailand's health statistics, number of health service personnel and area of specialization and number of hospitals

Price:	Thailand	1,200	baht
	ASEAN	90	US$
	Rest of the world	110	US$

Pocket Thailand in Figures 5th edition
Reference book on Thailand's socio-economic statistics

Price:	Thailand	350	baht
	ASEAN	20	US$
	Rest of the world	25	US$

Payment by a commercial bank draft payable to Alpha Research Co. ,Ltd.

* Price is inclusive of airmail postage.
For more information please contact:

Alpha Research Co.,Ltd.
289/8 Lad Prao 35 Rd., Jatujak, Bangkok 10900
Tel. 02-939-0764, 02-939-0765 Fax: 02-939-0763
e-mail:*info@alpharesearch.co.th*
web site:*www.thailandinfiguresupdate.com*

Order Now !

Thailand in Figures 2002-2003 8th edition

The most comprehensive reference book on Thailand's socio - economic statistics

8th edition
2002-2003

Contents:
* *Thailand at a glance* * *Geography* * *Population* * *Public health*
* *Education* * *Labor* * *Transport and communications* * *Energy*
* *Election* * *Gross domestic product* * *Agricultural production*
* *Manufactured production* * *Commercial banks*
* *International trade* * *Tourism* * *Price index* * *Household income*
* *Public finance* * *Province information*

Size :
21 X 30 cm., 988 pages

Price :
Thailand	ASEAN	Rest of the world
2,000 baht	120 US$	150 US$

* Inclusive of airmail postage

Alpha Research Co.,Ltd.
289/8 Lad Prao 35 Rd., Jatujak, Bangkok 10900
Tel. 02-939-0764, 02-939-0765 Fax: 02-939-0763
e-mail:*info@alpharesearch.co.th*
web site:*www.thailandinfiguresupdate.com*

COLLECTED
ESSAYS OF
Stuart
Grayson

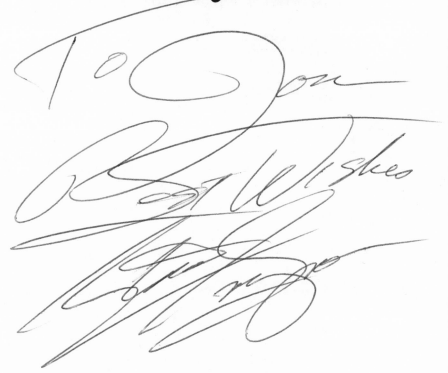

Mentors of New Thought Series

COLLECTED
ESSAYS OF
Stuart
Grayson

DEVORSS *Publications*

ISBN: 0-87516-679-2
Library of Congress Catalog Card Number: 95-068672

DeVorss & Company, Publisher
P.O. Box 550
Marina del Rey, CA 90294

Printed in the United States of America

Contents

COLLECTED
ESSAYS OF
Stuart
Grayson

Welcome to a New World

Is IT POSSIBLE to move into a new, truly fresh experience of life? Is it possible to move into a new world of consciousness? If you are studying the Science of Mind, you will probably answer in the affirmative. Yet how many responses will be based on a theoretical view of life rather than on solid faith built on spiritual understanding? In the final analysis, most of us will have a questionable expectancy of good. Fear and doubt rather than confidence and conviction tend to dominate human consciousness. And any expectancy of good is frequently limited by our experience of the past.

Whether we know it or not, each moment, day by day and hour by hour, we enter into a new world. The choice is ours as to our destination and the quality of our experience. We are always creating new worlds for ourselves through thought and feeling, and this through a complex consciousness: conscious and subconscious in silent collusion. Many have found themselves moved into experiences they don't like: worlds of problems and challenges that make for difficult living.

Students of the Science of Mind learn not to seek scapegoats for blame. Causation is never in the environment, other people, or childhood traumas; *it is always in the way we perceive our relationship to problems.* The facts of experience exist, but they are never the essential cause of difficulties. Too often we hug the disorders like a security blanket. We won't let them go because they give us a rationale for being and acting in ways that are self-sabotaging. *It is never a matter of blame, but rather of change.* What you don't like can be cleared through spiritually rational thinking.

The moment you go back to the basic Primal Cause of your existence—infinite and evolving Good—you have begun the dissolution of the blocks to harmonious living. It is entirely a metaphysical condition. Fundamentally everything is a projection of consciousness, since Mind is the underlying medium for all effect. Hence healing is always in a change of consciousness. And that change can begin anywhere at any time in anyone.

There is a Force for good in the Universe and It backs up all of us continually. It is the fundamental Resource sustaining and supporting Its creation. To recognize this and appreciate it on a personal level is to take control of one's existence. This means understanding our relationship to the grand, overarching Source of life we call God. It matters not what we label the Infinite Mind, Divine Urge or One-without-a-Second. It is That which enables us to live and relate and create our worlds of experience. Desire is part of this process, for no matter how good or fulfilling our lives have been, they can always be better—and a proper understanding of our relationship to God is the way to an enhanced quality of living.

The idea of experiencing a new world is possible because we are connected to an infinite Power. A divine imperative says, ''Go forth and do, go forth and be, go forth and become.'' You find this idea restated in both the Old and the New testaments. The biblical injunctions are symbols of states of consciousness. We seek to know what these states of consciousness are, what they are rooted in, where they come from, what they project, and the meaning of it all.

In 2 Corinthians Paul writes:

Therefore if any man be in Christ, he is a new creature;
old things are passed away; behold, all things are become
new. And all things are of God. . . . be ye reconciled to
God.

When Paul talks about being in Christ, he is describing a Principle that operated on, within, and through Jesus, the teacher,
who became the Christ, or was "Christed." Paul implies that
each person needs to become Christed. This means that you
have an enhanced understanding of yourself as a spiritual being,
living in a spiritual Universe and appearing in a physical form
and environment. This is the essence of the Science of Mind. As
you understand these truths, you become the new being as Paul
wrote and as a modern-day theologian, Paul Tillich, proposed.
A new consciousness always creates a new world. Further, Paul
asks us to be reconciled to God. He is talking about God as
Primal Cause and the Source of Being. We need to have the
spiritual understanding that enables individual consciousness
to connect itself to this Source. Then you become a special action of Life, evolving and manifesting something new in your
experience.

Our spiritual work is based on this eternal principle. The language is different from biblical descriptions but, in common
with the Bible, we affirm the presence of God expressing everywhere. Eventually this divine Presence must be manifest as a
new creation, a new experience, a new aspect of the ongoing, expanding life; a *new being.* Any mental rejections operating
through us are actually violations of the Law of Unfolding Evolution, which are paid for through painful human experience.

All of us at some time have looked to the past only to find
ourselves encapsulated by old thoughts or actions. The frequent
result is suffering. The Science of Mind proposes that we can exit
this mental trap through spiritual knowledge and self-work.

To attain freshness of being, you cannot relate to yesterday as the total truth of your life. If you do, the past becomes your present, and you become frozen in that. If this should occur, the way out is through spiritual understanding, which will dissolve any encapsulation. Then you can soar upward into the enlightened atmosphere of ongoing Good. You are complying with the laws of the Universe. And you will discover that this ensures harmony and guarantees a forward movement in life. Truly, *it is the creation of a new being.*

In his *Pensées*, the French philosopher Blaise Pascal wrote: "The last function of reason is to recognize that there is an infinity of things which surpass it." He is implying that we need to go beyond the factual world of reason, logic, and experience: to begin to think and reason from a higher viewpoint, for that is where the Primal Source and Cause exists. At that level we can direct the Law of Life, the Law of Cause and Effect, to eliminate the denials and inner blockages that have held us back from fulfilment.

The German philosopher Arthur Schopenhauer said something related to this idea in another way: "Every man takes the limits of his own field of vision for the limits of the world." How true this is! As you move upward in spiritual thinking, you see that if you think the physical world is all that exists, you eliminate the possibility of anything beyond it having caused, created, or produced this world. You look at Life from your vision and experience as a limited human being.

The "facts" of Life are always conditioned by the past. They are true only from a conditioned and relative point of view. Reality is always beyond this limited viewpoint. Reality has to do with infinite, ongoing Being. It is beyond limited concepts. We seek to know how to use this Principle of Reality so that It will produce something greater and better for us.

It is obvious, then, that we must become independent thinkers. This means not being influenced by the "factual," physical, material viewpoint. The first thing we have to do is what Jesus instructed those around him to do: "Judge not according to the appearance, but judge righteous judgment." The Science of Mind shows us how to do this and reveals the way to go. Through spiritual discrimination we judge rightly, and we begin to experience life from a new perspective.

Old thoughts can contain the new only potentially. It is not that they are worthless: there may be a potential in the old; but if you live in the potential, you never become the actual. The New Thought tradition contains the old as part of its heritage; but if it is dominated by the old, it is divorced from creativity: the dynamic energy is siphoned out of it, and it is like an empty shell with nothing in it. We understand that the old must be transformed, that we need to move forward into Truth. "Be ye transformed by the renewing of your mind." This idea has to do with not dwelling on or living in the old, instead seeing that there is always a potential in mind for moving into the dynamic of a fresh and new world.

Here are six points that will help you to access new experience:

1. Recognize the divine Potential within. It is the Universal Intelligence, present everywhere.

2. Understand that all things are possible if you have the consciousness for attainment of your desires.

3. Realize new possibilites are at work in the Creative Law, which is operating everywhere. It is the Law of Evolution.

4. Know that there is one Source of Life, Being, and Energy, and that you are a tributary. Therefore, you are a channel through which this energy flows.

5. Appreciate that Universal Intelligence is producing your life by means of your mind and the thoughts

which you direct. All fulfillment of needs is within you, ready to come forth into actuality. First you have to clear your consciousness of mental obstructions.

6. Accept the idea that your desires direct Creative Energy to express through your goals, talents and capabilities.

The study and practice of the Science of Mind will enable you to say, "I welcome my new life."

And as you move into a new and more fulfilled life, something will be saying. "Welcome to a new world!"

Breaking the
Barriers

THE MOST important possession you have is your "I"
(your essential self). God is the supreme "I" worshiped throughout the world under various names. And each individual, an
expression of the Supreme, has a personal "I" that can be com-
muned with, understood, experienced and expanded in a rewarding way. It has nothing whatever to do with the egotistical sense
of "I," in which one is not concerned about others or the riches
of nature. Your true "I" refers to your essential being. To deny
your "I" is to deny yourself and the divine Nature.

You were created to experience Life and to express Life's
abundance. You have a right to be free, a right to reflect the af-
fluence of the Spirit which is expressed on every level—mind,
emotion, body, and relationships. In studying the Science of
Mind, you can expect to find a new awareness and expression
of the "I," your essential being.

To begin a program of self-clarification, ask yourself three
questions: How do I look at life? How do I see myself? Do I think
from a restricted or limited point of view? After examining your
answers, ask: Am I letting the "I" of the past, the conditioned
self, direct my life? Most of us do. Most of us are much more

7

related to the past than to the present or future, because we are famitar with the past. It has a measurable existence. Then you might say about your life experience: "Well, that is the way I am and how things are." Or "That it what I have done and must do." If you think about these statements, you will see that they are all related to the past, your conditioning, and how you have lived. Our present is frequently robbed by these past experiences and attitudes. Some of the experience is valuable; all of it is an inescapable fact. If you see clearly and want to be a positive individual, desiring to break the barriers of restriction and limited thinking, you will realize that you are manipulated, conditioned, and distorted by thoughts, feelings, and memories of the past.

Each of us needs to focus on the present and live in the present. Ernest Holmes has written: "Break the bonds of apparent necessity and see life as one continuous expression of the Infinite Self."* You were born with potential talents and capabilities, but you need to work with them, go beyond them, and develop yourself in a new and special way. *You do not have to be a victim of the past.* You can make Dr. Holmes' statement a reality in your life.

You can release past experiences, because in reality they no longer function in the present. Your inner perceptions, based on Truth, manifest outwardly because the external experience always reflects the inner demand of thought. *Every* experience demands something of you. You cannot escape demand. Every thought is active, vital, alive, and ever functioning in consciousness. These thoughts manifest and influence your life. And every time a healing action occurs, it means the bonds of apparent necessity have been broken.

---

* *The Science of Mind*, p. 288.

Some scientists say that what one observes is changed by the observer. You, the observer, are always in some way influencing not only yourself, but everything you observe. Thought is dynamic. It is like a pebble that is dropped into a pond. As you observe, you see the ripples spread outward. This is a metaphor for human action and its rippling effect throughout life. Each ripple signifies a further change from some previous causation. You do not live in a vacuum. Your outer life always reflects an internal action. This inner demand of thought often appears as change from or toward an outer action. Thus one can understand the power of consciousness. Thoughts do produce things, and they change and influence them.

There is something called Universal Spirit that is beyond the functioning of your mind and thought: It can bring about change in your world. The more you think in terms of harmony, goodness, and freedom—expressing these in loving relationships, attitudes, and viewpoints—the more you align yourself with Universal Spirit. It gives you the ability to think, to reason. When you align yourself with this universal Source, you are better able to express your essential nature. What is that essential nature? It is simply the Life that is whole, good, pure. Like universal Spirit or Mind, thought really is limitless and ongoing. You can never be without thought, because it reflects and expresses the universal Mind Principle.

Ask yourself: What am I thinking and how am I thinking? What do I do with my thoughts? Do I let my thoughts run away with me? Thoughts may rise up from the subconscious or from a person's remark to you. Often these thoughts begin to manipulate your life. *Observe the action and source of your thoughts.* Where do they come from and what are they doing to your life?

Limitation of any kind is ignorance. We do not see that Mind is limitless, thought is limitless, and the potential within to create through directed consciousness is also limitless. *Begin to think in a new way.* The action of thought is an action of Creative Intelligence, the ongoing Principle of Life. It has no restrictions or limitations. It does not know about barriers. *We* create barriers. *We* restrict, limit, and encapsulate thought in our conditioning, in memories of the past. These try to manipulate our present and future. Through Spiritual Mind Treatment we break the apparent necessity of having these thoughts. Remember that we cannot think a thought and not experience the result. *We cannot think a thought without our experience becoming filled with the reverberation of it.*

All of this concern with thought, the Mind Principle, and experience implies a creative process to which each of us is intimately connected. And it means that your individual being is potentially in control of your world. A plan for progress, then, is what is needed.

Dr. Ernest Holmes writes: ''Anything you can dream of is not too great for you to undertake, if it hurts no man and brings happiness and good into your life.''* When your thoughts are filled with anger, hatred, or greed, they are contrary to the Principle of Life. There is a boomerang effect, and these thoughts work against you.

Begin to understand that the Universal Principle is Absolute Life, Love, Beauty, Order, and Harmony. Meditate upon these ideas. Live and act from this point of view.

Here are five steps to help toward personal fulfillment:

1. Conceive of the ultimate goal, whether it is better health, a loving relationship, or a new direction for creative self-expression. *Don't focus on the process.* You have to know about the process, but *focus only on the ultimate goal.*

---

* *The Science of Mind,* p. 288.

2. Think of your image or the idea of the goal as the very thing itself. You will begin to see how thought makes a demand upon life; that it has a ripple effect like the pebble dropped in the pond; and that some outer experience will take place. In a natural way, the Law of Life will begin to produce in your world of experience.

3. Erase any thoughts, doubts, or fears that might prevent you from demonstrating your goal. This is done through the method of *Spiritual Mind Treatment*. Treatment is the recognition and acceptance of right ideas. It denies all thought that you cannot achieve your goal. Deny, affirm, and release this treatment to Creative Law. Always remember, you are not the *creator*; you are the *director* of your thoughts, images, and the forces that produce your goal. *You* do not produce it. The Principle of Mind is always the producer. You *direct the flow* of the creative current, which always reaches its destination.

4. Eliminate the time factor. The whole subconscious realm is timeless and spaceless. Whatever you thought in the past is living in you on an unconscious level today. You need to eliminate the *belief* in time as a determiner of experience, because the subconscious knows nothing about time. It is the creative part of you that says *it is all here and now*. It is always ready to move into a new manifestation.

5. Stick with the idea of your goal until the demonstration is made. It is easy to affirm good. But inwardly you may be denying it or believing its opposite. The Science of Mind helps you to become affirmative and to understand what affirmative and constructive living means. You understand where you have come from as consciousness and where you are going. You can bring into your

experience whatever you desire *if* you *think* correctly. This is never done by "holding thoughts," but by *knowing* the Truth—because Truth is the universal Presence, Substance, and Power.

It is up to us to learn how to think more effectively. Consciousness always expresses at the level of our spiritual awakening and understanding of the Life-force, the action of Universal Spirit. It is the way to break the barriers of limitation. It is the way to live a life of fulfillment and peace.

The Open Secret

THE "CONCEPT of unity is the mystical secret of the ages, the key to spiritual wisdom and to the teaching of Jesus," writes Ernest Holmes.* Oneness is the great teaching that many mystics have experienced and that institutionalized religion has implied most human beings could not accept. It is the ultimate realization of those who have sought the truth about God and humankind, Life and its manifestations. The great open secret of Being is the concept of unity. It was thought to be too secret a doctrine to be taught to ordinary people. And so it was the "hidden" or occult teaching reserved for inner circles of students pursuing spiritual studies.

From time to time, a teacher would appear to reveal the esoteric ideas of oneness. Frequently, close students would quickly surround the teacher, school, or group with a shroud of secrecy that would cover up the liberating ideas once again. This was the history and experience of the so-called inner work on these special ideas up to recent times. But the spiritual evolution of the race has now prepared consciousness for the next inreach to Infinity.

Since the mid-nineteenth century in America a new and liberating expression of what Aldous Huxley labeled the "Perennial

* *The Science of Mind*, p. 69.

13

Philosophy'' began to manifest. It moved through the Transcendentalist philosophers of New England and certain teachers of what was called mental or metaphysical science. It was a triumph of the independent spirit of America, for it asserted that each human being had direct access to the Source of Being; that through changed thinking based on a new awareness of the oneness of God and humankind, transformation of the person took place. It was a teaching for all people, freeing thought from the shackles of old religious and theological ideas. It showed individuals how to take conscious control of their thoughts. It resulted in healed minds, bodies, and circumstances.

The revolutionary ideas that impacted the thought of those early times were:

1. Our divine nature is the seed of perfection within.
2. As we claim this good, our beliefs change from those of a sinner doomed to suffering to a recognition of our divine heritage.
3. We have a right to health, peace, and happiness: this is God's will or desire for us.

From these and other related concepts an entire methodology of thinking and practice quickly developed. Many persons were healed of various physical and mental disorders. Harmony and prosperity became a natural event. This movement, native to America, has influenced millions. It is the underlying thrust of New Thought organizations, and it is the major influence on many New Age groups.

Today, through the advanced teaching of Religious Science, every human being of whatever ethnic, social, or religious background can find the seed of perfect beauty and order within. Through the practice of the Science of Mind, anyone can learn to pray effectively. And a healing consciousness will be developed as the student understands the open secret:

There is a Power and Presence for good in the Universe, and everyone can use it.

Circles and Cycles

In his book *The Archetype and the Unconscious*, Swiss psychiatrist Dr. Carl Jung made a very provocative and interesting statement: "Thinking existed long before man was able to say I am conscious of thinking." Thinking is a process, but as such it is an emanation of a universal Principle of Mind, and it "surfaces" in consciousness as an individual expression of that Mind Principle.

Thinking is an essential part of this development of life. Thinking is fundamental; it is basic. Thinking is the foundation underlying and moving in and through all life. It moves specifically through the expression of Life called humanity. Thinking can be described as an expression of the Principle of Mind as It moves through the level of energy called the human.

From this point of view, you are a special expression of the Law of Evolution in its movement of onward, unfolding action. You have been brought to a point in awareness where you have the ability to say, "I think. I am. I relate to myself. I relate to my universe."

But how are you using your ability to think? We find that the entire demonstration of any individual's life experience is dependent on the quality of consciousness—that is, through the

15

ability of the individual to think, and the actual thinking process itself. In other words, *you become what you think.* Then some important questions arise: How are you using your ability to think? What are you doing with this capacity? Are you using your thought simply to repeat the circle of evidence and eventuality? Are you using your thought to repeat the circle of everything that you already see, hear, and know? Does your history continually repeat itself? Are you a circle that repeats the same tape loop, giving the same message over and over again?

Or do you use your thinking ability to move *upward* and *forward* on the scale of being? Though it may appear to be a circle, it is then really a *cycle,* in the sense of *a circular movement lifting you to the next level of awareness.* It is a breakthrough into eternal things and creative ideas. Your job as a human being is to live your life. But how do you live your life? By going over the past in an endless circle of defeat? Or is it rather by moving through the cycle of evolutionary unfoldment like a spiral winding upward?

If we were meant to repeat the past, to live in a restricted circle, then we would be like the lower forms of life. They repeat the identical experience from generation to generation. They echo the patterns and performance of their progenitors. Whether ant or antelope, there is no development beyond a defined level. It is repetition typical of instinctive action. Is that what you are? Is that what you see as the experience of your life?

Each of us is the individualization of an unfolding continuity, able to take the past and move it into the future at a new level or cycle. This can be described as a spiral of unfolding good. Nature reveals that we are not meant to follow a repetitive circle but an evolutionary cycle or action of life. If we live only on the dimension of the circle, we repeat past actions in the present. Our future becomes a modified continuity of the past. And we never move out of that repetitive circle of experience. We are entrapped by it.

But our desire to be free moves us out of this trap. It gets us to see ourselves as empowered by the Spirit Itself, by God. This means spiritual growth, insight, and awareness of our potential and possibilities for the creative use of thought. One is able to make constructive decisions and to move forward. I use the word *cycle* for a series coming to an end at full turn, having now reached a higher level, a level above what has been before.

I call this the *Spiral of Infinity*. All of us basically and essentially follow the Spiral of Infinity. It is the creative process ever giving rise to something new and better. But it comes out of what has gone before; it does not just happen or fall out of the sky. The creative process in life—in you, in me, in those who we perceive as creative—always brings forth, through consciousness, something *more*, something beyond previous levels.

The basic rule, dictum, or imperative in life is "Go forth and multiply." It simply means *to become consciously the spiral of action*, the Spiral of Infinity—to let the Life-force move through you to bring about something that is beyond you. It is an action from *within* you, yet *beyond* you, greater than what you are. We must see this as an action of thought, an action primarily of consciousness that is not related simply to the physical. Each one of us is a thinking individual, able to perceive and use the movement of Life as a *cycle*, not a circle.

We begin to see that prayer in all religions really represents this action of thought. It brings about a new cycle of experience through a change in consciousness. The prayer may be an appeal to what appears as an outside force—but actually we are directly using the Life Principle, which can be called Infinite Consciousness, Spirit, or God. This is a direct inner experience. But even those who use prayer wheels or pray by wind power as in Tibet, or invoke the intercession of saints and sages of the particular religions—all use the creative action of Mind. The prayer really is a movement of *thought* or *consciousness* that eventually expresses as an answer, as fulfillment.

In this sense, prayer that may start out as a *circle* of thought becomes a *cycle* when it is answered. Consciousness has moved up to the next level or evolute of being. This is the result of one circular action of Mind moving through an individual's thoughts and getting a response out of Life at a new level. This experience we can call divine Evolution. It is the difference between a *circular* action of life and the *cyclical* action of life. We need to understand that we can either live within the repetitive circle of all conventional thoughts, opinions, and beliefs, remaining stuck in the past—or, with inspired thought, we can risk taking a forward step into something new, greater, and better than anything we have known before. Life leaves it up to us. *We* must decide upon the direction of our lives.

The consciousness that desires to move forward is part of the Principle that provides the means and the way into the new experience. What we may call Spiritual Mind Treatment, or recognizing the Truth about ourselves, is simply understanding that thought is primary—that we cannot afford to allow our thoughts to remain in the impasse of past consciousness and experience. What we have to do is bring our thoughts into a new enrichment of mind and ideas, into an expectancy of more and better, knowing that there is a law of creativity ever at work. It is the Law of the Creative Process. We can know that positive, constructive thoughts and forward-looking vision will bring something greater and better into our experience. We may call it the demonstration of our "treatment" or the announcement of a Mind Principle. It is always the action of a Higher Power.

So it is up to you to examine your life. See whether you are living in circles—or in cycles of creative action. You know yourself best. Often, people appear to be one thing (even to themselves) but are in fact something else. You need to look into yourself, become meditative, become more self-aware. You must become sensitive to what you feel, desire, believe, or fear. There *is* a wonderful, marvelous gift of simple awareness; and once you gain a sense of who and what you are, and where you are in consciousness, you will be able to do something about you. *And you can do it at once.* You can change your thoughts, change your consciousness, change your way of thinking. Then you are using the Mind Principle constructively, creatively. You are not running in a circle like the dog chasing its own tail. Instead, you are moving up the spiral of awareness—knowing and recognizing that there is always more.

The Universe is the operation of an infinite Principle. It is an infinite action. You are connected to it. Therefore there must be, and always will be, more for you and for everyone. What that "more" is you don't always know; but you have your intentions, your desires and your goals. All of these are guides, signposts pointing in the direction of greater good. These are messages from an infinite action lying deep within you.

Remember: it may be the *same hour*, but it is a *new day*. It may be the *same corner*, but it is a *higher floor* with a *better view*. Spiritual evolution always means a new movement upward and forward. The circle is a symbol of the Infinite. In your experience, that circle may be the same hour returning—*but always in a new day*. It is another step forward, a point beyond where you were before. It is another level on the cyclical spiral of life. That movement upward and forward is the transforming, healing action residing in you. It is the potential for fulfillment within. It exists in a new thought, a renovated consciousness that moves you to the same point, but *another step higher*. The next step higher is a breakthrough into greater awareness, greater freedom, and a greater experience of the creative life.

You cannot go back to the past and still move forward. If you try—whether in thought or feeling—you will hold yourself back from a forward move. It is your job to see yourself in a clear, fresh way *in the present*. Of course, you will make constructive use of all that you have learned and experienced in the past. But keep your vision upward and forward-looking. Know that you are supported, sustained, promoted, and impelled by the Life-Principle, which is ever ongoing and forward-moving. That is the spiritual Law of Evolution in action. It is the cyclic action of your life. It is a force in you, ready to move you upward and onward. It all depends on your mindset: the way you think, conceive yourself, and feel about life; the way you look at your potential and possibilities. These are the factors that determine the quality of your experience.

Watch the state of your thinking! Observe the nuances of your thought! See where your vision is directed!

Then learn to act upon these insights and move forward.

Absolute Living

WHEN WE AFFIRM the idea that there is a transcendent principle in the Universe, we mean That which is above and beyond and goes over all. It is the Source and Force and Cause of all. It is beyond any individual, although it works *in* and *through* the individual by conferring Its attributes and qualities on the individual. We can talk about It as God, but It is the Principle of Being, and so we call It the Absolute.

It is unconditioned. That means there is nothing that in any way can condition It, can cause It to be anything other than what It is. It is the Cause of all, not the effect of anything. Therefore It is unconditioned. It is the Primal Force, the Primal Cause, and you can call It the One Self-Existence. Viewed another way, It is the One Existent Intelligence or Consciousness in the Universe, expressed through all form. Substance on the invisible plane is the form of ideas; and on the visible, the form of the material and physical world we see.

The Transcendent One we call also Immanent. That is, the Transcendent Immanent One is that which is over and beyond all, yet *in* all, *through* all, and manifesting *by means of* all. It does not mean that It is giving bits and pieces of Itself to every-one, but that Its whole Nature is operating *through* and *as* each individual while at the same time operating throughout Its Universe.

Ours is a metaphysical science, we say, which means that we are learning about this Absolute, this Principle, and learn-ing how to use It, how to make It truly "functional"—that is, the consciously functioning Life Principle in our worlds of ex-perience. God is always at work, the Absolute is always func-tioning, the Unconditioned One is always expressing. We as individuals with a high level of consciousness need to recognize that we live in the Spiritual Universe and that this Principle, no matter how we look at it—*even on the most materialistic level* —is a Law, an ever-present action or force. Principle simply *is*.

If we apply the word *spiritual* to this Principle, we can see that we live in Its *spiritual* Universe. Then we begin to perceive the intangible elements and aspects of our lives becoming tan-gible, visible through Law. That is, we see that this Principle is Consciousness and that It must be some infinite Mind princi-ple. We see that we also think with this Consciousness, this Mind, and that things happen to us through our own minds, our own consciousness.

That consciousness is backed up by *feeling*; and when we think in terms of feeling, we see that it too is an element or an aspect of this Source, Force, or Consciousness Principle. We can also see that It functions as a law in our worlds so that the way we think *and the way we feel* operates through us as a single force field of Mind-energy, yielding our world of experience. "Science" means learning about this Principle. It is learning about the Law of Life and how to use it, how to apply it in our own lives.

We have learned to experience this God Action in our lives. The Power must flow through us unobstructedly. *The Power is there, the Force is there, we are here, we are in It, we are part of It*. We have consciousness, we have thought, we have feeling. Yet because of thought/feeling, because of our consciousness, we can temporarily (and in a very superficial way, from the viewpoint of the Universe) obstruct the flow of this great energy, this divine Energy of Spirit, in our own lives.

This makes it all the more important, then, to see that through our spiritual awakening, through our spiritual awareness, through our spiritual understanding—and the thinking that is the product of this understanding—we have a Law infinite, eternal, ever producing for us. The way that we get rid of the obstruction of consciousness or thought is not by hacking at it in a physical, material way, but by gaining spiritual insight, spiritual awareness, spiritual understanding.

There is a way to have this spiritual insight, awareness, and realization—and to have it in fullness, so that we do not obstruct that Divine Flow through us: wherever we see difficulties, problems, disturbances, disorders of any kind, we can say: there is an order in the Universe, there is that Great Absolute, that Wholeness in the Universe; but here in my experience there seems to be some obstruction. Now do I have to cure God? Do I have to cure the Absolute? Do I have to "do something" about the Unconditioned One? Of course not! What I have to do is *try God*. What I have to do is get rid of these obstructive thoughts, feelings, attitudes, and points of view, by shifting my focus from the limited, material, sequential flow of events and situations and relationships and actions to a larger view of life—the view that "I and the Source are one." I'm in It, I have come out of It, I express It. Now I begin to understand that I am not just what appears to be. I am not just this little, puny, physical, material human being with all of its so-called problems, its ups and downs. *I am more than that.* I come from a divine majesty of Being, so I am literally the offspring of that divine majesty. I am a regent, representing, outpicturing, symbolizing, and expressing the Power and Presence of the Absolute.

When we begin to reason this through, to understand it and to resonate with it, we find that the Principle of the Universe, operating as a creative law in us, begins at once to dissolve the obstructions—not all in a single moment, but here a little, there a little, as we continue the pursuit of our own spiritual excellence.

Yes, as it says in the New Testament, all can be changed "in the twinkling of an eye."* There can be what the Zen Buddhists call the Aha! Moment—the moment of illumination, the moment when we say, "Aha! I see!" Haven't we all experienced that? Haven't you had the experience, in a situation of one kind or another, in which someone is explaining—or you have been pondering—some matter, and it doesn't seem that you can understand it—and then you say, "Oh! *That's* what they mean! *I see!*" What happens in that moment? Ignorance is dissolved in that moment, the obstruction is gone, and your saying "I see!" is simply an outer expression of the inner Aha! That's the way it is!

Science of Mind practice is related to very ordinary human experiences—and yet these are made to relate to Something far beyond the human and ordinary actions of life. We live in a Creative Intelligence and have this same Creative Intelligence at our disposal. It operates through our consciousness; It operates through our spiritual knowing, our spiritual understanding. That is why we revere yet another statement from the Bible: "With all thy getting, get understanding."†

Fortunately, through the study of the Science of Mind we learn a wonderful way to perceive the Absolute and "get understanding." We are not asked to believe in any creed or dogma or to have some superficial kind of faith. We are asked simply

---

* 1 Corinthians 15:52.
† Proverbs 4:7.

to think, to reason, to examine the rationale of what Life must be and how it must function *around* and therefore *within* us all if it is indeed a Life Principle. In fact, we are witnessing the Principle of Life everywhere, through all the levels of our life-experience.

Next, we see that each one of us is really *a mental atmosphere*. I am my own mental atmosphere, which came from my whole background—my education, understanding, thoughts, feelings, relationships, activities, experiences: these go to make up my mental atmosphere. You too have a mental atmosphere, and your mental atmosphere is composed of the same complex of elements. We may be related; we may have similar experiences; but no one is identical with another. We are all different, as that famous phrase captures it: "Unity in diversity."

Yes, we all come from the One, but we all particularize it. It is unique and different in each one of us. This is why you respect the human person and do not expect anyone to be cast in your own mold. You appreciate, respect, and honor the gift of the Spirit, God, the Absolute as It moves through others— through their personalities, their tastes, their particular way of thinking, their particular way of feeling. We are not taught just to honor others or respect human rights, we are not taught to do any external things—but to *believe*, because it is the right thing. We *believe*, we *practice*, we *experience*, we express— because we understand where life is coming from and therefore where everyone is coming from as a manifestation of the Absolute.

The success of our work, the success of using Principle, is directly related to your realizing the all-presence of that Principle. As it says in the Sanskrit:

One, without a second, everywhere present, that is always manifesting and always expressing through the Universe and through the individual.

Then we see that suffering is the result of some infringement of Law—something that you are doing to yourself related to the Principle of Life.

The moment we begin to wake up to what Life is and the way it functions, the Principle begins to move in a very full, rich, and rewarding way through us. That is *true* emancipation; then are we liberated through a new sense of Life and God—not through a new *life*, nor through a new God: we are emancipated through a new *sense* of Life and the Absolute, the Principle, or God. Nothing essential is changing except for your sense of Life, of who you are, what you are, where you are, where you have come from, and what you and your own life are all about. It is the sense of Life that is changed and that brings us freedom.

We talk about healing in the Science of Mind, and you can begin now to see that the healing process is simply becoming conscious of the truths that we are considering here: yourself in God; God moving through you; and your states of consciousness taking form. Your sense of you; your sense of Spirit or God or the Absolute; your sense of Nature; your sense of Law changing with your growing understanding of what Life is all about—these begin to produce in you, through the law of your own nature, something fresh, new, and wonderful. It will express the pattern of your particular state of consciousness or atmosphere of mind. That means your desire, your goals, your choice for the attainment of freedom and ease.

If you are thinking from a limited point of view, and because of that greed operates through you—a feeling that ''I've got to grab, I've got to get this before he or she gets it!''—then what happens? Nothing really *happens*, except that there is *obstruction* in your consciousness. The flow of the magnificent divine Energy trickles through a little here, a little there—because, although your total consciousness is not blocking, many areas of it are blocking; so that you don't attain or achieve, because you feel that you *can't* attain, that you are not *worthy* of it; somebody else is getting it, or someone else is worthy of it— but not you.

This relates to a question of basic self-esteem—not egotism or even egoism. Nor has it to do with ego inflation ("I am an exceptional person, I must have this, I must be there, I must do that"). That kind of ego manipulation of oneself is blockage. When you realize that there is enough of the Infinite Supply, the Infinite Substance, for infinite activity, then you begin to realize that there is enough for you and for everyone. This begins to dissolve that blockage where you feel something akin to "I missed the boat; I may not be able to get it; there may not be enough." In the Absolute there is *no end* to the good, there is *no end* to the potentiality and possibility for becoming—that is, for the evolution of the Life Principle.

We begin to see, then, that conditions are really not significant, conditions do not mean much. It is spiritual realization that is significant; spiritual awareness, spiritual awakening, spiritual understanding are what is vital. We need to get a sense of our own spiritual perfection. This means only that behind you and within you is *a spiritual idea of you*—a spiritual idea of *wholeness*, which is in the Absolute, in the Mind and Heart of God, in the Unconditioned One. Before the form, before the thing, there must be the idea behind it, there must be the mold, the prototype, the archetype, the pattern that then gets fulfilled in a particular way as your life experience and as your world.

What, then, do you really have to do? One thing only: learn to realize the state of wholeness of yourself—the state of wholeness that is in the Universe and the state of wholeness that is moving through you; *that* is what is important. Get this sense of it; get a realization of the wholeness in the Universe—behind you, around you, over you, within you, moving through you. You can't achieve good in any other way; you can't "send out" or "hold" thoughts. Thoughts, especially good thoughts, are wonderful—but they are limited. Spiritual realization is something that impacts the great creative Law of Mind. "Holding thoughts"—which no one can really do—would not accomplish much. "Sending out" thoughts—also which no one really can do—would again not accomplish much.

We begin to realize that causation is from within us where we "contact" Omnipresence; that is the universal Presence of God. If you seek outside, if you look outside, try to make it work outside—you are asking for frustration. You may attain a little here and there; but if you focus "out there" for the Source and Cause of all that is, of your life and experience, you are not only seeking but *finding* frustration.

Remember, there is one transcendent Principle—the Absolute. It is Wholeness Itself. It is Infinite Substance, Infinite Supply. It is unconditioned. As you get a sense of your connection to this vastness around and within you—and begin to use a very simple technique called Spiritual Mind Treatment—you will find a new life, a new birth, a new experience of living, a new quality that will make you step back and look at your life in awe. And from that awe, from that source of consciousness, is where all the hymns of praise and glory to the Highest originate; that's where they have come from.

And they sing of Absolute living.

Grace

THE TRADITIONAL CONCEPT of Grace—in most traditions, but we are thinking in terms of Western Christianity—is "unmerited love and favor of God toward man." This is the religious "mainstream" way of talking about what we in our teaching would regard as a joyous action—the infinite, eternal, joyful activity of a transcendent Presence and Power that is also immanent. There is at the depth of your being, no matter how despondent you might feel, a joyous action taking place. It is permanently established—because you didn't establish yourself, you didn't create yourself. You were created by a creative force, by the divine Impulse—God, Spirit; but it is a force that operates in a complex way, bringing about evolution on Planet Earth and developing us to the point of being human.

Deep within, at the seed center of you and of me, is this joyous action going on. It is unconcerned about you, unconcerned about your thoughts or feelings. *It is there*—working, functioning. Then we begin to realize that it is up to us to do something about it—to clear our thinking and our consciousness of all of the negativity with which we fill ourselves personally and that fills us from the collective consciousness of humankind. It says

No to life. *No* to good, *no* to joy, *no* to harmony: it has us focus only on the physical, the material—what we call the tangible reality of experience. Then we learn, as we proceed in our spiritual studies, that the so-called realities—tangible, physical experiences—are only partially real. They are symbols, and very often faulty, incomplete symbols, of that which is much greater, of that Higher Force, Power, Action, or Intelligence.

In Religious Science we learn that Grace *is*. We live in Grace, we move in Grace; Grace is operating within us as the giving-ness of God, operating within you and me, now and always. We cannot escape it. It is there and it is permanent. We were born with it—established in God's Grace. We learn through our studies that Grace appears to be given us to the degree of our acceptance of it, to the degree that we recognize this Truth and realize that, because of Law, it is operating in our lives according to our thoughts and feelings about it.

This Creative Law operates in the Universe, acting on our belief. Just as there are psychological laws that we see on the human level, operating according to beliefs, thoughts, and feelings, so this Great Law operates according to the way we understand it, accept it. That is the transcendent Grace, Force, Power. It will sometimes be very small in its expression, so much so that we are hardly aware of its existence. At other times it will be very large in its expression. Fully recognized, it gives us a sense of fulfillment, a sense of awe at the divine majesty and magnificence of Being, of God.

This breakthrough into awareness, this divine bliss, is known among the Hindus and the Vedantins as Satchitananda: Being, Wisdom, and Absolute Bliss. The saints and sages of that tradition would say "I want a taste of that nectar and bliss," meaning that they wanted to get some sense of the Reality in a very tangible way, *in* and *through* and *as* their lives.

We see, then, that blessings are ever given. You and I are

blessed right now—richly blessed. The giving is there already; we don't even have to earn it. If we want to experience it, though, we have to do something about it. We must "open it up" and take out all the beauties that are packed in there. But *we* didn't pack them. The divine Parent did the packing, sent us off, and told us to have a good time

We come with the bag, and most of us don't open it, though it's not even locked. So that is why we study the Science of Mind—to learn to lift up the lid and pull out the demonstrations of good that can take place in our lives.

The blessings are given. Actually, we measure the *extent* by our *receptivity*—by what we do with ourselves; but they are there. God's gifts are there *for* us, *in* us, right now—and we didn't earn them. Isn't that wonderful? But we have to do something about them. We have been given—as the child, the offspring of the Highest—intelligence to use, a mind to use, to see Life in its fullness on a material plane, on a psychological plane, and on what is called a spiritual plane. That really means on a plane or level of high, transcendent ideas—beautiful ideas.

We are talking here about something that is very basic to our metaphysical science—that is, the Law of Mental Equivalents, which says that what you believe you experience. What you are in consciousness, you receive in your life. Further, this Law of Mental Equivalents means that you can receive *more*, that you can *enlarge* that Mental Equivalent. We sometimes call it an *embodiment* of an idea or a state of thought. You can increase your positive, constructive beliefs, or embodiments, and therefore receive more good into your life, because the good comes *to* you *through* you. That is Grace. Think about it: *that* is Grace—that which is there all the time and is ever pouring through you; but you experience it *as* you and to the degree that you are *aware* of it, *accept* it. That is called receptivity also; and that is Grace.

Theoretically, you can demonstrate any good you desire.

Why do I say good? Because Good is the process of Life, the process of God, the process of the Transcendent and Its evolving action through all forms and functions of Life and life experience.

Practically, though, we experience only to the extent of the beliefs accepted—only to the extent that our consciousness is expanded. But we can always accept more and more of this divine beneficence. That is way God is called the All-Merciful, the All-Benevolent One. That All-Merciful, All-Benevolent One is giving to us right now. If we could just realize that, truly realize that, make it real for us for a moment: we would experience a fantastic transformation. Maybe not a *total* transformation— because we are complex beings and we need to *experience* it now and again, here and there and in yet other moments and areas of this transforming action.

Many of us have experienced this transformation in wonderful healings, physical, mental, emotional, relational, financial— call it what you will. It doesn't matter what the thing is that is transformed, because that is an expression of some state of belief and consciousness. What does matter is that the Grace is there and that we are being receptive to it. In the East, there is a wonderful statement that ''The winds of God are blowing.'' The implied directive is: *Unfurl your sails.* You see, we *have* got something to do with it. The winds are there, they are blowing. *Unfurl your sails and let it blow you forward.* The great Hindu saint Sri Ramakrishna used to say to his disciples all the time: *These winds of God are blowing; unfurl your sails, move forward.* This is what we are considering here: a mental embodiment or acceptance that *the winds of God are blowing.*

But there is also a spiritual embodiment, and this spiritual embodiment has to do with our study, our learning more and more about the ways of Spirit—the way Spirit functions as Life, the way Spirit functions in our life now, and how It functions in the realm of pure Spirit unfolding Itself to Itself. When we begin to understand *that*, think about *that*, it is what I would call *spiritual embodiment*. When you *think* about It as being in your physical, tangible, material, human world, then it is *mental embodiment*. We need both mental and spiritual embodiment.

Spiritual disciplines are important, but they do not influence God or God's Grace. It is only your mind which can be moved, and you can open it more and yet more to new beliefs in good, new beliefs in life energy, new beliefs in wholeness, new beliefs in harmony. Each one of us receives directly from the Source and not through any channel or saint or sage, not through any church, any baptism, communion, not through any particular good. We receive directly because *It* is there already. We say there are no *special people*, only those who *specialize the Spirit*. *Specialize*, meaning that they get a sense of their connection to the Great One Source of Being and of Nature.

We have to learn to surrender—surrender what is talked about in Eastern and Western spiritual disciplines: as the petty ego, this inflated I, I, I,—"I am this," "I am that," "I am the other thing." Realize that the only Reality in this I is God, giving us life, energy, intelligence with which to work. We have to learn to surrender every objection to, or negation of, this Truth. We are always objecting to it and always negating. We may deny this and protest that we love this teaching. We may love it indeed—but we are always negating it, because we focus too much on the physical, limited human experience, thinking that it is the be-all and the end-all; for isn't the Science of Mind for demonstrating good here? we ask. It is; but we can only demonstrate the good *here* if we see that it comes from *there*. Coming from *there* doesn't mean "out there" in cosmic realms beyond the beyond. *There* means *supramental*—from the transcendent Mind and Power and Force and Action within.

We face and harbor many fears about life and experience and our place here and what is going to happen to us. If you think about it, fears are simply thoughts—*thoughts of limitation*.

Think about it. Fears are misplaced faith—in disorder instead of order, in lack instead of supply, in limitation instead of this ever-unfolding abundant good that is in the Universe, that is in you and in me.

We have to get back to this idea that Life, the Principle of Being, withholds nothing from us. Sadly, though, what we believe in is not Life Divine, but what I call the 3 L's—lack, loss, limitation: that is what we believe in. Yet there is an inner voice in each one of us. It is the voice of freedom: freedom to be yourself, to be one with Being, to be a child of the Universe, to be part of that transcendent Presence.

This brings us to Love—Love that is so vast, so tremendous that we can't describe It. It is an infinite Giver, an infinite Principle that cannot be described. We use the Word *Love*, and right away we get the sense of a human kind of giving. But this human giving is only a faint shadow of the Love that is there in the Fount of Being, which is not only around each one of us, but *deep within us*. It is in us living fully, functioning fully, and giving to us all the time. If you want to use the human description of it (which some sages and saints have done) as waiting for you: then God is waiting for you, as it were, to accept the divine Benevolence, the divine Supply that is there.

The great question is: What are you doing with *you*? What are you doing with your mind? with your thinking? with your feeling? with your reasoning? This is very important. We talk a great deal about thinking and feeling; what are you doing with your thinking, with your feeling? What are you doing with your reasoning?

Aren't we reasoning from the vantage point of the physical, human, material limitation, lack, and loss *most* of the time?— and *every once in a while* from a little higher point of view, call it a more spiritual point of view (although *everything* is spiritual, because nothing is outside the realm of Spirit, God). What we need to do is learn to reason, more appropriately and properly, from the altitude and vantage point of the Great Spirit that is the Source and Cause of your being and my being and all of us.

The reason that you can demonstrate good in your life, the reason negatives can be neutralized, is that any state of consciousness that is not in line with the Cosmic Evolution can be changed. It can be changed through right reasoning. This is using the thinking process, but it is not just *thinking*: it is *reasoning* from the *appropriate* point of view, the *appropriate* standpoint— that of the Great Spirit—and not from the point of view of the puny material world. That kind of reasoning spells the difference between being a victim and being a victor.

Think about it: God is the Universal Presence of Love, the winds are blowing, the Grace is there. It is always giving, never punishing; It doesn't know about punishing—It only knows about loving, giving, nurturing, caring. We need to know how to get behind these appearances that say *no* and say *limitation*, *disease*, *disorder*, and *distress*—how to get behind these; how to receive. *There is only one way, and that is to look through appearances to cause*—to the Source—and learn to receive directly from the divine Providence that is always bestowing the gift.

Think about all the wonderful goodies in that bag that the Father-Mother Source has given to you and sent you off with— wonderful surprises that you can't even imagine; marvelous potentialities and inventions and possibilities for being and becoming. What we need to do is get rid of the reasoning that lack is necessary and get into a new sense of what we can call divine Provision. In the moment when you get that suggestion of *no*, say: "I am provided for, I have a divine Provision." Look within yourself and say: "I am open and receptive to this wonderful flowing forth from within me of all the gifts that the divine, transcendent Principle of Life gave me when I became who I am on Planet Earth."

This recognition, this awareness, this realization is Grace.

What Is Reality for You?

ONE OF THE FIRST things we have to realize is that everything is real—that is, that everything is real *as far as it goes.* The great problem is that *we don't go far enough.* Everything is real—is real as far as it goes—but you and I and most human beings don't go far enough in learning about that reality in analyzing it and perceiving it. When you *do* go far enough, you are thinking back to Principle.

There is nothing in our study that tells you to deny life, deny the material world, deny experience. We see that everything is as real as it could possibly be—*as far as it goes.* But *we* need to go back further to perceive, to appreciate, to recognize, to understand the Principle that is behind all existence, indwelling all existence, and that is working through us all the time. We do this through our study of the Science of Mind; that is what our study is all about: getting us to see back to Principle, to the Essential Nature; to get on the right track; to go home to heaven, harmony.

We begin to see that our perception of life, our perception of things, of relationships, of the material world is what really matters. Is our perception, our evaluation, our judgment on the level of merely the physical, material outer experience and its implications? Or do we go back further to what is behind it all—to the essential reality, the essential Principle behind it all?

We begin to find ourselves moving in a world of symbology; indeed, most of the religions of the world are simply symbolical methods of expressing these truths. Sometimes they express them only in part. Sometimes they express them totally; but they seem to be covered up by human articulation—human words, phrases, and ideas that appear to cover up the essential truth.

Going back to the ancients we see that the mystical number three has played a huge role, from the triangle of the pyramid to the essential Trinity that appears in many different religions. Three is the symbol of spiritual synthesis and the symbol of spiritual action. Thinking back far enough to Principle, however, we don't get lost in the three. We don't get lost in the pyramid, we don't get lost in the Trinity, or in any external expression of the mystical impulse.

I mention this because there seems to be a fundamental synthesis of all the energies that comprise life and the potential of human experience and awareness. In our study we see that there are three realities, and we begin to learn about them: the material reality, the reality of our material world of experience; the psychological reality, which has to do with our world of consciousness and with the interplay between the conscious and the subconscious parts of our minds; and the spiritual reality.

On the material level we are dealing with the realm of the unconscious because when we think in terms of just the physical, material world, we are thinking in terms of the kind of instinct that we see in the animal world and in ourselves—instincts and impulses that well up from an unconscious level. On the psychological level, however, we are dealing in terms of the realms of consciousness. We now begin to perceive the interaction between the conscious and the subconscious areas of this mind that we appear to have.

The third reality is the reality that most religions talk about but seldom can communicate to anyone. Religions seem to stay in the realm of religion, and only a few mystics within every discipline here or there move beyond religion to the spiritual idea and the spiritual function. The third realm—the spiritual realm —is where we say there is one God or Spirit, and It expresses as Its Creation. In our teachings we would say, with Ernest Holmes, *God as man, in man, is man**—a very mystical statement that requires study. The result of that study, and its attendant mental breakthrough, brings us to what we call the spiritual—or even the superconscious realm of mind, the superconscious realm of experience, the superconscious realm of realization. We rarely use the word *superconscious* in our study, because we recognize it as one aspect of consciousness. When you begin to orient too much to a word or expression like *superconscious*, you begin to isolate it and make it something objective ''out there'' that you can attain or achieve in some way.

We realize that there is only one Consciousness and Consciousness Principle. Whatever is called *superconscious* is *in* you and moving *through* you right now, as well as what we call conscious mind and subconscious mind. Your perception of it, your awareness, your realization of it, its interplay and functioning, is what spells the difference for you between being a director and being a passive puppet in a world of power and experience. Then we begin to understand this third world, this spiritual realm or superconscious realm. And we begin to see that we are not the puppet of anyone or anything but ourselves; we are not a victim of anything but our own perception or misperception of Truth, the reality of Being.

* *The Science of Mind*, p. 482.

To recapitulate: there are three realities: the material, physical realm; the psychological—the realm of consciousness and the interplay of conscious and subconscious; and the spiritual, which is the cosmic realm, the realm of the celestial, the realm that seems to be above and beyond us—yet is *deep within us* and *moving through us.* Jesus states it this way: the Kingdom of Heaven is within you. Did he picture a Kingdom of Heaven "up there," with all kinds of lovely external, objective people and events? No. The Kingdom of Heaven, as this great teacher said, is in the spiritual realm that is within you. All the instructions coming from this special teacher were to go within, go to the Father within, pray within—for that which is within you will reward you outwardly, externally.

Here we are beginning to get the hint, in the teaching of Jesus, of the spiritual side, which we call the Science of Mind. Going to that Reality within, and working in that spiritual realm within, we can expect to see a change in another realm—the external and "lesser" realm called the physical or material world. The true nature of Reality is always expressed through the symbol of three. We call it Spirit, Soul, and Body. Many religions of the world may not use exactly those words, but that is what they are talking about—Spirit, Soul, and Form, if you will. We say that these represent (1) conscious intelligence; (2) subjective Law, i.e. subconscious Law—something *within*, or *under*, which is Law; and (3) form—the outpicturing of the interplay of conscious intelligence and subjective Law.

Remember that the form is first within before it is external. If you want external wholeness in your life, you first have to have the form, within, of wholeness. If you want supply in your experience outwardly, you first have to have the form of substance and supply inwardly. Form is always first inward and then through Law it appears outwardly. Spirit, Soul, and Body: conscious intelligence, subjective Law, and form.

Ernest Holmes makes a very interesting statement in the

Science of Mind textbook. He says this: "The nature of Reality is such that Universal Mind has unlimited power but so far as man is concerned It has only the power which he gives to It."* Unlimited power—but for you, only as much experience of power in your life as you give to it, as you allow to happen in you and through you: through your awareness, through your awakening, through your spiritual recognition and realization. You are not creating power; there is a higher Power, a greater Power. But for you in your life, that Power functions as you stop rebelling, as you stop resisting and rejecting It. At the point at which you begin to recognize, appreciate, and realize It, It begins to flow through you in a fuller and a greater way.

We are considering states of consciousness that are reflected back to the individual as experience. Your state of consciousness is always reflected back to you through your world as people, places, things, situations, and events. This harks back to the Principle of Reflection, where the Spirit is always thinking about Itself and "reflecting" Its thought in creation. In you and in me is the image and likeness of God. This manifests as our ability to think, to have conscious, intelligent thoughts, conscious desires, and our ability to know that the subconscious is operating as a receiver of those thoughts and desires—a reactor to them and, through reaction, a reflector of them into our experience as our consciousness in form.

When you think about all this, you realize that *choice* is the prerogative and the nature of personal consciousness. You have the right to choose, the right to select, because that is part of the nature of this Great Spirit that is thinking about Itself and always unfolding Itself, always reflecting upon Itself. In you and in me It appears as what we label *choice*—the ability to select, to think: to think anew, to think more, to think in a larger way; or, if we are manipulated by distorted mental suggestion, to

* *The Science of Mind*, p. 396.

think in a negative way, in a petty way, in a destructive way. The basic human instinct, the basic human right, is to choose— the ability to select.

Law always manifests, and this is what is known as Omnipotence—a synonym in many religions for God. This ability to choose *and to know that Law is reacting and producing* comes from Power—and the only essential Power is Omnipotence, the Power of God. People call It the Higher Power. This is not such a good term, because it begins to orient you to a Higher Power "out there." Better not to orient to a Higher Power "out there" but to *Omnipotence*—which is really Omnipresence—ever present *within you*. The Kingdom of Heaven is *within you*, not "out there" somewhere. And we begin to see that if you misuse the Power, suffering is the result. On the other hand, if you use the Power in what we call the correct way, a way that is using Mind constructively and positively, the result automatically is fulfillment. Fulfillment: the attainment and achievement of something good in your life and in your world.

What do we conclude from this? What do we find? Suffering, pain, disease, disorder, distress, disturbance—these are not Principle; they are the result of *a use* of Principle, of Universal Law, the Law of Mind. And that Law is always operating. It is part of the basic Reality, and It creates *our* reality. Reality for us will outpicture in our world at the level of our ignorance of this Truth, or at the level of our spiritual recognition and understanding of the One Power and the One Eternal ongoing Reality and Good that is the *essential* nature of our life.

Spiritual Mind Treatment, which is our practice, is the use of the only Power there is—Omnipotence. In using the action of God, we awake to the Reality that is created for us. That is, we see the experience that is created for us through our recognition and use of the Power inwardly, and that inner Power moving always outwardly as our experience. Everything is made from this consciousness—of God, of Spirit, of Omnipotence,

Omnipresence—for everything is consciousness. Everything comes out of it and expresses it all the time.

Our reality is our consciousness of Life. Our reality is our consciousness of the One Being around and within us. Our reality is our recognition of this Presence which creates our world of forms, our world of experiences. Within and without, we are always experiencing the Divine Nature. Can we get outside of God? Never. We are always experiencing the Divine Nature and the Divine Consciousness. Always.

How are we experiencing? That is the question. At what level are we expressing It? At the level of the puny? At the level of the limited? Or is it at the level of the eternal ongoing experience, the expanding universal action, of the Great Spirit of Life? How *are* we experiencing the Spirit of Life? Is it bringing us freedom or bondage? That's for each of us to answer.

When you are experiencing more and more freedom, you know that you are working with the Law, working with Life, with the Great Spirit, with Nature. When you find lack, loss, limitation, bondage, and restriction, you know that something is awry. You are working against Life in some way. Not that you are a sinner or that you stand condemned; it's that you are doing something to yourself. Yes, you are doing *something*. Find out what that something is. It's sure to be external cause that you are focusing on, saying it's real, that's where it's at, that's what it's all about. Materially and physically it may seem so—but not from the highest standpoint of spiritual recognition. The Principle of Life is freedom.

We choose our reality. It cannot be escaped. The great question always is What is Reality for *you*? The limited, apparent world of physical illusion, delusion, and the experience? Or the Principle of Harmony, Wholeness, Right Action—the Principle of Divine Order that is ever operating in you—?

Make the latter your answer.

Oneness

THERE IS a Single Reality. It is universal and ever present. Is this the vantage point from which you view life? What do you believe about the cause behind all situations? Where do discouragement, fear, doubt, calamity come from? They cannot proceed from the eternal Source, that perfect fount of Life, the inexhaustible One. They must come from within your own consciousness. Therefore you must set yourself right with the Universe. You must find the Source if you are to be supplied. You must sense that you express the life of God if you wish to realize the Spirit in your life.

Oneness is the key to life and existence. It is the Single Reality. It is what we need to recognize again and again. Think in terms of a single Reality, not a dual Reality. Many may find that an idea within them—usually coming from some past teaching, past acceptance, or what psychologists would call conditioning —prevents them from really embracing this concept and moving forward. There is something that makes them resist it. They would like to hear an echo of the old conditioning, perhaps a familiar religious concept or idea. This is even true of those who never went to a church or participated in any kind of spiritual background.

Our society is permeated by a religious point of view—a state of mind with really makes one think not so much of a single Reality as of a dualism, of a God "up there" somewhere and a person "down here" somewhere, and maybe a still lower level with somebody else "down there" with a pitchfork. We laugh and we joke and say, "Oh, isn't that quaint?" But many people accept these concepts almost literally. And while others do not accept them at all, still, their minds are set in that dualistic framework.

What we are trying to do here is to get a sense of oneness that will enable us to break the conditioning of the past and move us forward in life. We need an understanding of the universal Principle and the way it functions. We have to break the cocoon of the past. We must not remain in the same state of mind. If we do, we frustrate all possibility of personal evolution to a higher awareness and greater freedom.

Many of us respect the marvelous breakthrough in the science of physics attained by Albert Einstein. He was a rare genius who through his Theory of Relativity opened up a new world. Yet even Einstein did not move forward. He remained in his own realm of thought, while certain other scientists began to talk about the "paradigm shift," a shift in the pattern of thought, of consciousness, of energy, which was yet another forward movement in physical theory. These people began to describe very interesting phenomena that they had observed. One particular scientist, Werner Heisenberg, talked about a Principle of Uncertainty. Einstein could not accept many of these ideas, which were based on quantum mechanics. He was frozen in his old realm of thinking.

This shows how conditioning can enslave even a brilliant mind like Einstein's—because he could not move forward into the novel concept of what is now called the "new physics."

None of this is meant to disparage Einstein, who was obviously gifted with a magnificent mind and who contributed to life almost more than anyone else in modern times. On the other hand, you have to recognize, in terms of human consciousness, the way all of us can limit ourselves. Even a great man like Einstein limited himself in some degree.

As we examine life, we begin to recognize a oneness, or Single Reality, in the Universe. We can say there is one God, one Life, one Mind, one Power, one Presence, one divine Nature. It is around us and within us, behind us and moving through us all the time. It is not static. It expresses itself as dynamic energy, and we see it throughout the material universe. But more than that, the material universe is a symbol of something much bigger and much larger: that is, the vastness that truly is beyond the material universe. It is cosmos. It is infinite ongoingness, the unfolding greatness of life. This theme of oneness in Life we understand as the theme of our own intimate and personal life experience.

The great Spirit of Life, the Single Reality, must be in you right now as the creative Principle. And it is your individual, personal connection to God. You were created. You know that you are here. You have consciousness. The Great Spirit of Life gave you consciousness and is reflecting Itself some way in you. You reflect all that God is. You—as a physical human being, as mind, as emotions, as a person—reflect the creative imagination of that Mind Principle, which is another term we can use for God or the Great Spirit.

Here is a way to look at this idea: Take a glob of clay. Divide it among three friends. One is given the task of molding the piece of clay into a figure. The second is asked to sculpt a boat. The third friend is to shape the clay into a house. Each gives of him- or herself in some creative way when performing the task. The person is not in the figure, boat, or house; but the person's imagination, vision, or mind is in the creative process and its expression. Each object reflects the consciousness of the person molding the clay.

In our study, working with the creative Law of Mind, each person is centered in the One. The Single Reality expresses *in*, *through*, and *as* every living being and object. It is one Substance manifesting or expressing Itself in a variety of forms, one Energy appearing through all kinds of energy in the Universe. In our transformational work, we recognize that the Energy is in each of us. Through techniques we can learn, the Energy is used in such a way as to neutralize and dissolve whatever blockage there may be in a particular person's consciousness and experience. This brings about a new experience of Energy. The individual is literally energized by a Higher Power.

We call it "being healed" or "demonstrating the principle of wholeness," or the Law of Mind in action, the Law of Creative Energy, the expression of the Single Reality. Such healing is a matter of opening oneself to an awareness that there is one Substance in the Universe, one Energy, one Power, one Presence; that wherever you are, and under whatever conditions, you can use it. *Wherever you are*, It moves in and through you, and It will transform you inwardly and outwardly.

The interesting fact that we have found in over a hundred years of working with this Principle is that there is no separation or fragmentation in the Universe. Life isn't fragmented. The same Principle works as your creative opportunities for self-expression, in your health, and even as your ability to make money, because money is simply a symbol of a spiritual substance and supply. It works in interpersonal relationships, in the mind, and in the emotions. It works in every area and in every aspect of your life, because it is a Single Reality, one Substance and Energy. You can particularize It and use It according to your creative thinking, according to what you think you need. Then it begins to move into different areas of your life-experience as a creative force. All of this requires study and practice in order to learn how to use the Principle. It is easier when you work with the process each day.

In the New Testament Letter to the Ephesians, Paul writes to his students about oneness:

> There is . . . one Spirit, even as ye are called in one hope of your calling; one Lord, one faith, one baptism, one God and Father of all, who is above all, and through all, and in you all. . . . Till we all come in the unity of the faith . . . unto a perfect man. . . . Put off . . . the old man, which is corrupt according to the deceitful lusts; and be renewed in the spirit of your mind; and that ye put on the new man, which after God is created in righteousness and true holiness.

Paul, of course, is talking about the oneness expressed as the true idea, as the perfect man. He is telling his students to get an understanding that each is the child of the One. That is, "to put on the new man" means that you are recognizing and realizing that you are the child of the One which is absolute Substance, absolute wholeness, absolute harmony, absolute perfectibility of being, absolute beauty, absolute order. *Absolute*, in that it is beyond the physical, conditioned world: that it is the infinite Principle of Life and Being. We have to realize that this One created us, is backing us up, and has implanted in us the energy we need to manifest the attributes of God, such as beauty, harmony, wholeness, creativeness and joy—and also the potential for working with the Law of Consciousness.

This is the creative process of the One: always producing something greater, larger, better, more fulfilled, more harmonious, more abundant than has been experienced. Paul's letter is filled with the injunction that we put on the new man, that we experience *the new*. One must really be careful never to judge by outer appearances. Look at the outside to see if there might be a disorder, disability, difficulty, or a problem; but then immediately look within for the solution. Look *within* to see what needs changing.

The objective side is always the expression of a subjective pattern. That is, the physical, material world is always a painting or a representation of what we are in the mental, emotional, and inner spiritual world. The spiritual world is the way we think about life, about ourselves, about our potentiality, and about the possibility of being and becoming something better.

To heal problems, we need to get a sense of our unity with the One. We need to begin to see and conceive of wholeness as the Principle of Life moving through all of life, including ourselves. There is no separation in the One or from Its attributes or expressions. This is a holistic science of Being. Holistic medicine claims that one has to be aware of the whole person, including mind and the emotions, which affect the body—and the body, which affects the mind and the emotions. We are holistic people, holistic beings, and we can never escape being involved with the whole person.

Why is this valid? Why is our essential nature whole? Because it is a minute mirror of the holism that is the Universe. Life is one. Life is whole, and healing through our technique of mental and spiritual treatment is based on recognizing our unity with the Source of all Being. This awareness must be cultivated, and the result—*healing*—is always the experience of understanding and realizing that "I and the Source are one." Remember, there is only one Reality. God is the One, Spirit is the One, Source is the One, perfect Wholeness is the One that expresses through the many forms of existence.

You have the right to assert your divinity, to assert that you are the child of the One, the child of wholeness, the child of harmony, the expression of the single Reality, that which IS. When you do this through the inspiration that comes from spiritual understanding and the growing awareness of this truth, you arrive at the point of realization and transformation—literally being transformed through a renewal of your mind. You go through change—inwardly in your thought, your feeling, and your whole consciousness; outwardly, as a manifestation of healing. Oneness is the theme of Life. The understanding of oneness is the way to the solution of every problem. Oneness is the open road to healing.

A consciousness of oneness is the way to live.

Subjectivity or Objectivity

Some years ago when jobs were scarce and the inflationary economy made mortgages tight, a friend was presented with a fantastic opportunity on the opposite coast. His family was excited about the move. He had plans for experiencing a new quality of life. Opportunity was knocking on all doors and windows. Even his exploratory visit presented him with a beautiful new home which he was able to obtain with ease. Soon after the move, his new employers expressed their delight at the innovative contributions he was making to their organization. Sad to say, when the first weeks of the honeymoon period were over, nothing seemed right. Even the climate of this salubrious region met with disfavor. Everything felt wrong about the move, and my friend was in despair.

During a brief phone talk it became clear that my friend had lost all objectivity related to the move, the job, and his new life. Everything in his previous world was appealing: the inadequate house, the old job, outgrown things and experiences. He was living straight out of subjectivity. He could not see the new with objective eyes, but only through the lens of the past. This un-

50

healthy state of mind was producing a disturbed mental, emotional, and physical environment. And he was wallowing in it. But he began to see that he was being manipulated by old subconscious patterns that were actually taking over his present existence and coloring every aspect of his new life, and this "seeing" enabled him to get a handle on the causation of all his misery. Through recognizing his divine right to enjoy each day as a fresh experience in creativity, my friend was able to dissolve past patterns that were blocking the expression of new ideas and their forms. Spiritual Mind Treatment dissolved these subjective patterns—time-bombs ready to explode into depression and difficulty. They were defused through a realization that the power and presence of Universal Intelligence had removed all blocks to a fulfilled life.

Frequently when we undertake "new beginnings," there is the challenge of change. Adaptation to new climates of experience, friends, and colleagues presents us with the stress and anxiety of the unknown. In these moments we become vulnerable to unresolved aspects of our past that are circulating in the depths of consciousness. My friend's experience is not uncommon. Most people are unaware of the potential for crisis or cure resident in the unconscious.

For those studying the Science of Mind, a new turn in the state of consciousness is an ever-present possibility. It is a matter of decision and choice. The moment one begins to raise thought to a higher point of view, the energy of Universal Intelligence backs up the effort. Then, recognizing and appreciating one's ability to cooperate with the universal Law of Cause and Effect, old patterns of resistance are removed; a complete acceptance of the forward action of life is realized; the morbid hold of the past is eliminated.

And life moves on in an ordered and beautiful way.

When Push
Comes to Shove

How MANY of us have heard or spoken the cliché "If push comes to shove, then I will do this, or I will do that"? When people use that term, they simply express something in which all of us are involved all the time—that is, manipulation, or, more precisely, *trying* to manipulate. If you are brutally honest in examining your life, you will see that much of it is really an action of manipulation. Often it is being manipulated by people, events, situations, or things. You are not working constructively with the Law of Life if you are living in a consciousness of manipulation.

Yet everyone feels put upon. Everyone is in the midst of some stressful action of life. Often, it is the need to say something to a special person regarding an event or situation which you are reluctant to bring up or about which you feel tense.

Stress is *the* hot topic today. There isn't a popular magazine that doesn't have some new "Ten Steps to Eliminate Stress" or "Four Ways to Look at Your Stressful Life." Certainly, the phrase "when push comes to shove" represents just the tip of the iceberg. Here, we really need to have a clear idea about what stress is and what it does to us, and then about a way out of stress that is meta-psychological—a way that gets us above and beyond simple psychology.

To begin, we must observe the problems that develop from stress. The "Stress Press" talks about headaches and sleep disorders, digestive problems, increased susceptibility to germs present everywhere, unpredictable mood swings, underarm odor, sexual difficulties, slipping dentures, back pains, bad breath, muscle spasms, incontinence, cold hands and feet, headache, inability to concentrate, shortness of breath, insomnia, a short fuse with the kids, a vocabulary to shock your mother. When that sounds familiar, you are a bona fide member of the Stress Club.

But all of us are part of this club. Turn on your television set and you are bombarded by the sales pitches for ways to release or reduce the effects of "everyday" stress. Stress comes from feeling that you do not have control over your circumstances, your environment, or what you do. So people say, "I just don't have enough time. I am overloaded. They dump this or that on me in the office. Then I go home and the kids are after me, or my wife demands [or my husband expects] . . . We have those house payments to make . . . not enough time . . . not enough energy."

Never enough to meet the demands of life! Or to function in a balanced way, either. One of the important points to remember is that *stress comes largely from feeling that you have little control over your circumstances or environment, no matter what you do.*

Stress is a $150 billion industry. These billions are spent by business and various organizations on stress-related costs that include everything from seminars and workshops by self-proclaimed "stress evaluators" and stress experts, to medical expenses, costs of absenteeism, and employee turnover. This $150 billion per year is larger than the 1985 after-tax profits of all the Fortune 500 companies combined! Little wonder, then, that we have so many problems in our lives—in our bodies, in our minds and emotions, in the world! I firmly believe that most of the world's problems are the result of this inner, stress-related disordering of consciousness.

Basic to all stress-related problems is what psychologists describe as the "fight/flight response mechanism." Fight/flight is an innate animal response to an experience that confronts you. It is a reaction to a present challenge through the mirror of the past—through a screen of memories. This includes not only our individual experience of life but the entire past history of the race. We tend to react to present challenges with a caveman mentality, thinking and feeling that the unknown predator is about to jump out of the bush and strike us down.

This deep, living subjective pattern is within everyone, although there are no longer any predatory animals in our lives. We have no need for such a strong reaction to ordinary experiences. Yet there it is, inescapable, as we react to the boss, to our employee, to what the doctor says, or to some other challenge of human relationship. Even attitudes toward finances or mortgage payments may come from a deep-seated fight/flight conflict within us that seems always to be at work.

What happens when you are continually and repeatedly undergoing this stress action in life? Physically, adrenalin shoots through the body. This comes from the endocrine glands, and within six seconds the body responds to danger signals received by the brain. Every function has changed in the neurological and hormonal systems.

The result is constriction and dilation of various blood vessels and acceleration of the heart. Digestion ceases, the blood-clotting factor increases, and cholesterol is released into the bloodstream through the liver so the body can perform under stress. The liver, aided by the pancreas, produces insulin, which combines with sugar that has been released by the liver to infiltrate the bloodstream. The pupils of the eyes dilate, muscles tighten. Other physical reactions take place, and in brief time you have been literally transmuted, transformed. You are a changed being.

This is not an extraordinary experience. When push comes to shove—and so many of us find ourselves in this kind of emotional syndrome—all of these physical things happen. It would be all right if they happened once in a rare while, when we were prepared to meet a real crisis. But major crises do not happen in our lives that frequently. Important things do take place, great challenges do arise, but they are not crises. It is only when we face a real crisis that we need a total hormonal and physiological change. But when every small encounter brings about these strong reactions, the result is a vast array of potential health problems facing the average man or woman.

All the biofeedback methods and the seminars, workshops, and other activities that are offered the public simply enable the individual to combat daily stress. They try to confer upon the individual a little more personal control of the life experience. One can be trained so that when one feels inner turbulence, one can become still, getting centered so that there is an experience of self-control.

One of the health problems that we see consistently on television and in other advertising is "tension headaches." We are told they are caused by an increase in the blood supplied to the brain, resulting in a tightening of the muscles around the cranium. Muscle tension builds, which is manifested as tension in the scalp, in the back, and in the neck. All of this combines to disable many people.

Ulcers are another problem. Usually, they are a result of increased acid in the stomach because of a decrease in the blood supply to the digestive system. Then there are cardiac and hypertension problems. Elevated blood pressure is often the result of constant stress. Sometimes this builds up in those who are resisting certain aspects of their experience.

And we cannot overlook our familiar friend cholesterol, the perennial villain for every health newsletter and popular magazine. It is difficult to pick up a newspaper or periodical that doesn't have something about cholesterol in it. Certainly, our diets need to be under intelligent control. But cholesterol becomes a problem when it is released by the liver in excess and stays in the bloodstream, causing blockages in the veins and arteries. With an increase in the clotting factor during stress, there is a greater risk of stroke or heart attack.

Since we are frequently in a push-comes-to-shove mentality or experience in some area of our lives—financially, or in personal relationships, on the job, asking for that raise, getting an employee to do something—we find ourselves disturbed, in a state of imbalance, needing some kind of clarification. So the question is: what is a truly effective program for life and for your personal experience? I mean a *truly* effective program—more than a momentary panacea, more than just a way to sense the tension and then try to do something about it. We need a larger and deeper program to get at the root cause of stress and tension.

What might such a really effective program be? I have found from years of research and counseling, combined with years of study in the metaphysics of healing, that there is only one eventual answer: *spiritual understanding.* That is what builds the necessary inner conviction about life, the self, one's personal being, and control. It is only spiritual understanding that builds this conviction, that neutralizes the buildup of stress which blocks freedom and ease in living. When push comes to shove, listen to your deepest, innermost self.

When I am faced with a challenge, even though I don't like it, even though I have to face it and deal with it, I also see something else happening which I believe is the result of the accumulated buildup of self-knowledge and the growing spiritual understanding that I have set as a goal in my own life. (Believe me, we all need as much spiritual understanding as we can get.

The search and study must be an ongoing thing. For me, it is constant. It never ceases.) But when I am faced with a challenge, something happens in me that makes me sharper, clearer. The challenge is there, the stress begins to appear, *and then somehow I get clearer, I get stronger.* I am able to say, "Okay, I can face it."

It is the spiritual understanding, the spiritual foundation built up over years of study and self-work that supports the conviction within. It is this which reduces the blockage—or what could become a blockage—immediately. After that first fear reaction, something from within that is greater and more powerful pours forth. *When things look the worst, then we can depend upon our inner resources to rise to the occasion, to control ourselves, our lives and, eventually, our experience.*

This comes about through a spiritual understanding which depends on learning about the way life really works on the most profound level, on a deep, unconscious level as well as on the level of conscious thought. Spiritual understanding includes how consciousness can be guided and directed and used to change the action of the Law of Life.

Almost automatically, the subconscious mind goes to work on our thoughts and feelings. It is a universal creative principle within us all. It operates as law. And that is why psychologists explain that this is the creative area of mind. The moment you think and feel emotion, the subconscious part of you responds. That is why there is always hope for change and improvement of experience. It all depends upon the nature or quality of our thought and feeling. Consciousness is the name we use for this action. And consciousness is an integral part of each person's experience. It is the universal support system undergirding you at all times. Use it constructively, and it must automatically respond to your state of mind and emotion. It can change your life and your world. It all depends upon your understanding of these ideas, your use and acceptance of them.

If, when you work with this idea, you demonstrate a better experience but then have some kind of relapse into the old condition, or if you have only demonstrated the principle in part and too little is happening, you may become disappointed. This is a warning signal. It is simply revealing that your spiritual understanding needs expansion. You are too restricted or limited in your awareness of the unlimited potential within you and the principle of Life.

Principle goes on forever. It is without limitation or restriction. Principle is the Law of Life and the underlying foundation of existence. It is eternal. It is infinite. It is ongoing. It is the creative energy in the Universe. It goes on however you relate to It. It doesn't need your attention or support, although It has created us all to be self-expressed, reflecting Its own nature and action.

The Principle of life goes on. If we are disappointed, let us never be disappointed in the Principle, but only for the moment in our limited understanding of It. Then say, "I am not going to be disappointed. I am simply going to know that I have to deal with myself, deal with the challenge, deal with my spiritual understanding, expand my consciousness, learn more about the principle of creativity, more about what thoughts do in consciousness to produce new things in life, or how they distort things or invert the good and produce what appears to be bad. I will continue to work on myself."

You can reject life if you wish. Some people even go to the extreme of thinking that by taking their own life they are rejecting it, getting out of it. But they are not; for Life never rejects *you*. Life is yesterday, today, forever an ongoing principle of creative intelligence, and you will simply meet Life again as your consciousness moves on—not on this level of energy but, as Life evolves, on a yet higher level of awareness.

Life always supports itself. It always supports its own creation, which is *you*. So watch where you put your reliance, because reliance really indicates your deepest trust. If you put your reliance in the passing fancies of the human mind, in the phantasms of the imagination, in the limited, physical, material world and its experiences, then how secure, how permanent is the focus of your reliance? Thus it is for *you* to choose what to trust. Will it be the passing moment or will it be the underlying Substance, Supply, Intelligence, Life-force that is supportiveness undying—ever living, ever ongoing—that is in the Universe and in you and in me and in all—?

Where *is* that trust? If you see life and yourself from the universal point of view, your doubts begin to go. If you contain yourself in a universal attitude, universal viewpoint, the doubts will go more and more quickly. Then you will begin to work with yourself in a way that is truly miraculous. If the first new mental treatment for yourself doesn't work, are you going to be disappointed? Will you feel that your spiritual work is not producing the instant and miraculous change you want?

To have a new experience, we are required to reinvest in the idea; not to give up, but to continue self-effort. Call it scientific prayer, call it Spiritual Mind Treatment—the label does not matter. We must continue to clarify consciousness again and again. Until we demonstrate the results that we want, we need to clarify our consciousness one more time. Each time we perform this act of mind, we are on the verge of a complete inner and outer transformation and change. But if it doesn't seem to happen, we go on again.

So when "push comes to shove," when things look the worst, when you are in a corner, when you have to face the challenge, say, "All right! What I need to do is understand more of who and what I really am and how I can go on in life, taking control and directing my consciousness and, eventually, my experience."

This is the only way to permanent freedom.

The Law of Averages

ALL OF US live more or less under the consensus of human opinion. You live under that consensus until you wake up—and most people are hardly awake at all. Most people are manipulated and unhappy. They never accomplish what they feel. They never realize their desires for the good life, the fulfilled life, or the satisfied life. They know no contentment because they always have some contention operating in their experience.

People who live under the consensus of opinion, belief, and passive acceptance do things that they really do not want to do. They feel unfulfilled and frustrated, as though they had missed out on life. In counseling individuals through the years, I have been amazed at the number of people who are disappointed with their lives, with what life has to offer them, and with what they are doing.

I attempt to point out to these people that they are living under the consensus of others' opinions and beliefs. *They do not have to do that.* This does not mean that you must go out and act counter to everything that everyone else does, believes, says, indicates, and perceives in life. But you can begin to think in a different way—think in a new way about life and about yourself. Such thinking draws on energies within you that operate through the law of action, also in you, to begin functioning as a form of intelligence at work.

As this intelligence operates in our lives, we see it as a kind of guidance or direction from a larger power, a larger force, a larger intelligence, the Higher Mind, the Infinite Mind, or One, or Principle. We are beginning to wake up—to see, think, and feel in a new and fresh way. Actions begin to conform to this, but they are actions under an inner direction, and that is why it is not a matter of going out and performing some rash act.

We are all subject to certain invisible forces. These invisible forces—what I call "the Law of Averages"—are the collective consciousness of the race. A term that is very important to understand is *race-suggestion*. It does not refer to any particular racial group, but to humankind, the human race, *homo sapiens*, from the time of the evolution of the human brain and its ability to think, take responsibility, act, believe, fear, prognosticate, anticipate—because intelligence within the human mind enables the individual to prognosticate and anticipate based on history, based on the experiences of the past.

Race-suggestion is also the collective consciousness of the race on both a conscious and unconscious level. We are saturated in the beliefs of our human race, in the beliefs of humans since time immemorial. These operate within us and through us and upon us. Even on a conscious level we easily see them in what the media sell us and in what our friends, neighbors, parents, and teachers tell and teach us. The Law of Averages is the grand pot into which we put all of this. It is a boiling cauldron, always cooking, always ready to bubble up into some particular thought, feeling, attitude, or action in us and in our world of experience.

This Law of Averages operates as a tendency in you to do or not to do, to be or not to be, to experience or not to experience. The Law of Averages plus your tendencies adds up to a memory field that lies within you. It includes your personal memory on a subconscious level and the memory field of the collective consciousness. We might label this memory field "soul." When you ask, "What is my soul?" think of your inner mind, your inner self, the inner patterns of your memory field. You have thought these things unconsciously, because they have come to you on a subtle, subliminal level from the human point of view, and also from the vast energy of the collective consciousness.

All of us use the same Law, the same Principle, the same Life Principle, the same Mind Principle, and we use it two ways. One way appears to be special to us; but then we get lost in supposing that it is impossible for us to be using the same Law, the same Mind Principle, as someone else. For on the conscious level, we seem to be separate, very different. But although individuality does reside there, it is the *same action* that is at work. On the conscious level we do have choices; but there is something else working in us at a level of which we are not aware—the subconscious.

We all use one law—the one Law of Mind—on two levels. The level that is so filled with influence is the subconscious level. That is subjected to the consensus of what is generally believed, experienced, expected to happen at a particular time, under particular circumstances. All of this is opinion. Opinion influences us at the level of the belief structures, the thoughts, feelings, and messages from the subconscious.

On the other side—the conscious—we have choices; we can assert ourselves and our spiritual individuality. We can assert that which enables us to choose despite appearances and opinions. In other words, we begin to live out from the level of that wonderful statement ''Judge not according to appearances, but judge righteous judgment."* Righteous judgment simply means the assertion of spiritual individuality. It is recognizing who and what you are as a chooser in a world of possible choice, backed up by a principle of Mind that is infinite Intelligence ever at work and that can give you the impulses, insights, and energies to begin to think in a very clear and a very wise way. Your spiritual individuality is your real nature and being, always in motion, always in action. Your spiritual individuality moves you from limited ideas about yourself to a life independent of circumstances. You begin to perceive that you can live according to the ways the mystics have taught for all time and through all time: that you can be in the world, but not of the world. You can live *in* the world as a human individuality, thinking, feeling, being, asserting yourself; but not *of* the world as a victim of the world's opinions and beliefs, the "they say" of the so-called authorities of this world.

Don't complain about life. Don't complain about situations or circumstances. One lives most and learns most through resistance and difficulties, just as physical resistance helps us build muscles and strength. And in order to grow in strength, we increase the resistance.

There is a legend that appears in the tales and the myths of most cultures. It is of the night sea-journey. In our Western tradition we know it from the Old Testament as Jonah's being swallowed by the whale. It is about the individual who, in a night sea-journey, is overwhelmed by consciousness. For a period of time race-beliefs and race-suggestions from the subconscious and the conscious awareness rule, overwhelm, and swallow the individual, who is then manipulated by these forces. Finally, with time comes freedom—liberation from that encapsulated action and experience. This is a rebirth experience

* John 7:24.

—a new awareness, a new sense of self, a knowledge that one *is* a self and that one can *assert* that self.

Watch how you may be swallowed by the world's opinions and belief systems. Often they tell you who you are and what you are and where you are in life and what you may experience. *Much of the time they limit your experience.* The result is that you begin to move into lack and restriction, and often into loss. We begin to find ourselves in a world that we don't want, a world that is unhappy, a world without any direction or goal that promises any kind of fulfillment. If we allow the world's opinion to control our thinking, then that will be our demonstration.

A *demonstration* is the exhibition and representation in our lives of our consciousness. It can be a breakthrough in consciousness, in awareness, showing itself outwardly in healing. The inner transformation brings outer healing. It can be in personal relationships as well as in your body, mind, or finances. But if we allow the world's opinions to control our thinking, then that limitation will be our demonstration. The question is, can we rise superior to the world, can we create a new pattern? Metaphysics means "above and beyond the physical." It refers to the capability to rise superior to the world's opinions and beliefs. It means that you can use the power of an idea to catapult yourself to a new level of experience. And metaphysics underlies all life.

We know this to be true. Every human invention, attainment, and achievement that has brought us to this level of existence with so much ability to live in command of life has derived from the power of an idea. It is true that we are still victimized inwardly and outwardly; but the invention of man is magnificent. It is always some idea that has catapulted someone, that has made a breakthrough for a person who has perhaps been able to inspire some others, and then together they make that breakthrough, that new invention, that new way of functioning—some new experience in life that brings to the billions greater freedom and ease. The same principle that works individually in us is saying, "Get the idea, and the idea will catapult you into something new and fresh and greater and larger and better."

We must establish a certain kind of self-sufficiency. If you don't have it, you will remain a victim in life. Self-sufficiency means to be oriented to something beyond race-consciousness or the Law of Averages—something that enables you truly to banish the Law of Averages from your life as an active experience manipulating you. The way you become self-sufficient is through depending on the higher Principle of life, the Principle of God. Having become truly dependent on God, you then yourself experience these worderful attributes, your understanding of Spirit or God, and become able to function as a self-sufficient individual. Then you are independent of the world's opinions and beliefs. You have begun to get a new sense of self-esteem, of self-acceptance, of the value of you *as you*—as a *self*.

Dr. Carl Jung wrote in a letter to a patient and friend:

> The value of a person is never expressed in his relation to others, but consists in itself. Therefore, we should never let our self-confidence or self-esteem depend on the behavior of another person, however much we may be humanly related to him. Everything that happens to us properly understood leads us back to ourselves and makes us dependent on ourselves. This is because dependence on the behavior of others is a last vestige of childhood which we think we can't do without.

Being dependent on another's point of view, on the value in the relationship of others to you, is an immature or infantile way of thinking of yourself and of life. If you don't feel self-sufficient, if you don't have the self-esteem that you need, then begin with yourself, think and act in life as if you do.

However, if you try to do that without having the foundation of a metaphysical point of view, it is not going to last. You will find instead that it is manipulation, basically illogical and unsustainable. But if you begin to understand your right to *spiritual individuality* as an individualization of all the power, presence, action, beauty, and balance of the Divine that created you, you see that you are an avenue, a vehicle, a channel through which creative energy flows—that there is Something about you greater than appears to be.

Then you can begin to act with self-confidence and self-esteem. You begin to think from a different point of view, knowing that the Law—meaning the Principle of Life—backs you up. It is backing up your thinking, backing up your feeling. It is supporting you and sustaining you in this action. It *does* back you up *as you believe*. You are thrown right back into the basic Christian teaching: "It is done unto as you believe." But you can believe only when you begin to understand the Source of your existence, to understand who and what you are as an expression of that Source. Through that you literally, instantaneously begin to banish the Law of Averages.

In life, all of us are on the Damascus Road like Saul. The transformation of Saul to Paul can happen to each of us if we begin to recognize a higher Nature and Power and Presence working in our lives. But we need to work toward a revelation of freedom from the past. This means freedom from world opinion and belief, and from all our own beliefs that are less than we would desire for ourselves or anyone we love. Mind will bring about a new, rejuvenated, renovated you.

The love you can have for yourself is the same love that you can have for everyone. It is the essential reality and nature that has been given to you out of the infinite Source. It has been given to everyone. This is God's perfect action, the gift of life from the infinite Principle of Life. There isn't anyone who cannot in some small way—because it builds upon itself, step by step—banish the Law of Averages from his or her life forever and begin to live under the aegis, the inspiration, and the direction of a larger creative Intelligence. As you begin to experiment in little ways in your life, you gain the confidence to act in big ways, and in still bigger ways. Your confidence begins to enlarge, and you realize that the principle that says that you do not have to be under the Law of Averages is a viable one.

Surely we work step by step, moment by moment in progression, in the unfoldment of good. We do not attain complete freedom in a single leap. But as we grow in our understanding of Life and our participation in it—as we begin to understand God, the Great Spirit—we begin to sense that spiritual individualism which is the Principle of Life. We begin to become more rational about ourselves and about our relationship to the infinite Source. We begin to see that it is indeed a resource for us and for anyone who will begin to recognize this truth. Then we will realize that we are already moving through this awareness in the flow of Intelligence, toward an ever greater awareness of Intelligence in our life.

All of this spells freedom: freedom to be, freedom to become —*and freedom to banish the Law of Averages.*

On Your Own

CLARITY OF MIND is essential to the successful practice of the Science of Mind. For this, we need consistently to review the essentials and fundamentals of Religious Science. The easiest method is through a daily study of the writings of Ernest Holmes. In them, consciousness is dissected, analyzed, and explained so that the ordinary person can understand the ways of thought and the power of Mind. Quickly we learn that our thoughts and words become gods to our personal world.

Each of us communicates through language composed of vocabulary, grammar, syntax, and other symbols and instruments of meaning. It all comes down to the use of *words*. However, our words portray feelings that are rooted in our conditioning, mindset, and attitude about life. Actually, we are always living out our state of mind or thinking process. This gives dimension to our lives. So it should be obvious that thoughts are vital elements to living. They symbolize who and what we are. Yet this consciousness is not static but ever changing. The Science of Mind enables us to mold thought, which in turn modifies our world of experience.

Many people practice affirmations, which are nothing more

than positive statements about the truth of our spiritual nature. These may be helpful superficially, but they usually have little permanent effect. Through understanding and utilizing the process of Mind as a universal intelligence system personally applied, we can substantially change inner patterns and outer experience. It is a matter of dissolving the ignorance which has sustained a limited view of our nature and life experience.

Through spiritual insight and awareness we can bring about profound changes in our minds, bodies, and circumstances. It is as if we reconnect ourselves to the primal impulse and purpose in the Universe. Of course, nothing of the sort happens. We have never been disconnected, nor can we ever be outside the divine embrace. But the physical senses and human experience lead us to believe that our edifice of being is assaulted, disordered, or in a process of decay.

The truths of being reside in the depths of our nature. We are not *independent* beings but *individualized* beings. Quite a difference! So it becomes important to understand that the material world is real as far as it goes. It is not an independent reality or function of reality. It is intimately connected to the Mind Principle and our use of it. In experience, the physical world always reflects our state of consciousness.

Since the material senses cannot be trusted to communicate reality, we must forever be alert to the various illusions that appear as substantial and the truth. Proper discrimination based on spiritual knowing will keep us from being deluded by the world of human observation, opinion, and belief. We keep our focus on the truth of our spiritual nature. We know that out of the infinite Invisible has emerged all that we are or could ever be. And we appreciate and praise this One Power and Presence which sustains and maintains us eternally.

One of the important truths in our work is that you cannot perceive the spiritual Energy or Force and its action with the physical senses. That is why we are careful about imaging, practicing visualization, or creative imagination. Obviously, it is far better to use imagination and practice visualization of wholeness, harmony, and abundant supply than it is to be shackled by the fear of disorder, lack, and limitation. It is advantageous, of course, to imagine good rather than bad, health instead of disease. But through Science of Mind inner work you learn to move beyond material limitation to the metaphysical orientation to life. This view is beyond, above, and deeper than the surface physical presentation of experience.

This is why we say it is impossible to evaluate anything solely on the level of sense experience. There is always something more going on. Our spiritual work and studies are for the purpose of giving us an insight into deeper realms of being. This insight enables us to understand the symbolical nature of human experience. We want a happy, healthy, rich life. We know it is right for us to experience these earthly or material benefits. Why? Because the physical experience is a symbol of something greater, called the metaphysical. The object of our spiritual study is to gain a greater insight into the nature of our existence.

We understand that existence is composed of spiritual substance—spiritual ideas that are the seed elements for everything that could possibly grow into being. We work with these ideas. We learn how to plant them into the fertile field of mind-energy for our welfare. Then we step back in thought and observe. That is what happens when we release these ideas in treatment to the creative process in the universe.

This Mind-action operates in us on a subconscious level. It takes over these ideas and produces their outer growth in our world of experience. Each one of us is a spiritual nurturer. We support our desires, goals, and ideas with the nourishment of spiritual understanding. *We do not produce the nourishment. It is there.* We begin to perceive and appropriate it through our understanding of metaphysical truths. We say, "There is a Life, a Power and a Presence in the Universe that is Absolute Good. It is around me and within me and moving through me and manifesting by means of me now in every action and every relationship.''

When we do this, we are nurturing ourselves with spiritual knowing and with ideas that we did not create. They exist because of the One Intelligence. The joy and wonder of the Science of Mind is to perceive this truth and bask in its light. Then we see the beauty, order, and magnificence of the divine Presence and Power in our lives.

Go for It!

THROUGH THE YEARS I have been told that I speak well. Sometimes I have even been told that I am eloquent! Every time I hear this, while I understand what is being said, part of me goes back to when I was a little boy, or to my teens, when I was a young man struggling to make it in the business world and to grow as a self-aware person.

No matter what happens to us, some part of us is always tied into the seemingly "other" person that we were. But it *is* us. No matter what happens to you or how you develop, you are still part of that youth, part of that immature period, part of that earlier point in your evolution as a human being. Something in you still remembers that you are one, you are a unity, you are a single being as one person. You just can't say, "What I was in the past is cut off, is gone forever." The *negations* may be gone forever, the *experiences* may be gone forever—but the *result* of these experiences, *the patterns in consciousness*, are there; and that is what motivates us.

Every time someone tells me that I speak well, or that what I have said is good, something in me says, "*Really?!?*" Often, people don't see the years of self-work, they don't see what you went through. But in fact I have been working on myself to develop what is called eloquence for years.

I first joined a Church of Religious Science in 1960 and went through the training and studies offered there. In 1965 the pastor of our church, Dr. Raymond Charles Barker, asked me to become the associate minister, telling me that on occasion I would have to speak publicly, that I would have to teach publicly, and so forth. I had always been painfully shy and a very private person. I thought I could never be a public figure, a public speaker, *ever*.

But I had been working on myself. When Dr. Barker asked me—although I was still quite shy and inner- rather than outer-oriented—I went for it. I said *Yes*, and the moment I said it, I thought, *"What have I done?!? I will never be able to get up there and speak!"* Nevertheless I *did* set myself to the task, and I *did* go for it, realizing that I had to extend myself and work on myself more and more diligently to be able to prepare myself for the work that I knew I would have to do.

Most people who hear from a friend, or say to themselves, "Go for it!" experience a certain amount of fear and trepidation, sometimes of doubt, or reluctance—a mental holding back. But they are rightly told to "Go for it!" We *all* need to *go for it*—for life, more life, the good life, the abundant life, the healthy life, the joyous life, the creative life, the life of Love in action. We all need to go for it *all the time*. What it means is to go with the evolutionary principle, *go with Life*.

But there is something very important to keep in mind: *never compete with anyone*. Excel! Work on yourself! Be! Become! Grow! Expand! Excel in your particular area of expertise, or work, or whatever your goals or choice may be! Excel in your process of getting there! Excel in doing that! Or being that! Or accomplishing or experiencing something! But never compete with a person, a place, a thing, a situation, or an event. Never compare or despair. Create! Produce! Present!

This whole idea of "going for it" comes from the concept of the evolutionary principle which is always *going for it*, always evolving more and more and more and more. Since Life itself is always expressing more and more, then the idea of "going with it," going with life, accomplishing, need never involve competition. Realize that one doesn't need to compare or despair if things aren't going right at any particular moment, but that the only goal is to *create, produce,* and *present*—to accept your role in the creative process, of which you are a part all the time. Allow this creative process to produce through you, and let it be presented in your particular world of experience. We need to remake our minds! You can remake your mind by changing your thought and then watching your world change. Watch your world unfold! Watch you world evolve!

I can think of many good examples of people who *have* really "gone for it." People who have really moved forward and accomplished. Here are two of them:

Ms. magazine gave one of its Woman-of-the-Year awards to a 90-year-old lady, Marjorie Stoneman Douglas, who for many, many years has been working continually to keep the earth green. This lady has been combatting the devastation of the earth's resources, including what has been called the "greenhouse effect," through which we seem to be working towards terminating life on this planet—something that will surely happen if we continue functioning as we are now. Ms. Douglas has been fighting this by continually working, for many years, to make the earth green. She was still *going for it* at 98 years of age and deservedly received this wonderful award.

The second person I would like to cite is a former college president, as well as the former chairman of the board of a Federal Reserve bank. He is a labor economist and an author. He has worked at many odd jobs and is now an innkeeper in Vermont. He tells us this: "Go where your heart and head tell you to go.

If you have an urge to walk in the woods for a long time, go do it.'' At age 54, before taking up his job as a college president, he spent a period of time in New Mexico working as a garbage man. Thus the work he has done has not been only as a president or a labor economist or in some other grandiose job or activity. He has done all kinds of odd and peculiar jobs because he ''went for it.'' He *needed* and *wanted* to have the experience. He wanted to *go for it*!

When you look at life and all its wonderful benefits, you see that we have them because somebody ''went for it.'' Somebody said, ''I'll try. Let's go on further.'' We need to remember that this is what life is. We need to know about people who *go for it*, because it is very easy to slip down into what we call the ''race-consciousness''—the collective belief that people have about ego or background or education or job or self that induces them to become crystallized in an old pattern or that holds them back from moving forward.

You can find the results of this life process everywhere. Since 1962, for example, we have seen a switch from manual typewriters to electric typewriters to the Selectric, then to the electronic, and now to word-processors. Today, most offices have personal computers. That is amazing when you consider that just a few years ago, people resisted them as oddities an occasional person here or there might have and use. This is a far cry from having to use carbons to make copies with onionskin paper. Do you remember how we used to do that? Do you remember the inky black mimeograph, the ditto machine, those early photocopiers with special paper and chemicals? By 1987–88, there were 457,000 FAX machines installed. There were almost a half-million FAX machines in 1988. One year later, there were 1,000,000 FAX machines in place. It looks like somebody ''went for it''!

This ongoing action—what is it, really? What is the key to

it? To "go for it": what does that really mean, and what is the
key to the whole thing? It is attaining a consciousness, culturing a desire, and then working with that desire as a spiritual
quality. We can call it our spiritual independence, for it is an
ability to *choose*, to *select*, to *move beyond what has been*. It
means moving beyond group conditioning, moving into something new. All of this spells "progress," and progress is the law
of life. Progress happens when you decide not to be a victim of
conditioning and to *go for it* instead—when you decide to move
forward—when you decide to move into the new.

All of this has to do with Principle, with Law, with *you*,
working in *your life*. It is the functioning of Life Itself—functioning as Principle. The Law through which we operate is infinite,
but *we* appear to be finite. That is, we have not yet evolved to
a complete understanding of ourselves. We are unfolding from
a limitless potential, but we can bring into our experience only
that which we can conceive. There is no limit to the Law, but
there appears to be a limit to our understanding of it. As our
understanding unfolds, our possibilities of attainment will
increase.

Spiritual awareness enables us to see that we are *in* and *of*
the Law, but we need to have a complete *reliance on it*, a *trust
in it*. This is trusting in the Spirit of Life, the Law of Life that
is within each of us. Wherever we seem to be out of it, or working against it, or in some kind of inversion of it, that is where
we are seeing negation happen, or destructive action in our
experiences. Changing your mind changes your thoughts and
consciousness—and, finally, your world of outer experience.

It all has to do with learning to *trust*. Trust in Life. Remember that when you don't trust in yourself, you trust in chance,
in luck. When you don't trust in yourself, in the whole nature
of your being, then you are going to trust in the external, you
are going to look for something *out there* to grasp, to hold on

to—and very often the concept you will find is luck. Recognize that there is no power for ill in the Universe, no power to work against anyone.

The next thing we have to do is to get our thoughts and our consciousness clear, to think and learn about the Source of life, of existence and the Principle through which it works. We come to trust through culturing trust. We *learn* to trust. We learn *how* to trust; and so we can begin not only to *trust* Life and ourselves, but to believe in Life and to believe in ourselves, to believe in our potential. We begin to see that in essence there is a single reality. In essence, my real self must be God. That is, whatever there is to my real self must be God, or of God, or from God. It comes from that source of creativity.

David Macaulay, in his book *The Way Things Work*, says: "To any machine, work is a matter of principle, because everything a machine does is in accordance with a set of principles or scientific laws." He points out that machines are subordinate to principles and powers that have always existed. To which I say that the human being is "the Divine Machine": we use laws that enable us to go *for it*, meaning to work with the Law—the Law of Evolution that moves us forward. We see how it has worked in a generalized, collective way, moving us from human and animal muscle—attaining, achieving—to waterwheels and windmills, to steam, electric, nuclear power, etc.; and I have to add "etc.," because we do not know what is yet to come.

If you doubt that you *can* "go for it," that simply means you have not grown into the understanding that there is a "gift" already built into you, and that is *the gift of choice*: to obtain from the Universe all that you could possibly need for fulfillment. What you have obtained from the Universe first and foremost is an idea, or a collection of ideas, operating through thought that makes you begin to ruminate in your consciousness; that enables you to decide—and then go *for it*, based on a change in your mind, a change of your consciousness that moves you forward. Ernest Holmes, one of the great contemporary metaphysical teachers, points our that "We do not have to drive or push but we must accept and believe."*

There is a sequence of three actions that brings all of this about:

First of all, we need *mental assertion*.

Second, we need *mental attention*.

Third, we need *mental acceptance*, which has to do with conviction.

I say *mental*, meaning that at first everything is thought; at first everything is a state of mind and an attitude of consciousness, a poised mentality. *Everything*. There isn't a thing that is done that isn't done through consciousness—even if it is done on the level of the unconscious. You may say of some action, "Well, I wasn't aware of it. It just happened. I just did it." Consciously, of course, you were not aware of it; but is that all there is to consciousness? There are people performing things, doing things right now in other parts of this nation and of the world. You are not conscious of it, but does that mean that it is not happening? It *is* happening, but it is not happening for *you* at the moment. It can happen for you, however, if you learn about it. How can you learn about it? You don't have to be there these days, because other people "went for it." You can turn on your television and see it happening. You can see what is going on elsewhere.

Everything happens through consciousness. It is all a movement of power. You may not be conscious of everything, but there is a side of you—the unconscious side of you—that is always operating in consciousness. So the primal teaching here is that everything is thought, or, in a larger sense, *everything is consciousness.*

---

* *The Science of Mind*, p. 58.

We need to use consciousness.

We need to assert that truth. To assert every element and aspect of consciousness—and to pay attention to what we are asserting. This is not concentration so much as it is "flowing with it," "going with it," and, of course, *going for it.*

Then we need a spiritual understanding, a deeper understanding of life, that gives us the quality of consciousness which is labeled *conviction*, which is simply accepting that there is a principle that operates the "Divine Machine" that each of us is. There is a Principle operating in the experience of mankind and in nature and in the evolving Universe. That Principle moves through the consciousness of every individual.

God is not a reluctant God. God is the giver of life, of nature. That is why in the religions of the world it is either said or implied—and it is the epitome of the Christian idea of Spirit in its purity—that God is Love, the Divine Giver. From this we draw the necessary and only possible conclusion that *God wants you to have everything.* That is an audacious statement, but it is the truth about life, about nature, and about the Principle of existence. All you need to do is learn about the laws of life, apply them appropriately and correctly, and you can attain and achieve.

"All that I have is thine," says the biblical Sage, and he is simply asserting that the Spirit of Life, around and within each one of us, is saying right now, "It is all there. It is in you. Think! Don't just sit. Think! Use your consciousness. Use your talents. Use your thought. And then: *Go for it!*"

Science of Mind: A Veritable Science of the Mind

I WOULD LIKE to dwell a little on Religious Science. The best way I know how is to begin with a statement from Ernest Holmes. He says that Religious Science is a correlation of the laws of science, the opinions of philosophy, and the revelations of religion applied to human needs and aspirations.

Now in our work we don't teach or even study (except in special class work) comparative religions or comparative philosophy. Nor do we get involved in the different domains and disciplines of science and the laws that operate within them. What we do is see the *interrelationship*, which is really what Ernest Holmes means by *correlation*: the interrelationships between these three areas—science, philosophy, religion—and ourselves in this vast panorama of our search for meaning, for what existence really is, and for fulfillment, satisfaction, and the achievement of greater freedom and ease in life, in being.

Religious Science exists for one purpose only and that is to relate us to our universe, and to the world; to relate us to our needs and requirements for happy, healthy fulfillment; to relate us to ourselves and to others. To this end, we study the Science of Mind. The Science of Mind is different from a "science of the mind." Sometimes you hear people say "I am studying 'science of the mind' "—and they are when they study with us; but I am not sure they understand that they are saying something a little different from saying, "I study the Science of Mind."

We teach both.

The Science of Mind is the methodology related to the philosophy of Religious Science. It teaches a Universal Mind, Presence, and Power that is One Mind common to all, underlying, overarching, indwelling, and relating to everyone. One Mind Principle operating in the Universe, functioning around and within us all: that is Spirit. It is sometimes called God.

When we think of a "science of the mind," we are thinking about our individual use of this Mind Principle and of our very own psyches—that is, our conscious mind, our subconscious mind, the interrelationship between the two, and how this mind of ours is related to the Over-Mind, the Supernal Mind, the Universal Mind that exists everywhere. We in our tradition study the Science of Mind, and we study a science of the mind as well—and all of this is related to the great and wonderful correlation of science, philosophy, and religion that we call Religious Science. It gives us an easy way to comprehend the search for meaning.

Religious Science is directed to who we are and to what we are as discoverers of ourselves, discoverers of the laws of Life, of the Divine Nature that operates through all nature; and this only serves to empower us. That is the object, the goal of our work: to attain a state of awareness or realization that seems to bestow on us *power*.

But as we study the Science of Mind, we begin to realize that no power *is* ever bestowed on us. *The power is already there in us.* We were created with this power; we were created with talent; we were created with this spiritual genius that enables us to think clearly and to understand the ways of Life and then to act intelligently, relating ourselves to our clear thinking and our spiritual understanding of the way Life functions and works. It enables us to act from that point of view and therefore to produce in our lives and in our world something greater, better —something more fulfilling, something more enlivening for us than has ever before been our experience.

Our life is enriched through our enriched thinking, through our enriched awareness—and that is what enlivens us. That is what gets us this wonderful ability to stand tall, to look forward, to look through all of the good, bad, and indifferent of the world. To look through all of the challenges, not to be hooked by any of them, not to be encapsulated by any of them, but to see clearly, to analyze wisely, and to be able to move through life in charge.

When we are absorbed by any person, place, thing, situation, or event—when we are absorbed by a particular challenge—we lose our ability to be ourselves, to be in charge. That absorption is not only a mental focusing on some particular, or thing or event or joy or problem—it is more than that: it is *being absorbed by it*. That is more than focusing. It means that we are *taken over by it*. If we examine our lives really honestly, we will see that there have been times in our experience when, despite ourselves, we have been so absorbed by the negative (or by the positive) that we lost our balance.

We lose sight of what is going on in life and of where we are and of who we are and of *what* we are. We get lost in that absorption, in the process also losing sight that this is only part of an ongoing stream, part of the passing flow or passing parade of the many events of life unfolding right now, through us, on Planet Earth in this experience, and ongoing.

Our job in the study of Religious Science is to try to break out of narrow absorptions by correlating all of the different concepts of religion, science, and philosophy relative to the way life functions and how to live a good life. Many religious symbols, for example—even of ideas like crucifixion and salvation—are all part of the human striving for awareness of a higher Truth than the truth we know as merely ordinary human experience. This is where Religious Science brings in the revelations of religion. We begin to see that there is only one religion, and that is Truth—seeking Truth and understanding Truth—"Truth" meaning the truth of Nature and of Being expressing through all of us as we perceive life and search for a greater meaning than just this material, physical existence.

We begin to see that there is this one Truth, this one religion that expresses through individuals, seeking and finding for themselves particular ways of mental and emotional development and relationship to the Universe, and a relationship to a Higher Power. We perceive all the religions of the world as being more or less expressions of Truth—the Truth for that particular prophet or saint, expressed in that particular religion.

We encourage everyone to follow their own way, to follow their own unfoldment. Those who walk with us are basically individuals seeking—and hopefully finding—the wonderful amalgam of science, philosophy, and religion that is given to us in a science of the mind that the individual can perceive as *the* Science of Mind: a conscious identification with this Truth and Higher Power which, through awareness and realization, brings about the enlivening and empowerment that we want to experience.

This is our Religious Science: coming together to review basic ideas that we find in the world's various religions, sciences, and philosophies—ideas which are then focused within a methodology that we call Spiritual Mind Treatment—our form of "prayer" and the way we connect ourselves through our minds with the Over-Mind so that we may be open and receptive to the upflow from within, from the Power that is already there.

What It Does

SOME PEOPLE seem to have absolutely no interest in life—at least as far as one can see. They are oriented only to fulfilling their physical senses in the material world and to nothing beyond that; not even a single speculative thought ever enters their mind. It is as if they were oriented entirely to the material universe.

People so oriented are not receptive to the Creative Intelligence in a conscious way and, in consequence, they are unable to make conscious use of the infinite Power that is. Our job is to learn how to use this Power consciously for the enhancement and the benefit of our own lives. This means physical, mental, emotional, interpersonal, financial healing. Healing is a natural part of the infrastructure of the universe, when you understand the universe and use it as it is.

No one else can know God for you, no one else can know the Law of Creativity or the Law of Nature for you. You have to know it for yourself. You have to want it, you have to desire it— to seek and to search. But, indeed, you *will* find it, because the seeking and the searching is already part of the finding. It makes you a receptive mentality, a receptive consciousness, a receptive vessel for Something greater than you are that is "out there," but that is also *in you*—that created you and that enabled you to think in the first place.

You can know and consciously become what you really are. That is, you can know and consciously become the God-Self. Of course, the concomitant experience will follow: you will begin to experience the result of this in consciously recognizing, knowing, resonating with the God-Power, the God-Source, the essence of Nature and of Being.

Through this recognition—it is a mental thing, it is something of consciousness—you literally, consciously, become Godlike. You are inherently Godlike because that is what we are, that is how we have been created. But we need to become *consciously* Godlike as well, for that empowers us and gives us the ability to really know the Truth that liberates and makes us free. The Principle of Life *as a principle* must be universal, and all of us can use It. *To understand that much is already to use It.* And we *can* use It because we come from It. It has made us what we are and given us what we have, as well as our ability to think and to be conscious and aware of It, Its nature, and Its being.

So that which created us gave to each one of us the means of understanding It and ourselves. What we have learned is that to the extent we understand It—Its divine Nature and our divine Nature—we experience It. We experience It in a tangible and in a concrete way in our lives.

Mind is the means, mind is the method, and our mind expresses the Mind of God. Our mind *must* express the Mind of God, since this is the Mind Principle in the Universe. It is all that we have that could possibly give us consciousness and give us the ability of mind, if you will. Mind—Infinite Mind, Universal Mind, Eternal Mind, the Mind that is—is Intelligence Itself and is meant to be used by us, and in fact it *is* used by us in knowing, seeking, and experiencing any particular area of life.

Therefore we say that the Creative Intelligence used by us can be known on any level: philosophical, scientific, humanitarian, or metaphysical. We know that Mind connotes consciousness, which means ideas and thoughts. It also means your belief structures—those which make up the body of what you believe in and what you believe about yourself and experience.

Therefore you must watch your beliefs. Your beliefs are part of mind; your beliefs are part of this Creative Intelligence. *Watch your beliefs.* They either limit you or they can release from limitation your vision and your experience of the Law of Creativity. Our beliefs are really outer symbols of our consciousness and our thoughts. These determine the extent or the limit of our physical and human—as well as our mental, emotional, interpersonal, and material—experiences of life.

We think, and when we think, we are immediately choosing. If you turn it around the other way and say, ''I choose,'' then the moment you are choosing, you are thinking. *You are choosing by means of some thought.* It may be a physical thing, in the material world; but the *thing* is the vivid *symbol* of the *thought*, of the *consciousness.* We think/choose and the Creative Law of the Universe around you and within you projects this state of consciousness.

Spiritual Mind Treatment is a method of encapsulating all of this view of life into the concrete use of the Creative Intelligence, so that we become coworkers with the positive, constructive, forward-moving action in the Universe. Spiritual Mind Treatment, then, is part of you, part of me, part of humankind. It is an innate part of our nature. It is our personal use of the universal Principle of Consciousness, the universal Principle of Mind.

What happens when we do this is a *demonstration*—an exhibition, a materialization of the consciousness of what we are projecting into Universal Mind, of the way we are thinking about Life and about ourselves, relative to our goals and choices.

This demonstration is really the effect of Mind Action. It is an aspect of what we may call meditation, but which is quite different from what most people mean by meditation, because it is specific reasoning—that is, specific *thinking* and the directing of thought energy toward a choice or goal. That choice or goal can be anything that means fulfillment for you.

It means the enrichment of your life, not only spiritually (which you can get through classical meditation and in the wonderful impulse of centeredness and peace, as well as sometimes in spiritual ideas) but materially as well. It is the attainment of the creative nature in your life—that is, your ability to be inventive, to work better, to attack problems in a truly intelligent way, to solve problems, and to move forward in your experience.

Spiritual treatment is putting yourself into alignment with that which is the Creative Intelligence. In fact, we are already in alignment with It; but what a treatment does is make us recognize It, make us understand and accept that in Truth we already are where we want to be. That is what treatment is all about.

Treatment is the action of the Creative Intelligence that works around and within us all. What It really does is supply the energy. It never changes of Itself, for It is always there—although it will change form. What *you* do is provide the concept or the mold or the avenue for the constant that is the divine Energy. Your part is a variable, changing with different choices, different desires, different forms, different goals that you may make at any particular time. What the Creative Intelligence does is constant. It is absolute energy that is ever pouring forth, forever expressing.

We say that we create the mold through our mind. We fit the mold according to our goal through the subconscious Law that is ever active in and through the mind of the individual. God provides both this great subconscious field and the great subcon-

scious action, supplying the latter with the energy through Law.
God is actually expressed in, through, and as the *Law* of God,
or the Law of Creativity, or the Law of the Creative Intelligence.
Your responsibility, then, is to know yourself, to know what you
want.

So many people want good, but they don't really know *what*
good they want. They say, "Oh, I just want a better life." What
kind of better life? *What do you mean?* What are you talking
about? God is infinite Intelligence giving *you* intelligence with
which to think and to work on yourself and on your life. You
are not an infant. In the metaphor of the Bible, you are the image and likeness of God, a child of the Universe, meaning an
offspring—not an *infant*. As the image and likeness of God, you
are the perfect reflection of an infinite Creative Intelligence. We
then need to use it, to assert it, and to be secure in who and what
we are. It is our own responsibility to know what we want. But
our faith in the Law, our faith in this great Creative Intelligence,
is absolutely essential. For faith is really the expression of
spiritual understanding.

If we do treatment work not based on understanding, and it
is simply words, then it is only superficial, and nothing much
can happen. If your treatment work is not working for you, examine your beliefs, examine where your faith is, examine what
your understanding of Life and Law and self is, and what and
who you are.

Faith is vital. Faith can be created. How wonderful that faith
can be created! You don't have to wait for something to emerge
from somewhere in outer space. *It can be created by learning.*
How do we learn? Through study. We learn the theory of Mind
Action. We learn through applying the theory—through applying Principle and then observing the effect.

We have come to understand that statements of truth, moving through the Law of Creative Mind, must be *definite* and
specific to be effective. What happens is that the specificity and

definiteness of our thought—that is, our goal, choice, or desire —works through a law of reaction from the grand and great Principle within us, bringing forth that which causes a change in our experience.

If doubt, fear, or discouragement appears in our minds, then what we must do is deny these denials of truth, because they are the denials of the essential Reality. Then we reaffirm the Truth that we are learning and knowing about: the Truth that frees us. A new state of consciousness emerges, and that new state of consciousness, being established, will then proceed to move through the Law of Creativity and appear in our world of experience.

This is the way of the Law and what it does. The Law, remember, is an attribute of the eternal Principle that is ever creating. Consciousness is a basic element, the mover of the Principle. Your consciousness can direct the Principle for your life in a specific and definite way that you may call *demonstration of the Law of Mind*, of achievement, of attainment of the goal.

Through your thought—that is, your consciousness or your intelligence—you direct a universal, impersonal Principle of Life *in a personal and a particular way*. It is infinite, omniactive, ever-present Good, and it is up to each of us to learn more about it, to accept it, and to use it.

What Is
Spiritual Healing?

THE FUNDAMENTAL ASPECT and the fundamental focus of all metaphysical teaching is probably spiritual healing. What, really, *is* spiritual healing? Most people think of spiritual healing as faith healing, but it is not. Faith healing has to do with an unquestioned belief in some great God "out there" or some vast power—also "out there." Sometimes it takes the form of a shaman, a person who is empowered to produce extraordinary, magical effects in the world of the person who believes in him. All this is variously called shamanistic healing, psychic healing, or faith healing.

In Africa, the Philippines, and other parts of the world there have been individuals who perform a kind of faith or psychic healing called *psychic surgery*. In psychic surgery, the operator, usually a medium, appears to perform all kinds of alleged surgery on the so-called etheric body—an aspect of the body that is supposedly above or within the physical body. This is an interesting phenomenon, but it is not spiritual healing as we understand it. There is no element of the rational mind or of the logical consciousness brought into the situation.

Spiritual healing is the restoration of wholeness or wellness to one's experience. It is recognizing, accepting, and realizing the atmosphere of God, or the perfect spiritual idea of being, in the individual. It removes the toxins of distorted self-acceptance that appear to have separated the person from wholeness.

In the spiritual mind healing process, we do not deal with unquestioned belief in any holy person, religious rite, sacred place or object. We deal directly with the truth of Being. We should understand that Truth is something we perceive and accept as part of the underlying Reality of Life. Spiritual Mind Treatment is the way to neutralize and dissolve inner patterns that bring about outer experiences of disorder, disease, and disturbance of the human condition. Universal Law is the process which brings about health. It is the result of the Law being used in the correct way. Disease is always the result of using the Law of the Creative Process in a distorted way. The inner patterns of consciousness inevitably appear as an outer world of experience.

In spiritual healing you become conscious of the truth that your life is the Life of God, or the Great Spirit. You know that there is an infinite, eternal, ongoing creative Intelligence that moves through a creative process that produced you. It is a human being's destiny to be creative. Much use of the Creative Law is constructive, but too frequently it is negative and destructive.

How can we uncover the essential Truth? Through recognizing, understanding, and appreciating the logic of a primal Harmony. When we perceive the reality of wholeness, then Truth takes over our lives. Mental/spiritual treatment must come after a spiritual awakening. We are the administrators of Truth in our own lives. And Truth is always the sovereign and total remedy for all apparent difficulties, problems—and, yes, inharmony.

The magnificent ancient Chinese classic *I Ching*, or *Book of Changes*, makes a penetrating statement: "Even a single passion still lurking in the heart has power to obscure reason." A single distorted opinion, or belief and acceptance, can express as an attitude or way of relating to life that will cover the Truth within and adulterate the purity of the Mind-force within the individual. We are all splendid entities through which the Power and Presence of Truth called the Great Spirit can flow and express Itself.

What follows can be called *seven essentials* in the practice of Spiritual Mind Healing. I am not describing the treatment technique but seven essentials that you can incorporate in your thinking before you practice Spiritual Mind Treatment. Then you will move from "faith" healing, or a blind belief comprised of hope and fear, to confidence, assurance, and a state of mind that says "Yes" to life.

1. *The recognition of a personal union with the Divine Spirit.*
You can't escape this truth, because it is what you have come from and where you function and exist both now and always.

2. *There can be no compromises, no negotiations with so-called evil.*
Evil means denial of good. It is the negative and destructive use of thoughts, feelings, and emotions that must be dissolved.

3. *Face up to your shortcomings.*
This is absolutely essential. Your shortcomings are the illogical and irrational experiences of states of consciousness and feeling. Don't gloss over things and situations. Face them. Take time to observe yourself in relationship to everyone and everything.

4. *Don't fight the negatives or evil. Realize Truth.*
By knowing the Truth, you get rid of mental entanglements and blocks such as anger, resentment, grudges, jealousies, etc.

5. *Practice continued self-examination.*
Observe your mood swings and states of thought and feeling. These are the guideposts for self-work. They are describing areas of vulnerability to negative belief systems.

6. *Don't look outside for the source of your problems.*
Don't blame, but look within yourself for causes of outer distress. Realize and state that there are no enemies in your world and no battles to be undertaken. Look within yourself and address yourself to whatever patterns may exist to be dissolved in treatment. As you neutralize the cause, you will get rid of the disordered effects.

7. *See internal negatives as simply inversions of good.*
Don't be fearful and don't get angry. Face these "inversions" honestly. Then perceive the Truth in which you recognize and affirm the good. Then you will understand that good comes from the great Source of all Life within you. Through this practice you appropriate and distribute spiritual power.

So it is up to you. The time is always favorable. It is never too late or too early to begin. Power is there. Wholeness is there. They are the very essence of your being. And the techniques of Spiritual Mind Treatment are easily learned. As you progress, you will begin to feel empowered. You will become your own shaman, as it were. You will become your own means of internal and external change or transformation.

Then you will begin to experience spiritual healing every day of your life.

Repeat Twice a Day

IN TREATMENT, we acknowledge a great creative Mind and Life-force and Spirit in the Universe that is whole and complete. We acknowledge that It is *our* life *right now*. We express It. We individualize It. We can use It. And we continue the treatment process with affirmations of Life and denials of everything that would say "No." We must deny these denials of good, wholeness, harmony.

We state that they are distorted thinking. We must deny the idea that we really can't attain or achieve the great good fortune that we would like for our lives. That great good fortune, of course, can be healing of the body, healing of the mind and the emotions, or the healing of one's relationships and affairs. There are five aspects of this treatment process that we have to be aware of:

1. The first is *neutralization*. We need to learn that, through our minds, our thoughts, and our feelings, we can neutralize a belief in the necessity for a disease, for a disturbed, lacking, losing condition of life. As we learn about the belief, we can really dissolve the belief through denial of the conditioned world and

its lack, loss, limitation, disease, distress, and disorder. That is the first step in treatment work.

2. We have to *translate the physical disorder*—the lack, the loss, the disease, the distress, the physical condition—*into a state of consciousness.* We have to release our attachment to the senses, the person, the place, the thing, the situation or the event "out there." All of us tend to get captured by the illusions, delusions, and simple facts of human existence. You can be working on yourself for years and years; then something happens, and you are right back there in the physical with that person or thing or event, and it becomes once more the rule of your life.

We have to be prepared to face these situations so that we can say, "Oh no! This is a state of consciousness first before it is something physical 'out there.' " *We can learn how to translate everything that happens in our world into a state of consciousness*—that is, into a state of thought and feeling, a state of awareness. Then we move on from there.

3. *See every disorder as impersonal.* No one is after you. You don't have bad luck. It is simply an impersonal action, a denial of Life or a state of ignorance. However we label it, it is a state of the negative that is impersonal, coming from the ignorance, the negativity, or the denial of good that make up so much of human life. Nevertheless, even though it is a lie, you can suffer from a lie; you can be killed by a lie; you can die because of a lie. We have seen that in the history of humankind. The lie and the ignorance have tremendous power. We must face the lie and reverse it. We must see correctly. We must change consciousness.

4. *Recognize the invulnerability of the essential self.* Say this to yourself:

Something in me is beyond anything physical, beyond this disorder, beyond that person, beyond this situation that seems to exist. This is not the essential me, the essential self. The essential Reality is there. It is heaven within, God within, the Spirit of Truth within me. This is the reality. It is infinite, eternal, and universal because it is a principle of Life within me.

We begin to relate to that essential Self. It is Wholeness. It is Harmony. It underlies all life and all existence.

5. *Accept with gratitude and true thanksgiving the fulfillment of what spiritual/mental treatment does.* We become grateful for the good that is accomplished in our lives through understanding the truth about Life and Being. This wonderful technique of treatment that we can use, simple to learn and easy to review, brings about inner and outer changes

Do you know what the problem is for most people everywhere? They do not sustain the vision. They drop it. When they start out, they seem to catch the ball, they run with it to the goalpost, and then they drop it. "Forget it! It's too far away. I can't get there. I will *never* get there! There will be no touchdown. Forget it! It's over!" They don't sustain the vision. But any great achiever—whether it is in sports or in any other field —who attains the goal is someone who follows through, whose vision is attainment despite the challenges, despite all the people around, despite everything that says, "No! Impossible!" They follow through.

When you find yourself in the position where you feel as though you cannot sustain the vision, or cannot believe or accept the truth that you are studying and meditating over, then repeat the affirmative thought or the affirmative truth. Meditate further on the meaning, on the implications. If you are trying to do the mental work—the Spiritual Mind Treatment—and you cannot sustain the vision, cannot believe in it, accept it, then make an affirmation about what you are doing. State something positive and definite; then simply think about it. Meditate over it. Ruminate over it. Think about its meaning and implications, for in that way you will begin to clarify your consciousness and to develop you understanding. This is really a prescription that needs to be followed daily.

What happens when you take the thought, reason about it, analyze it, and think about it is that it begins to penetrate different layers of your mind. It goes beyond the conscious into the subconscious. It opens up areas of the subconscious and begins to touch the deep, unconscious areas of your being. That is where the pure Self resides—the essential Self, the pure Reality. Your essential Self begins to find an aperture to move through and express as your life. You move into your inner nature, which is beginning to express through you. You are uncovering the treasure that is the Truth, which now comes forth through you. This uncovering of the Truth is a natural, normal thing. We can't force it. All we can do is meditate, contemplate, and reason about the Truth. Think over these ideas. Let these ideas go deep into yourself. That within you which responds to these ideas will begin to move into and through your life experience.

All of this is the movement of your spiritual understanding. It directs a process of life, a process of your mind. It allows an inner creative law—the Law of Mind in Action—to move through you and do the work, to express your life. This is spiritual training. It needs to be done daily, as in the attainment of any goal, for proficiency in anything takes daily training, daily practice. A proficient violinist doesn't just pick up a violin once in a while and play it. Every day—for hours every day—the musician goes over basic exercises that are boring. But the artist improves technique and begins to fine-tune hearing in this way. Things are heard that need to be changed. All of a sudden the exercises have improved capability and artistry.

The talent is there: we have been given the talent—but we have to use it. We have to develop what we have. *The talent is there.* But we must improve the way we use this talent that we have. We learn more and more how to reveal the inner treasure, and then we take the inner treasure and use it.

We have learned that wholeness on every level of life is at the level of an inner consciousness or inner understanding of what Life is. Therefore we say that it is *brought forth*. We don't put it on. We don't take it and put it on ourselves. *We bring it forth from within ourselves.* The wholeness and the wellness is within. Our spiritual understanding is able to bring it forth through us with our words in *treatment*.

Our spiritual position is that the nature of everyone and everything is a divine unity. Each one of us—each person—is rooted in this universal Life Principle. Each one of us needs to become aware or conscious of this great essence of Life that is within all, recognizing that it is infinite abundance, infinite good, infinite beauty, infinite order, infinite balance, infinite intelligence, and infinite wholeness.

With this understanding, we see that wellness is a principle of Life. With spiritual understanding and acceptance, we can say, "I am whole now. Every area of my life is good, harmonious, and well."

The Harvest
of Healing

HEALING IS the *way* of consciousness—as is illness or derangement of affairs. Our problems do not come from superficial negative thinking, although states of thought play an important role in our life-experiences. We are all products of a complex consciousness composed of personal conscious elements, the subconscious patterns that lie below the threshold of awareness, and the deeper unconscious factors that come from the collective or race mind.

To be a student of Religious Science and to experience healing through the Science of Mind, we need to reach an understanding that illuminates consciousness and brings about a realization of the personal with the Universal Consciousness that is Wholeness Itself. It is this spiritual realization that automatically—through Law—brings about what is called a healing experience.

Recently, CBS Television Evening News covered the work going on in our church in New York City.* It was a very com-

* First Church of Religious Science, 14 E. 48th St., New York, NY 10017
—*Ed.*

100

plimentary report. Among the interviews with our students were the following recorded excerpts from their reports of healing:

Student #1: "I started to get very ill, extremely ill, so that I couldn't walk. . . ." This was an individual who began a wholehearted study of the Science of Mind and, with the help of a practitioner, found both inner and outer transformation. The result of this spiritual treatment work was a spectacular change from the inability to move about to complete freedom and ease. "It changed my life; it changed my life!"

Student #2: "I was between life and death. I went to the hospital with infected gall stones. . ." In this instance, the student decided to bring in the help of medical science. "And the surgeon said, 'We took out the gall bladder and opened it up. There wasn't a gall stone! You were riddled with them, but there wasn't a gall stone!' " What is remarkable is the profound *before* and *after* evidence of Spiritual Mind Healing. There is nothing that can resist the power of specific spiritual knowing.

Student #3: "The doctor decided to do a bone scan, and that turned up positive. At this time, I was extremely distressed." Spiritual treatment was then given by a practitioner to support the student's spiritual work. The disorder which appeared to be bone cancer was completely reversed through spiritual treatment. "The doctor said to me, 'I am surprised; it's negative. You don't have cancer.' " The subject in this case was a registered nurse in an acute-care hospital with access to top medical diagnostics and insight. She saw that cancer does not exist in God's universe of wholeness—that this universe was her total experience of body.

Student #4: "I was blind. Through treatment work and working with myself and with Dr. Grayson and Religious Science, I regained my sight." This is another remarkable case of incontrovertible healing through Science of Mind spiritual work. This was literally a move in consciousness and in body from darkness into light.

Student #5: ". . . my front teeth were on the floor and my whole upper jaw fractured. . . ." The young man in question was a student in the junior church. "They did treatment work for me, and within about two weeks, the X rays were totally clear." Today, this student is a successful businessman, practicing the precepts of Religious Science. He is in exuberant good health.

You can visit churches of Religious Science around the world and meet individuals who have had experiences similar to the foregoing. Although ministries are different because of the individual expressions of the ministers, the basic ideas of Science of Mind are taught and practiced. It is a teaching which recognizes the inextricable connection of the individual to the Universal. God is understood to be truly "closer than breathing, nearer than hands and feet." A realization of this truth operates through a divine law of cause and effect that always creates a new world of experience.

The extraordinary work of Religious Science goes on without fanfare or claims of miracles. Each experience is seen as the act of divine Law, which every human being can direct and use for his or her welfare. Religious Science is for all people. It is a matter of personal choice and effort. And on that personal note, I am grateful for innumerable experiences of physical healing through the spiritual work called Science of Mind treatment.

Keeping Spiritually Fit

MORE THAN 400 years ago, St. Ignatius of Loyola composed his famous *Spiritual Exercises*. These were instructions he gave those who were under his spiritual direction. The program took four weeks. The exercises included visualization, prayer, meditation, and personal observation of one's self. It is interesting to learn that certain aspects of his instruction are similar to Science of Mind practices.

The 19th-century Indian saint Sri Ramakrishna has been an inspiration to millions of Hindus in India and to many others throughout the world. He was able to attain the highest realization of God through various practices drawn from many different religions. He was a living example of the Vedic declaration "Truth is one; men call it by various names."

One of the teachers of spiritual exercises and philosophy based on the Vedantic tradition was a disciple of Sri Ramakrishna, the renowned Swami Vivekananda. In 1893 he presented the great Vedanta truths to the World's Parliament of Religions in Chicago. Here was one of the outstanding individuals in spiritual history who brought the liberating idea of the Absolute to the Western world. Although New Thought was already in full flower when Swami Vivekananda came to Chicago, he contributed many liberating ideas to its followers. Swami Vivekananda suggested repeating the Sanskrit expression *Soham* ("I am He"). He said this constant recognition of one's unity with God in addition to performing good works would produce a spiritually integrated person.

Swiss philosopher-psychiatrist Dr. Carl G. Jung gives a simple formula for spiritual integration and discipline. He says that introversion, introspection, meditation, and the careful investigation of desires and their motives are the real means through which you can work on yourself.

Although brief, this review of different spiritual exercises and the need to keep spiritually fit enables us to understand the tremendous value of the Science of Mind. What we actually do through this investigative study of world religions and philosophy is validate for ourselves the richness and practical vision of Ernest Holmes.

Through Science of Mind practice, keeping spiritually fit becomes a method of *spiritual discrimination*. It means discovering who and what we are as a child of the Universe—the expression or manifestation of God. When one says: "I am an expression of the Infinite Mind," this is remembering our essential nature. It is recognizing that clear thinking vitalizes the entire being. Taking conscious responsibility for one's thought and directing consciousness toward a particular constructive goal is what spiritual discipline is all about. For students of the Science of Mind, it becomes *the* spiritual exercise. We learn how to discriminate between the false "facts" of the world and Truth, the essential Reality, expressed as divine order and perfect right action.

Keeping spiritually fit means reviewing spiritual ideas again and again. Always think them through to a logical conclusion.

This "reviewing" is devotion to Truth. It always produces a happy and fulfilled life experience. It means never losing inspiration and it brings a new enthusiasm to the daily study and practice of the Science of Mind.

A New You

As the expressions of the great Spirit, of the great Mind, of God, we have a conscious mind, we are able to choose and change our life's destiny. Truth, this Single Reality, expresses through its offspring by means of the life of the offspring. We call that expression the "human being" the image and likeness of God, who is perfect, whole, complete, harmonious, and free. Each one of us is an expression of this spiritual idea of the Single Reality of the Truth. The spiritual idea, or child of God, is an idea forever maintained in the Mind-Principle of the Universe. To realize this is to know "truth."

To know truth is not just to know *about* the truth. When you know the truth, it immediately dissolves the false illusion or apparent facts of experience. These may include disorder, physical malfunction or disability, various disturbances, distress, and disease. These begin to dissolve when you know "the truth that sets you free." The result is called healing. Metaphysical healing results from spiritual knowing. If you "know" the truth—not know *about* it—and can begin to understand it, you will begin to dissolve the blockage or inner pattern in consciousness that caused the disorder, physical dysfunction, or limitation.

There is danger in remaining theoretical about this idea and becoming absolutist. Saying that everything is good, whole, and harmonious, while true from an idealistic standpoint, is really staying on the *theoretical* level until you prove for yourself that it is true. Demonstration—the practical experience of healing or change—is the arbiter of truth for you. Your knowing the truth projects itself as transformation in your life. Then the particular good you experience is a direct result of your knowing the truth. If you do not experience enough good, there is no reason to be distressed, disappointed, or upset. It simply means that you have to gain a deeper awareness and realization of the Single Reality, which always expresses around you, within you, through you, and as your world of experience.

All conditions are dependent upon some cause. *Conditioning* means that something is in some way manipulating you; that you are related to something only passively. My "conditioned response" or "conditioned reflex" means that I am expressing something beyond my conscious thought. But new thoughts create new conditions, because conditions are always reflecting our state of consciousness. There is always a cause behind every material condition or experience. The Mind Principle of the Universe is the supreme Cause in the Universe. It can be called First Cause. It is the cause of life, of all being, and therefore of *you.*

To create the new, you need to think, feel, and see independently of the physical, material world of effects. You must see with a higher vision. You need to have a larger sense of being and of life. You need to connect yourself consciously with the Single Reality. You should be able to recognize and affirm that

There is one Power and one Presence, one Action in the

Universe. It is Wholeness Itself. It is Harmony Itself. I am at one with It, and It appears in me, through me, and as me. It is my human nature and individuality right now.

If you choose, you can begin to transform your consciousness and your world at any moment. Then Truth as your new awareness, consciousness, and realization moves into your world. You begin to experience something fresh and new and wonderful. We call this process of thinking *treatment* or *Spiritual Mind Treatment*, because it has to do with your mind —your consciousness and the way you think about yourself, reality, the material world, the world of conditioning. The way you think about potentiality and the possibilities of life depends on the state of your thought. And Spiritual Mind Treatment has to do with your thoughts, your consciousness, and the way you work on yourself.

You can "treat" for whatever you can think about. That does not mean that you are necessarily going to demonstrate an *immediate* change in your world, which would require a genuine breakthrough into the realization of Truth, the essential reality behind the thing you are treating about. But at least you can begin the process with hope, confidence, and energy. And you may indeed begin with a very real breakthrough into the full awareness of a particular "truth" which instantly transforms your world of experience.

You can treat about any good thing, anything constructive, anything that is life-affirming. Why must it be good, constructive, and life-affirming? Because if you could treat negatively, it would be a negation of life and self-destructive. You wouldn't get anywhere. The forward, evolutionary movement of Life is always for the transformation of the individual; for bringing about something new, greater and better; for healing of the body, the mind, the emotions, the finances, the relationships—all of the blockages and patterns that seem to prevent one from having an opportunity to move forward. Healing means that you are evolving into greater freedom and greater ease.

Here is the sequence of how to do this:

First, *embrace the unseen cause which is a spiritual idea:* "I am perfect, whole, complete as an idea in the mind of God."

Second, *begin to see the unseen cause in the effect world:* "My world is a display of the Spirit—the display of an infinite array of spiritual ideas evolving, unfolding, and expressing through this world of material existence as harmony and wholeness and right action and divine order."

Then we begin to see the inner and outer transformation taking place.

Remember that all science, creativity, and invention begins on the unseen level first. Anything that has ever been attained or achieved in life was first in the consciousness of someone—first in their thought and feeling, in their vision, in their mental and emotional environment. Only later could the action take place to bring the necessary elements together so that the seen —the physical, tangible, and concrete—could unfold. The new you is available to you moment by moment by moment.

Then seize the moment! Seize the opportunity! It is your divine right.

Principle as Promise

IN YOUR READING of the Bible you will find that there are some very interesting promises in both the Old and New testaments. For example, there are many statements of the kind "He will not forsake thee"; "The Lord thy God is with thee wherever thou goest"; "Arise, shine, for thy light has come and the glory of the Lord is risen upon thee"; "All things are possible to him that believeth it"; "Whatsoever things that ye desire, when ye pray believe that ye receive them, and ye shall have them"; "Whatsoever ye shall ask, that will I do"; "Fear not for I am with thee"; "With God nothing shall be impossible"; "My Father which seeth in secret shall reward thee openly"; "Before they call I will answer, and while they are yet speaking, I will hear."

Now there isn't one statement here that is not directly related to the Principle of Life, directly related to the premise on which we place our metaphysical reasoning about existence and the demonstration that comes from that—the premise directly related to all these statements. We can take these rather anthropomorphic, simplistic statements about God's promises that we read in scriptures of all kinds, and especially in the Old and New testaments, and we can translate them into the action of a science of nature or Being. Perhaps the authors didn't have an insight into the science of Being. However, some of the prophets and some of the saints and sages did. They couldn't articulate it, and indeed they didn't articulate it, the way we do. But they had a sense of the connection of the individual to the Source. They had a sense of the Power that is, which could operate *within* and *through* the individual *as* the individual, *by means of* the individual, into the individual's world of experience.

They had this intuition or spiritual sense; of that there can be no doubt when you read the many promises you find in the Old and New testaments. Looking at these, and then moving on to the idea of *premise*, we realize that the premise of the Bible (and of almost all intelligent scriptures) and of what we study in the Science of Mind is that we are living in a perfect spiritual system. This means One Universal Presence, One Universal Power. And this in turn means that there is a universal subjectivity as we call it in our work: something below the threshold of awareness, by means of which we are reactive to an infinite source of power.

There is One Universal Presence. We can call it Universal Mind or anything we wish, but there is also a universal subjectivity, meaning that Its thoughts or energy action certainly has to go somewhere. Where does it go? Outside of It? Beyond It? If It is *universal*, meaning everywhere present, that implies infinite energy, eternal ongoingness. Can you get outside of God, outside of the Universe? Can you get outside of the Universal Presence? Never. Impossible. That is why we use the word *subjectivity* for that area in the Universal where all Its energy goes—where all the thoughts and feelings go that the Universal One—God—might have; where *your* thoughts and *your* feelings go; and it is always *here* and always *now*, never later and never earlier; it is always in *this moment*.

God is the God of the moment. Spirit is the Spirit of the moment. That is really all we have—this moment. No one knows what will happen in the next moment. We can project, we can reason and assume, through deductive and inductive reasoning, that the next moment and the moment after that will express in a certain pattern, and usually it does. But if we face the truth, if we live moment by moment, we do not know what the next moment will be, because we do not limit it.

In that great Subjective Law all of the impulses and energies, all of the consciousness that will project in the next moment and the next moment are resident, ready to be manifest. We begin to see that there is but one Presence and that there is no absence of that Presence anywhere. In your life there is no absence of the Presence of God, the Presence of good, of wholeness—no absence of the Presence of the One Mind, Power, and Mind-Action. Therefore as you think, your thought-impulse is going into the subjective part of life, and you receive accordingly.

We have seen that the subjective side of Life simply *receives* this impulse, whether it is God or the human being. It doesn't reject the impulse—it accepts it, because that is all it can do; and in accepting that impulse, it reacts by expressing. We say that God creates the Universe, God creates the Cosmos, because God the Infinite Thinker thinks into the subjective part of Itself, which acts as a law of creativity which, in reacting, produces the worlds. The same thing happens in you and in me, in that "part" of us we call the subconscious: it reacts and expresses in the human experience.

Your experience is the result of Mind-Action, and you can't escape that. It is a mirror of what is going on in the Universe. That is why we always say in our work that there is no process in healing. There is a process *of* healing, which has to do with the thinking and the feeling and the knowing that we have in our conscious minds, which move immediately into the subjective part of ourselves, which then accepts and reacts. *It is a mirroring of what the Universal Presence does as the Power of Creativity in us.*

We derive from the Universe; we cannot have any qualities that are not of the Universal Intelligence, Mind, Presence, Power, which we replicate in our little way. There is no other God, no other Power; all we can do is be the children of God, the heirs of the Highest. All we can do is express what God is in our own individual and little lives. We do that in every way, including the way of our minds and the way of our subjective selves.

The *whole method* is what we are after, and the method is simply conversion of thought, conversion of consciousness. That is, we move our thought from limited concepts and beliefs about ourselves, about the physical world, about material existence. We move our consciousness from these limited concepts to spiritual ideas, and we do that through affirmations and denials in what we call Spiritual Mind Treatment. These affirmations and denials, in our understanding of the premise of life, help us to create faith.

In many of the world's scriptures we see that faith and belief are essential for the good life. We attain that faith through moving the focus of our attention from the physical, limited, outer world of experience *backward, inward* to spiritual ideas. In that way we literally create faith, and we energize it. The whole basis for this is the One Presence, the Universal Presence, which most people call perfection. God is this Universal Perfection. Our thought of that must accept an essential *wholeness* in the Universe. And there is an energy inherent in that wholeness which is *action*. Universal Wholeness—or Perfection and Its Action—is perfect God, perfect Man, perfect Being. Nothing less is the theme of what we are studying and working with here.

It takes time to meditate over these ideas—time to analyze them in order to make them your own, in order to understand that *perfection* means *wholeness*. There is a basic underlying Wholeness in the Universe. It is the essence of the Universe, the essence of Life Itself. Therefore right reasoning on this very basis leads us to right conclusions, which means that we are already changing the state of our minds, already changing the focus of our attention. We are now reasoning, in a very rational and logical way, from the point of view of Universal Presence, the One and Only.

Again, your personal participation in this whole premise and idea is to refocus your attention from disorder to the innate order and underlying Wholeness within you. You cannot escape that Wholeness. True, you can do much on the surface to stop It from expressing, but It is still there. It is innate; It is a part of your very nature. It is the essential part of your being, and your personal participation in It is your recognition that within you is this very Wholeness—a harmony, a perfect order that is the Great Spirit of Life and the Universal Presence. Being everywhere present, It must be present within *you*.

The interesting thing about our participation is that when we make this recognition, we find that there is a change in our lives. This awakening, this realization appears to remold and remake the physical and material world of experience. And that is what we rightly want, what healing is all about. It is a kind of remolding: people think in terms of a clay that God is working with in the Creation; and in our minds we *are* molding a clay, creating our own forms. That is all right if it helps—but it is better to get away from that kind of physical representation and get into a sense of your thought molding and remolding and remaking the consciousness that expresses in your world of experience.

In a problem, when we are beset by a challenge, the first thing we need is spiritual discrimination. That is, we have to learn to clarify our thought, to clarify our consciousness. Yet this is something that anybody can learn. Anyone can study this process; anyone can learn how to clarify consciousness. For that is our basic need in a problem situation: we are thinking incorrectly; we are focusing in the wrong direction. We are allowing the whole group of thoughts, feelings, and attitudes from the world around us and from ourselves to operate through us and to present a problem to us.

But the problem that is presented can be changed *through* us, by means of us—that is, *by means of our thinking, by means of our clarified consciousness*. There are basic questions we have to ask. Any time you find yourself being clouded by a problem or in some way being confused by an issue, ask, "Who am I? Where am I? What am I? Who and what is speaking here through this so-called problem, this challenge? From where does it come?" This is the way to attain the solution. You will see that the answer to these questions always moves you back to Principle, back to the Source.

What is this Principle? It is Omnipresence, the Everywhere-Presence. It is Oneness. If It is everywhere present, nothing is outside It. Its oneness underlies, moves through, permeates—and expresses by means of—everything and everyone. This is one of the essential teachings of the Science of Mind: that there is a Oneness in the Universe and that *you* are at one with the One Presence. It is an ever-active Presence—active as Law. Law has to do with action and the experience of that action. The Oneness that you experience through your mind with the Principle of Life, the only Presence and Power that there is, brings about an action—an action that moves through consciousness and expresses in your world of affairs.

One of the major points we have to realize is that God is not limited. Universal Presence is unlimited, Universal Life is unlimited. We must be clear that the Presence and Power which is the Creative Force in the Universe is never limited by the forms It creates. It may limit the form as though to say, "This is an arm and not a leg." Therefore it is going to function as an arm through the image, concept, and thought that then "limits" it to that particular form. But that form in no wise limits the creator of the form. That form has only the life in it that the creator gives to it, whether the creator be God or you in your own little world of experience. God creates forms but is never limited by Its forms. Our goal is to think the way God thinks and not the way the limited, human mind thinks, with its belief in a limited, physical, material world of experience as the be-all and the end-all and the only.

We, then, as Ernest Holmes puts it, need to have *the* faith *of* God, not *a* faith *in* God. The Great Spirit is teaching us to have the faith of God, and all those scriptural promises are related to having the faith of God—to function from the altitude and attitude of the Great Spirit; not *looking up to God*—because that gets you into the weakness of *appeal*. That is what most religions do, don't they? They make an appeal to God. "O Lord, please help me; O Jesus, help me. Support me in this special time." The Lord (if the Lord could speak) and Jesus (if Jesus could speak) would be saying, "Think of the promises! What are you doing with *you*? What are you doing with your mind, with your consciousness?"

Why do we demonstrate good in our work? We demonstrate good because the Universal Principle of Life is a Universal Presence for good. It is always here, always now, always operating as a Law of Nature—divine Nature and human nature (which is simply a mirror of the divine Nature). We need to move into an awareness that Principle is unlimited. But how are we thinking? How are *you* thinking about the unlimited Principle that is the principle of *your* life, that is operating in *you* now—that operates *around you* and functions *by means of you* and expresses Itself in a very individualized way *as you*—? *How are you thinking about that*?

· "Oh, I don't know; It's out there somewhere." Well, if that's the way you think—and most people do—you had better begin to think in terms of Its being here *in you* also as well as "out there." I don't say It's not "out there," but It's also *in here*, in your life—and *for* your experience, *for* your demonstration, and *for* your fulfillment.

You have to address the issue of *you*, and that means the *in here* of you, and not "out there." You don't need philosophy or theology; you *do* need an experience, a *spiritual experience* of the here and the now functioning in you. That is what we are all really after. Because whatever we could possibly want "out there" must have a *spiritual idea* behind it.

All we see in the disorders of life are the distortions of this spiritual idea—through distorted consciousness, distorted thinking, distorted feelings, distorted acting, distorted attitudes. Again, when you are in a problem, when you are looking for a solution: go back to Principle; think back to the spiritual idea. *There is a spiritual idea behind everything that could possibly be.* Every cell, tissue, muscle, organ, function, action, reaction in your body and in the body of the world is first a spiritual idea. It would have to be, for there is only one Universal Presence, Power—call It God or Good or Love or Life or Light or Beauty—there is only one; and then you go back to those promises again.

Here is another mystical promise: "Before they call, I will answer." What does it mean? *The instant and constant responsiveness of the Law of Nature, of Life, of the Principle of Being.* The demonstration of good in your life: this is the essential teaching here. Your demonstration is not dependent on externals, on any person, place, thing, situation or event—however much they are labeled by the world as brilliant, as the only answer, as the only way out. *Nothing in your life is dependent on externals.* Everything is dependent on *you*: your understanding of life, your knowledge of the Principle, your acceptance of It.

You begin to see that all of us receive in life continuously. We receive at the level of our belief, of our consciousness, at the level of our understanding of life. Everybody is receiving all the time. The promises are kept, the answer is always there, and

God is always giving. The important factor here is that God or Spirit or Life can give to you only *through* you, through your consciousness *at the level of your consciousness*—the way you are.

Principle as Promise? Absolutely. "All that I have is thine." There you have it. So we have to go on, day by day, and learn more and more how to take in this glorious and wonderful Life that is there for us.

If we listen to the world, we will be at the level of the world and its myriad limitations.

But if we listen to the Inner Voice, the voice of Truth through spiritual discrimination, there will be a power and an action from the ever-present One working *in you* to produce *through you* the great, the good, and the better yet to be.

Depth Spirituality as a Transforming Experience

SPIRITUAL THINKING today is an accepted state of mind. The average person does not consider a spiritual adherent as a stange mystic or paranoid adventurer into the unknown. True, many sects, cults, and gurus have occupied the world scene and the minds of the millions, staking their ground outside the norms of life. Yet there seems to be a shallowness to the supposed in-reaches of Mind and Spirit by the popularized methods and sects of the swamis, masters and modern-day arhats.

Surely the time has come for solid thinking about the Erhards, Muktanandas, and Rajneeshes. These "Bhagavans" and their many ersatz copies are marketing age-old truths as though they were novelties, in our outlandish times. Often they hit the crises of the moment, collectively experienced or personally expressed as anxiety, superstress, and desolation of spirit.

Isn't it time that the spiritual seekers and surveyors of Promised Lands awakened to an essential truth: God is not new, but old; Truth is not a creation, but a revelation through each person; awakening is not "there" in a special person called a guru or in a special, communal, environment, but *here* and *now* and *everywhere*—if one truly wants it.

119

But most people seek excuses and various alibis for their lives or fears or experiences. Few will understand that *what happens* to *you happens* through *you and always* as *you in some unique way.*

Correction and change come about only through the brave mind. The challenge of existence is profound and life-threatening. The way to bring about an improved experience is through the consciousness that sees Spirit as underlying everyone and everything right now. The task is to face up to the suggestions and attacks of the so-called human experience and race consciousness while demolishing the very foundations of evil, or error, with a fresh inspiration from the *On-High Within.*

Life is not a gift to those who will not accept the reality of themselves. To them it becomes an arduous journey through "the slings and arrows of outrageous fortune." Truly it sounds like "a tale told by an idiot full of sound and fury." It then becomes understandable that the sensitive soul or the frightened furies of consciousness reject Life entirely or in part and rest in soporific security while cradled by the teachers and the communities that hold these unfortunates in the embrace of words like "commitment," "being with it," or devotion, enlightenment, liberation, and deliverance.

But all of this only echoes a shallow sound that mimics something greater and deeper and more profound: the penetration of Being in spiritual understanding and experience of the simple and direct relationship that we enjoy, under Law, with Reality.

Karma and Reincarnation

KARMA AND REINCARNATION: many are familiar with these words and with their descriptions. Actually *karma* is a Sanskrit word and it literally means "action."

In the East, particularly among the Hindus, karma has always related to the *activity* of the individual, the *action* of the individual; and from that they extrapolated, saying that it is really the duty of the person: Your *karma* is your *duty*. First and foremost that is what it means—your duty in life, your duty as a human being. We think in terms of karma, of action, of work; duty generally is thought of as *one's own* duty, not only to family or to life, but to the work that you must do through life.

One's duty yields the form of yoga that one practices. *Yoga* means "yoking" or "connecting." It really means yoking yourself to this larger force or power. There is a form of yoga called Karma Yoga, in which the individual relates him- or herself to duty, to work.

Everyone in some way is a karma yogi; that is, we are all working, all *doing* in some way. Just being in Life is to be *in action* in Life. We are all practicing some form of karma. Basically, karma is action and its effects in one's world—the results of action—the reaction to the action. Karma is simply cause and effect. When it talks about cause and effect, it is talking about the mental law in the Universe that is the Law of Action and Reaction, Cause and Effect.

Karma is sometimes coupled with another word: *reincarnation*. Reincarnation is a theory. There are several religions in the world that believe in the reincarnating soul, or self-essence of an individual. Reincarnation is the theory that life is repeated on earth in human flesh. Some believe that life is repeated on earth in possibly an animal form of embodiment. Reincarnation is the carnate payoff. What you are in life, what you do, is going to come back to you somehow, and it will "come back" very probably in this life experience. The reincarnationists see it coming back in a future life.

Some religions say that in that future life, if you are very animalistic in your perceptions, emotions, and actions, you will come back as a particular symbol, in the form of a related type of animal. Reincarnation usually means that one rebirths in the flesh in some family here on Planet Earth.

Reincarnation is a *theory*; karma is a *law*. Indeed, it is called the Law of Karma, and we can see that it is a valid law of cause and effect. The Law of Cause and Effect operates; reincarnation is a theory about *how* karma works. It all depends, really, on one's point of view: *scientifically*, there has been little evidence in support of this theory. There have been investigations, and there are some individuals who have tried to make scientific analyses of events that have taken place in their children's and others' lives—that they seem to be relating or repeating something they would not otherwise know or talk about: some part of a previous life or family experience in another village, say in India. This they claim to have observed from time to time.

If you think in terms of modern psychology, and particularly in terms of the Jungian orientation to mind and the collective consciousness, you begin to see that we are all part of one another and all part of life, which is the heart of Religious

Science teaching. It is not unusual to have a perception of another aspect of our lives elsewhere. We are all participating in consciousness, and in a consciousness of one another. In a very subtle way on an unconscious level, and usually in a very obvious way, we find that we are influencing other people and that people are influencing us. But when we take into account our subconscious mind, we see that reincarnation could be a misinterpretation of the way our psyches work, the way our consciousness operates.

The purpose of all of this—karma and reincarnation—is freedom: freedom of the person, freedom to be, to grow, to become; freedom from pain, sorrow, and affliction; freedom to grow in grace, into greater ease and ability to be oneself.

A very famous philosopher and analyzer of these ideas who came to this country in 1893 and introduced the Vedanta philosophy—the intellectual aspect of Hindu philosophy—was Swami Vivekananda.

He wrote:

> It is under the impulse of this tendency [to freedom] that the saint prays and the robber robs. When the line of action taken is proper and high we call it good. The impulse is the same—the struggle toward freedom.

The robber feels that he is not free—that he is lacking, limited in some way. By robbing, he is attaining, he is getting something to give him satisfaction, fulfillment, ease in life. *He is robbing to attain a certain kind of freedom.* The result is that the robber is not working on the level of the positive and constructive but on the level of the destructive and the negative; and karma being the Law of Cause and Effect, the robber's *action* comes back and hits him in some way. Cause and effect—a law—is the essence of karma; and the purpose is *freedom*.

For many years I have studied Eastern philosophy and religions; I have also studied Sanskrit in an attempt to get into the meaning of key words; and I have come to see that karma really has two sides to it: what you can call the exoteric side (the outer) and the esoteric side (the inner, or the hidden). When we look at it from the exoteric aspect, karma is the expectation, by the individual, of a reward—something from the outside that presents or bestows some good. This may also include the idea of reincarnation. That is, if I do all these good things in my life here—if I am prayerful and good and behave in a positive and constructive way—then it will be given me to reincarnate as some saint or sage in my next body. I will be free, and more than free: I shall be surrounded by disciples who will all be supporting me and sitting at my feet as I give them my pearls of wisdom in exchange for their love; and there will be wonderful mutual support. This is the supreme example of external reward, held out by some religions.

The esoteric idea of reincarnation, by way of contrast, would obviously be something operating not externally but *internally* —an inner action, an inner functioning, an inner fulfillment of the idea of freedom.

One of the greatest of all spiritual teachers—Gautama the Buddha—said this:

I do not care to know your various theories about God. What is the use of discussing all the subtle doctrines about the soul? Do good and be good and this will take you to freedom and to whatever Truth there is.

The Buddha was a great teacher, a great analyst, a great thinker, a great liberator of the individual from the confines of organized religion and from all of the stress that is put upon rules and regulations, and even from these ideas of karma and reincarnation. He is saying: Be good, do good, seek the Truth, and you will find it. Familiar, isn't it? We don't need to be constricted by the rules and regulations of human beings who in their anxiety and stress, and in their need, create hierarchies of power and elements of religious worship and ritual to try and make for some surcease from pain—from the anxiety and stress of just living as a human being on Planet Earth.

We can think in terms of Christianity and get another idea of this "esoteric" karma. You may remember that there was a great teacher of the Jews, Nicodemus, who went by night to the rabbi Jesus to solicit his teaching. In response, Jesus said that unless one is born again, which really means to be born anew, one cannot see the Kingdom of God. Jesus was talking about the esoteric, the hidden, the inner karma. But Nicodemus was talking about externals, and so he asked how one could be born again. How can you go back to your mother's womb? It is impossible.

Jesus then expressed this inner way, this internal meaning, symbolizing it by saying that you have to be washed in water and by the Spirit. He was talking in symbology of an inner experience that had nothing to do with going back into one's mother's womb and being physically born again or being reincarnated in some way.

We find that the Buddha and Jesus are talking about a creative law that is in the Universe. They are implying that it is a creative law of Mind—that consciousness, as causation, brings about effects in your life and world, both here and hereafter; so that whether they are talking about life here, or heaven, or another world of experience, it is all related to karma, all related to this law of consciousness—a Law of Thought, a Law of Cause and Effect.

In the Science of Mind, we say that the medium through which all this karmic law works is a medium of universal Soul —a creative Principle of Nature, the Law of Nature, which is really the Law of God, the Law of the Great Spirit around you, within you, and through you. The important point is that *we all use this system*: whether we know it or not, like it or not, choose to or not, *we are using it*. This is a system that is *law*: it is mechanical, it is impartial, it is impersonal, and it is always operating everywhere simultaneously and continually.

This Law of Karma, although *impersonal*, is used *personally* by the individual. But it is impartial in its working and mechanical in its operation and action, as is all law. All law is dependent on you, the user of the law: *you* personalize it, because you use it personally through your conscious mind, and then through your subconscious mind. We begin to see that consciousness, particularly the subconscious mind, creates a memory bank deep within you. This memory bank, ever operating, can speak out through you and into your life at any time—and it does so, often when we least expect it! It is like the Freudian slip: you say the word that you don't consciously want to say, while that memory bank expresses through you, by what you might say or do. We begin to see, then, that this Law is a law of consciousness, operating through our whole conscious and subconscious mechanism, and that it creates a bank of memory that is ever functioning.

Reincarnation is the acting out of these memory-bank impulses. They are there in you and in me right now, and they are acting out as *new experiences*. Good, bad, or indifferent, all are dependent on causation, all are dependent on what we have thought and done. They are there in the memory bank, and they are going to be eventually acting themselves out in our world of experience. This is what we call the Law in form—the Law becoming form in our lives through people, places, things, situations, and events *all of which are the result of what we are internally in consciousness*. By the way, this is pure Christian teaching, original Christianity.

We are always birthing and rebirthing ourselves, because of our thought, our feelings, our actions or non-action (which is always an action). Even *not to do* is nevertheless a *doing something*. The practical side of this is that there are limitless unborn possibilities for living, for experiencing, within you and me all the time—unborn possibilities within us, and we can elicit them. These unborn possibilities are seed thoughts we have deep within ourselves in the memory bank plus much more. Deep within us, our own particular memory bank is rooted in a greater memory bank of the collective consciousness of the race. And behind that lies the potential energy of the Divine, the Source of all that is, with a vast array of creative ideas. So there we are with all this unborn potential, which we can elicit through our *conscious use of consciousness*, a conscious use of the Law—the Law of Mind, the Law of Consciousness. This is what we call healing, the cure of what is called bad karma, negative karma, negative action through you.

How is this done? Through Spiritual Mind Treatment—the use of your consciousness in a very specific and directed way for the greater fulfillment of your life experience. It is our form of prayer. The difference is that most other prayer is a prayer of appeal, of seeking outside for some benefit from a god "out there." That doesn't relate to responsibility of the individual for his or her life. Instead, we neutralize and dissolve the negative patterns within and cease from outward action that is negative and or destructive.

This is the true sense of salvation. Salvation means *spiritual understanding*—spiritual realization of the truths that there is a Law in the Universe, a karmic law, that operates around the individual and within the individual; that you have a responsibility to become more conscious, more aware both of it and of yourself and then to use that Law in an aware way—to bring out the unborn possibilities of life for good and to neutralize and dissolve, both inwardly and outwardly, any negative patterns that would produce in your world a negative experience.

Then you reach the fulfillment of the realization that one reads about in 1 John in the third chapter: We are *already* the children of God, and *today* is the day of our highest good, the freedom to be.

Find and Use
Your Inner Power

MANY YEARS ago a struggling young artist in Paris was so poor that he could not buy a canvas on which to paint. Walking along the quays one day, he saw that an old painting of Napoleon III was for sale for a few sous. He bought it thinking he could remove the painting and use the canvas for his own work. As he cleaned off the surface paint, to his amazement he found another picture underneath. Examining it closely, he thought it looked like a fine Corot. Immediately he sought out experts, who verified that the painting was indeed a genuine Corot. His days of poverty were instantly over. His financial future was assured.

The story, told by Emmet Fox, is metaphorical of the nature of human beings. At the surface of life many people present imperfect images: lack, inharmony, limitation, and disease. These are the overlays resulting from past experiences and the opinions and beliefs of both individual and collective consciousness, which people have accepted. Our work in Religious Science consists of one basic purpose: to wipe away the false images and erroneous concepts of life which have been accepted as essential, real, and therefore a permanent condition. Underneath this overlay of human perception is the true and beautiful inner Being that has always been present.

Begin to remove these negative overlays and find your true nature. Ask yourself: "How do I define myself?" Much of the time we allow the world's opinions and beliefs to define us. No matter how hoary with age these views may be, the fact is we are permitting others to define our lives, natures, and often our future—and sometimes our past. Then we become victims of these views. And because of that, we often believe we are puny, limited, little beings who cannot expect much from life.

In actuality, it is as if we were hibernating superbeings in need of being awakened. How is that accomplished? Through the force and power of That which created us, but which is temporarily covered up and therefore inhibited by our beliefs and our acceptance of limitation.

Ernest Holmes in *The Science of Mind* says, "To learn how to think is to learn how to live."* This seems to be a simple statement, but it is so important that we need to think about it. We need to understand the divine Power within in order to awake from our hibernation. Remember, we create the springtime of our lives each time we recognize that we reside in the Great Spirit that created us. It is the power of this Supreme Nature that controls our lives. In the final analysis, Its Law of Mind is the Law of the Creative Process. And personal experience of power lies in the constructive and positive use of this Law. Eventually, constructive thinking will dissolve negative patterns and overlays of consciousness. Then Truth begins to move upward and forward from the depths of our beings. And this new thrust of creative energy makes our lives a delight.

The spiritual-force is our *Way* of life. It is the creative process we use to control or direct our environment. We use this Law

* P. 133.

of Mind to fulfill our lives. The process we call *treatment*. Treatment is for the purpose of guiding personal consciousness and directing our minds, thoughts, and feelings so that we can move forward in personal evolution. However, treatment is not just a process. There is power in the very treatment itself, and it derives from a person's spiritual awakening and realization. This power can be unleashed and released into the individual's life.

Here are some necessary questions to ask yourself before undertaking treatment:

1. *"Is what I treat about constructive and does it affirm the abundant life?"* Examine your goals and desire because thought is powerful. The Law of Mind operates on every thought. Is your consciousness really constructive, forward-moving, life-affirming?

2. *"Do I desire to manipulate or appropriate another's good?"* Be sure that in your efforts to direct your inner and outer environment you do not try to influence anyone selfishly. Be sure you do not try to attain your good through appropriating something that rightfully belongs to another.

Frank Buchman, the renowned spiritual leader and founder of Moral Re-Armament, said, "There is enough in the world for everybody's need, but not for everybody's greed." He followed this statement by saying, "If everybody cared enough and everybody shared enough, everybody would have enough." This is true love and cooperation. We should realize that abundance in the universe is an expression of the everlasting spiritual Substance and Supply; that there is always enough for you *and* your neighbors. You don't need your neighbors' good. You can create your own. And so can they!

Recognizing that Power is universal, we can see behind creation, knowing it is limitless. Any power we have must derive from this unlimited Resource. We can learn how to intensify and direct this Power in our lives; but first we must locate It before we can use It. We need to study the Science of Mind so that we understand the universal Law of Creativity within us. Indeed, each individual is the One Mind Principle in personal action. We must understand these truths so that we can fully embrace and use them. The power we experience from our studies will transform our lives. It comes from that inner Force which is universal and always is a quality of the divine Nature awaiting our personal recognition.

Ernest Holmes, in his famous affirmation of Being, says: "There is One Life, that Life is God, that Life is Perfect, that Life is my life now." Realization of this truth is acknowledging and using your inner Power. You can decide right now to discover and use this divine Power in a very personal way. It is the Life-force within you. It will bring about liberation from all human fear and negation. It will move you into real freedom and ease in living.

Are Thoughts
Human or Divine?

IT IS SAD but true that many students and teachers of the metaphysical way of life—with particular emphasis on Religious Science—feel the need to follow the followers. When Science of Mind first hit the modern New Thought movement it was a bombshell, stirring thought and revolutionizing timeworn concepts. That leaders and students flocked to Ernest Holmes is indication enough of his ground-breaking ideas. The consciousness of metaphysical students was being prepared for a new surge forward in the evolution of thought. The result: a greater ability to demonstrate the science of Being.

When the great laws of life were refined and reinterpreted by Dr. Holmes, phrases such as "mental equivalent," "mental correspondent," and "Spiritual Mind Treatment" became familiar buzz-words for many students. A revitalized, less restricted, more universal and efficacious teaching emerged as the Science of Mind. A magazine dedicated to the issues of metaphysical science and an institute for training in the philosophy and techniques of Spiritual Mind Treatment were created. An outreach developed into a worldwide movement through Religious Science International and the United Church of Religious Science. Millions have been influenced, although formal membership has never been huge. Nevertheless this work has had a very salutary influence on the metaphysical field; but it has also demonstrated a certain "reverse" effect.

As more psychologists, motivational speakers, therapists, and teachers of self-improvement and self-actualization were influenced by the application of Ernest Holmes' ideas, a strange reaction set in among many students and even some teachers of the Science of Mind. Instead of being encouraged and inspired by the wealth of potential applications of Dr. Holmes' concepts, some individuals took a nose-dive into psychology. The adoption of a mixed bag of psychological and other notions, ideas and methods—some of which were inspired, for good or ill, by interpretations of the original Holmesian thinking—became popular with some groups.

It is obvious that this "adoption of adaptations" reveals some people's insecurity about the Principle of Mind and its demonstrability in human experience. Surely a further study and a clearer understanding of the Science of Being is indicated. Wouldn't this only serve to encourage deeper thought and dedication to metaphysical truths rather than to merely fashionable and transient psychological panaceas for what are essentially spiritual and existential problems?

The demands of spiritual awareness require a disciplined mind, inspired thought, and commitment. Nothing less will do—for nothing less can do the job of breaking negative human belief patterns, whether personal or emerging from the collective consciousness of the race. While respecting the various "mind" disciplines, let us reach into ever *deeper* levels of spiritual understanding and connectedness to the One Life Principle. Let us be mindful of Ernest Holmes' great gift to mankind:

a Science of Mind and Spirit that goes beyond the concoctions of the human mind to the purity of Mind revealing Its Nature from the depths of individual consciousness.

This is the heritage of Religious Scientists. *This* is the demand echoing within the heart and mind of each growing student, teacher, and minister.

Caution: Hope May Be Habit-Forming

WE BELIEVE in hope, but this belief is based on understanding what hope is and what it means. We also believe in the continuity of change, and through it we expect the best. These are good and positive attitudes. People have learned through long experience that attitudes are vital. Today we understand how attitudes influence our lives while enhancing well-being. An attitude can either bring about good or it can act as a repellant of good.

Our objection to hope is that it is inadequate. Ernest Holmes called it "a subtle illusion." Clearly, you cannot live in hope. Ideas such as "Success is just around the corner" indicate a consciousness that is forever "in process." Fulfillment is always *going* to come "some day."

We have learned through our study of the mind-process about the vastness and power of the subconscious mind. All thoughts, feeling, and attitudes are received and reflected back into experience by this Mind-force within us. When you practice the spiritual techniques of the Science of Mind, you learn that hope is not only inadequate; it devitalizes your Spiritual Mind Treatment. Why? Because it involves a type of *speculation* which is

135

often fused with *doubt*. Although we appreciate hope, it has nothing to do with spiritual treatment. It is not a scientific use of Principle. Proper use of the Great Law is to recognize, appreciate, and affirm the eternal laws that are an integral part of life. They function continuously.

Our "work" is one of spiritual awareness and acceptance. It is the key to a correct use of Principle. It is a different concept totally from hope and the repetition of affirmations.* It operates on a different level of mind. To move beyond hope, you need to correctly answer the questions: *What is God? What does God do? What is God's will?* Through the study of Religious Science, we learn that God is Omnific Spirit. It is infinite Reality, which must be wholeness, harmony, creativity, beauty, and order. As Primal Consciousness, It can only desire wholeness and abundant good for us.

Religious Science gives you a philosophical understanding of life that helps you change your mindset and attitudes. Then you can say with conviction, "The perfect spiritual idea of what I desire already exists *in* me, *through* me, and *as* me, and it now appears in my world."

This is the basis of Spiritual Mind Treatment and spiritual healing as we understand and practice it. The entire process is based not on hope, but on a profound spiritual awareness.

In the depths of your consciousness right now is limitless power. That is your original connection to the Supreme Spirit and Source of Life. As you progress in spiritual understanding, you will accept your connection to this Source of being. When this happens, all things become new. You know the Truth that liberates from all limitation. You are transformed inwardly and outwardly. You are not "beyond hope"—you just don't need it any more.

---

* See pp. 68, 69.

Outline for Living

To LIVE dynamically one must have a philosophy and a plan: a way of life that contributes to a sense of purpose. When it is based on the idea that all living beings express a universal intelligence, we are moving in a Reality direction.

The religious experience is always functioning at the level of the subconscious. In our study we try to make the subconscious *conscious*. We "work" to be open and receptive to the flow of the Unconscious Energy as a conscious action. We can direct the Divine Energy because it is not something we have to apply to ourselves. It is something that already exists in us. But is must be elicited or drawn forth out of ourselves.

We need to see life from this divine perspective. It is true vision—not just a limited view of the material universe. This spiritual seeing brings not only a corrective to the human experience, but a healing. Looking at the universe and seeking for answers on a purely materialistic level brings only a temporary change or action. If you want a permanent change, you must look for a spiritual solution to your problems.

People are victimized by their belief structures. Thoughts

and feelings about a situation determine the quality of that situation in your life. Mere beliefs often create problems and difficulties. Whether an experience is going to be a tragedy or an opportunity for growth and development depends on the state of an individual's consciousness.

Here is a brief Outline for Living:

1. Live in the conscious recognition of the universal Principle of Life.

2. Realize that consciousness is the essence and the basis for all experience. It is the Reality in you expressing as you and your world.

3. Recognize that the spiritual you, the essential you, the true idea of you is whole, pure, perfect, complete. This recognition opens your consciousness to the healing power of Truth.

4. Intuition is God in you. When you understand this, then intuition directs you from within and can guide your every experience. Often you will get a feeling: do this, not that; go here, not there. This is the God-action operating as an innate intelligence through you. Get inspired by this idea, fired by it, enthusiastic about this wonder-potential within you.

5. All concepts of lack and limitation must go. Lack of any kind is a wrong use of the universal Law of Limitless Supply. It means that you have not understood the Creative Principle. It means that you have an erroneous view of yourself, life, and your potential experience.

6. You draw from Life what you think into it. So take charge of your thinking. Right thinking is perceiving

from the altitude of Truth. Thought uses the Creative Principle in you, which is subconscious mind. It is the creative energy within that responds to your mental states and feelings.

To be true to yourself, assert *That* in you which is the Infinite Consciousness. You can make your life bountiful, blissful, and blessed through this Outline for Living.

Limitless Living

MANY PEOPLE FIND themselves in a continual flow of problems. When one gets resolved, another seems to pop out of some corner of their experience. Life seems an ongoing challenge and worries never cease. It is as if they were calculating: So many problems down—an infinite number to go. The cycle moves from problem and worry to problem and worry. On and on.

Students of the Science of Mind look forward to the time when their studies will demonstrate perfect ease in every aspect of their life. But this happens infrequently. Why? Because of past conditioning. They have programmed themselves to brace for the next blow from life. Misguided attention feeds them with worry. Yet if these same people could swing consciousness to the worry-free level of spiritual understanding, an entirely new way of life would unfold.

Our goal is to move out of the mental complex that focuses attention on worries and problems. We learn how to dissolve inner patterns through Spiritual Mind Treatment. Wherever we live—in the city or in the serene country—there are always challenges. But if we learn to relate to the Principle of Being, It must express through us as a consciousness of harmony and power. Then we can direct It to bring about a better quality of life.

The world's old song—that life is tough and that the No's of experience abound—must be rejected. It is an old tune, sung by humans throughout all time, believed in as absolute truth and accepted by the deeper layers of mind that always react as subconscious power. This is what compels belief in the negative and engineers humankind to deny themselves fulfillment in life. However, the Science of Mind proves that this is not the truth, although it expresses as fact. The truth of Nature or Being always dissolves inner negative patterns that allow suggestions to flow through us and manifest as disturbed and disturbing experiences.

When we realize the truth of Nature, the truth of Life, the truth of Being, we obtain a transformation of consciousness. The Great Teacher was right when he said, ''Ye shall know the truth and the truth shall make you free.'' Our object is to learn more and more about this truth. When we do, we begin to disengage ourselves from everything that would try to sell us the idea of limitation. We attain objectivity. And we realize that we come from a limitless Source.

Ralph Waldo Emerson wrote, ''God offers to every mind its choice between truth and repose. You can never have both.'' That is exactly the Science of Mind. You can become a victor instead of a victim in your life experience. But for that to happen you cannot live in repose. You must live in the Truth.

At this point you have moved from worn-out thoughts and traditional concepts to the vantage point of spiritual understanding. This is the place in consciousness where all things do indeed become new.

This entire physical universe is the effect of an invisible Cause. We are rooted in that invisible Cause. At the subconscious level it is deep, vast, and endless. Everything emerges from this limitless power of Mind. It is the Totality which has given us life and is always producing through us. We recognize that It is Universal Law functioning as a law of Life, a law of Creativity. As our understanding grows and we consciously begin to use this Law of Life, It becomes the Creative Law of our own lives, a creative process working in and through us by means of our thoughts and feelings. These are always interrelated, moving together, and expressing by the way we use them.

A basic question seems to be, "Can you attain your goals from where you are?" If you always link the future to your past, you add still further challenges to the challenge that is already besetting you as you move toward your goal. We must watch that we are not misled by the past, the present outer picture, or an anticipation of the future. Through spiritual reasoning and thinking we can penetrate to the essential invisible Cause behind all visible experience. Out of this infinite Resource will come everything that is manifest as our world of experience.

When you think, you use the Universal Mind. Ask yourself what you think about the Great Source of Life, and how you think of yourself. Do you conceive of yourself as connected to an infinite Source that created and produced you, a total Good that is behind you, backing you up? Do you conceive of yourself as a success because of this Reality? Do you think of yourself as prosperous, healthy, and intelligent? Because you come from an infinite Source and Mind that reflects your use of It, you can claim these things. If you think of yourself as a pitiable sinner, or as a weak person and afraid, there is no way out. You are finished before you begin.

Our goal in life should be to experience the inner transformation that will bring about outer transformation. The Creative Power is always functioning and expressing. It does this through a personal act of consciousness which distributes the Divine Energy. The problem is that many times we make decisions through an unconscious action and get what we don't want!

The good news is that you can take conscious concern for your life and responsibility for the quality of your existence. This is done through reviewing and thinking through the basic questions that exist in each person's mind: Where have I come from? Who and what am I? What is the source of life? Where am I going? How am I using my consciousness? Is it possible to bring about a rich and satisfying existence?

Most people know that there are three essentials for success: performance, consistency, and stability. It is true of every business and it is true of those who achieve their goals. These qualities are elements of consciousness. They keep the individual vital and independent of the whirlpool of negative beliefs that rush about human life. Only through spiritual discrimination— separating the chaff of human experience from the wheat of metaphysical Truth—can real independence and freedom be achieved. Then Truth becomes a sheet anchor in the storms of life. We can hold to our spiritual understanding while problems move out of our world.

Another view of this process is to understand that we either *bloom or perish*—bloom when we attain a spiritual awareness of the nature of existence or perish under the stress and storms of experience. Recognizing that we are nourished by the nurturing soil of Nature, we become strengthened and encouraged to move onward to achievement and success. It all comes about through thought. It is the way we use consciousness.

Conscious mind directs the creative process within us. Actually, we are never limited. The creative subconscious projects restriction when we believe we are restricted. The dynamic technique of Spiritual Mind Treatment eventually produces new forms in our worlds. This demonstration is the pronouncement in our personal lives of a great Law operating at the level of physical fact that can always move us into new worlds of achievement. It can transform a belief in lack into the experience of continuing supply, loneliness into friendship and love.

This demonstration is made through a change in consciousness. It is the result of an improved mental concept backed up by spiritual realization. It is a way of thinking about yourself, cultivating desire, and envisioning the good you would have in your life. It is entirely a matter of choice. Creative Mind always responds. You are responsible for the quality of your consciousness. Be sure it is in line with the good, the beautiful, the whole.

Frequently what we desire is blocked because of a mix of good elements with much of the world's negative opinions and beliefs. Through Science of Mind study and self-work we can cultivate and refine constructive thinking, desires, and goals. This is the way we evolve, by means of the Single Reality that is forever operating around and through us. The responsibility to use It is ours. We possess a potential and power that is very special. Appreciate yourself. Recognize what it means to be a human consciousness.

Are you choosing a life of extraordinary fulfillment, or one of ordinary living, functioning, and relating? We are free to think any way we wish. It is up to you to accept the responsibility of directing your life. Everything in the Universe is for you. Nothing is against you. The totality of an infinite Resource is behind you. That is what is implied by the metaphysical axiom "One with God is a majority."

Limitless living can be yours. It's all up to you.

Strategies for Living

STRATEGIES FOR LIVING have to do with spiritual awakening, awareness, acceptance, and realization. They are always wedded to action: to the analysis of the human condition and to activities that will move one forward into a more fulfilled life.

Here are some insights and guidelines for strategic thinking and living:

1. *Never let circumstances manipulate you.* Often we say, "There is no other way. This is the way it is." Although a situation is presently valid as a human fact, it does not have to be accepted as the profile of your life. You can bring about change. The important first step is to say, "I will not let circumstances manipulate me."

2. *Know that you are worthy.* Understand that you come from the Highest. You are not a sinner; you are a child of the Universe. Through metaphysical study, thousands of people have proven that they are worthy of the best. They have demonstrated it in many areas of their lives.

145

3. *Recognize that your desire is primarily an idea.* Everything is first an idea before it takes form as a thing, event, or action. Your desire for good and the new is always first a mental concept or movement of consciousness.

4. *Everything is energy.* Know that ideas are like nuclear power: they produce an action of some kind. They are in you and they function to your detriment if you suppress them. You may feel unworthy and that you can't have what you want, hence the resistance. You may become bitter and resentful instead of recognizing that ideas are spiritual energy and that they can manifest form. Assert that you are now allowing constructive ideas to express as concrete experiences in your life.

5. *See this whole action as Law.* It is the Universal Creative Process, and it always operates and is forever active as cause producing effect.

6. *Do not outline, but plan.* In *planning* you know exactly what you want and you know that the Law of the Creative Process brings it about through the right people, places, things, situations, and events. *Outlining* is telling the Universe that what you want must come *only* through situation *A*, not *B*—that your good can only manifest in a particular way. Planning is a divine Creative action; outlining is a coercive movement of the human will that can be counterproductive to the spiritual movement of your life.

7. *Appreciate and praise the good wherever you see it.* Praise your talents, your ability to give, and your ac-

complishments. Appreciate the wonders of life. Look for the good in all.

8. *Do something each day to help or assist others.* Contribute to their life experience. Remember that a Law of giving and receiving means circulating the good.

9. *Take time to be quiet.* Listen to your thoughts and write them down as they emerge out of the depths of your nature. You can receive inner guidance and direction from the Intelligence within you.

10. *Do your Spiritual Mind Treatment each day.*

If these strategies for living are thoughtfully followed, they will produce a wonderful experience of creative living.

I Recognize My Harvest of Good

A SPIRITUAL TREATMENT

THERE IS a supporting Intelligence in the Universe. It is God. It is the infinite and eternally ongoing Good. Operating as a Creative Process, It created me and my world of experience. I live as an ever-unfolding action of God, expressing harmony in every way.

Whatever I need, wherever I turn, the Divine Presence of Supply is there. I accept this reality now. Any beliefs in the necessity of lack, restriction, or loss are dissolved through this spiritual treatment. The pattern of Original Harmony is the foundation of life, and It expresses through me, manifesting in my world of affairs. I am at peace and experience opulence in every way.

Each day is God's perfect day. I recognize this truth as the foundation of my existence. Moment by moment, I see the glory and grandeur of the Law of Divine Right Action at work. It brings about everything necessary for my greater good.

Through reason and intuition, I perceive spiritual concepts with new understanding. I embrace positive and constructive

148

ideas. In this day of God is revealed only the beautiful, the good, and the true. I am inspired by these thoughts and they now become concrete experiences. Therefore, I realize that I live always on the cutting edge of greatness.

Spirit produced me with talents, capabilities, and potentials to create a fulfilled life. Each day, in diverse ways, I see my spiritual nature with clearer vision. This increased awareness of my connection to God enables me to assert my spiritual integrity in every situation.

Any limited opinion I have about my potential or ability to achieve is now erased through this positive spiritual consciousness. I am a center of affirmative knowing in the One Mind that is forever affirming Itself by means of me. I attain my goals. I achieve optimum results with each undertaking. I rejoice in the greatness of God manifesting through me.